190 Barf & (its deer)
194 # of people on earth
1 to 1 million before Adam
died

LETTERS TO THE
EDITOR

Virtually all Scripture references are quoted from the King James translation of the Holy Bible.

Letters To The Editor

Copyright ©2000 by Arno Froese
West Columbia, South Carolina 29170
Published by The Olive Press, a division of Midnight Call Ministries
Columbia, SC 29228 U.S.A.

Copy typist:	Lynn Jeffcoat, Kathy Roland
Copy Editor:	Susanna Cancassi
Proofreaders:	Angie Peters, Susanna Cancassi
Layout/Design:	Michelle Kim
Lithography:	Simon Froese
Cover Design:	Michelle Kim

Library of Congress Cataloging in – Publication Data
Froese, Arno
   Letters To The Editor
   ISBN# 0-937422-49-5

   1. Prophecy

Printed in the United States of America

*This book is humbly dedicated to the
Church of Jesus Christ worldwide.*

*The primary intention of this work is
to reveal the general knowledge of Bible doctrine
within the Church today.
It is our hope that this publication will contribute
toward a better understanding of God's counsel to man
based on the Holy Scriptures.*

*The letters have been randomly selected from those
published in our Midnight Call magazine.*

*All letters are original. Names have been substituted
with initials in order to protect privacy.*

*The author does not benefit from royalties or any
proceeds from the sale of this book. All funds
are reinvested into the worldwide
furtherance of the Gospel.*

C O N T E N T S

CHAPTER 4   57

AUTHORITY OF SCRIPTURE

Keep Ten Commandments • Keep The Law • Ten Commandments To End? • Sabbath Or Sunday? • This Generation • Will Christ Take Back The Earth? • Temple Destroyed Twice? • Endtime Events • Holy Spirit Removed? • Ease My Mind • Enoch And Elijah • Tribulation In Two Parts? • Temple Restoration • Future Dates • The Last Generation • Two Witnesses • Die Twice? • Tribulation Saints • Special Revelation • Lamb And Lion • Integration • Resurrection • Fallen Angels Deceived?

CHAPTER 5   91

SPIRITUAL FUNDAMENTALS

Messiah And Savior • Jesus In The Old Testament • Divine Blood • Pray To The Holy Spirit? • In Jesus' Name • Trinity • Jesus' Return And Trinity • Genealogy • Resurrection Time • Doctrine • Predestination • Name Of God • The Name Of Jesus • Spirit And Soul

CHAPTER 6   115

PRAYER AND SALVATION

More Prayer Makes It Worse • Written Prayers • Prayer Changes God? • Satan Hinders My Prayers • Date Of Salvation • Losing Your Salvation? • Doubting Salvation • Saved In The Great Tribulation • Rebirth Versus Conversion • Saved By Water? • Redeemed Or Saved? • Unsure Of Salvation • Can Sin Cancel Salvation? • Exact Bible Words • Disciples Converted?

INTRODUCTION

Letters To The Editor is a book that is true to its title, and one which I consider the voice of the Church. Because our letter writers are not only national, but international, we can assume that virtually all churches and denominations are represented. Therefore, opinions and views will vary due to the influence of denominational guidelines. However, it is fair to say that a large percentage of our writers are concerned readers who have been motivated to respond, in agreement or disagreement, to certain issues that have been addressed in our *Midnight Call* magazine. Therefore, we have taken great pains to publish virtually all letters in their entirety. Thus, the largest contributors to this book are our letter writers, a voice that will be heard throughout these pages.

Although we have changed the names and initials of the writers to protect their privacy, all letters are original, with minor editorial revisions having been made only when necessary for clarity or grammatical purposes.

The variety of letter writers representing many different backgrounds and nationalities is what makes this book so unique. With this in mind, I would like to thank those who wrote for being my teachers. This is important to emphasize because it was the letter writer who caused me to search the Scriptures and find answers to numerous questions. They prompted me to refine my answers, seek additional scriptural proof and ground my understanding deeper into the eternal Word of God. The way they responded to my answers enriched me with their views.

Of the thousands of letters I have received since I entered the ministry in 1968 under the leadership of the late Dr. Wim Malgo, this book represents only a small fraction; however, the letters selected represent a unified voice of the Church expressing various opinions.

I am humbled to admit that in some cases my answers may come across as impolite, sarcastic, or somewhat self-righteous. However, this was never the true intention of my heart. Rarely have I ever replied to someone without revising my response before putting it in the mail. The motive behind all my answers, as well as that behind my life and ministry, is to proclaim the truth of the Bible to the best of my knowledge and ability. I have done my utmost to base my answers on the simplicity of Scripture, the ultimate authority for all Christians.

As mentioned earlier, the letters published in this book have been selected from several years of letters which have appeared in *Midnight Call* magazine. We have attempted to categorize them according to their various subjects. Each letter is titled according to subject matter and content. Although a number of letters deal with the same subject, each letter has been answered on an individual basis, without reference to, or comparison with previous answers.

My response to each question or opinion has not been based on the framework of certain theological seminaries or popular schools of thought, but, as already mentioned, I have attempted to let the Bible speak for itself. The knowledge I have gained since entering the ministry by answering thousands of letters is really quite impossible for me to comprehend. One thing is absolutely clear: I have learned a great deal from my readers, friends and foes alike, who have often caused me to change my view on certain subjects at certain times, and at others, have helped me to gain a deeper insight by further intense study. However, I have never changed my mind regarding the truth of Scripture; it is plain and clear in context and in no need of interpretation or further analysis.

Although according to Bible prophecy, knowledge is being increased and the speed of accumulating scientific knowledge, particularly in electronics, is explosive, I have adhered to the motto of Midnight Call Ministry founder, Dr. Wim Malgo, "The Bible is the best commentary to the Bible."

In conclusion, I must highlight one more important point, namely, the uniqueness of each person as created in the image of God. This uniqueness enables us to see various things from different perspectives. Therefore, we shouldn't expect to agree on everything. Even members of the first church and the apostles amongst themselves did not always agree on all matters at all times. We know that

Paul had to correct Peter and bluntly told him that he was in error. When reading the book of Acts, we notice that Paul and Barnabas "...*had no small dissension and disputation*" with certain disciples from Judea. Verse 7 says, "...*there had been much disputing.*" On this occasion, the apostle James took the lead and said, "...*Simeon hath declared how God at the first did visit the Gentiles, to take out of them a people for his name. And to this agree the words of the prophets; as it is written*" (Acts 15:14-15). Thus we see that the answer to the disputation was "*the words of the prophets,*" the written Word of God. Even great co-workers in the kingdom of God such as Paul and Barnabas had a difference of opinions, "*And the contention was so sharp between them, that they departed asunder one from the other: and so Barnabas took Mark, and sailed unto Cyprus*" (verse 39). Therefore, living together in peaceful harmony at all times is not necessarily required and this truth is clearly shown to us in the example given in Scripture.

We may have differences of opinions, and our interpretations of difficult Scriptures will vary; however, regardless of our differences as believers, the direction of our unity must never be solely on a person-to-person level. Instead, the direction we must take in order to arrive at perfect unity must be vertical. We are one in Him and only in Him are we one.

Addressing the Church, Paul made the following statement, "*Now the God of patience and consolation grant you to be likeminded one toward another according to Christ Jesus: That ye may with one mind and one mouth glorify God, even the Father of our Lord Jesus Christ.*

Wherefore receive ye one another, as Christ also received us to the glory of God" (Romans 15:5-7). It is absolutely essential that our desire for unity is centered on one person, *"...likeminded one toward another with one mind receive ye one another"* and is built upon the foundation *"...as Christ also received us to the glory of God."* Jesus made this unity of the Church clear in His high priestly prayer, *"...that they may be one, even as we are one: I in them, and thou in me, that they may be made perfect in one"* (John 17:22-23). Therefore, unity in Jesus must be the goal of our lives, the Church, our ministry and this book.

I pray that the pages of this book will contribute to fulfilling Paul's admonition to his spiritual son Timothy, *"reprove, rebuke, exhort with all longsuffering and doctrine"* (2nd Timothy 4:2).

CHAPTER 1

CREATION/EVOLUTION

GENESIS CONTRADICTION?

Mr. Froese,

Considering that you believe in the infallibility of the Scripture, I want to prove that Genesis chapters 1 and 2 are contradictory, and [were written] by two different authors. The first chapter states that animals were created before man, but chapter 2 reads that animals were created after man. It should be apparent that these creation accounts can't both be right.

All versions of the Bible, with the exception of the NIV, include two contradictory stories of creation. I have enclosed a portion of the Hebrew-English NIV [translation] of Genesis 2. The English version is a deception. In Genesis 2:19, this version inserts the word "HAD" to give the reader the idea that the creation of animals took place earlier than the creation of man. If you read Genesis 2:19 in the Hebrew, from right to left, it clearly states "NOW HE FORMED," which means that right then and there animals were formed so Adam (the man) could find a help-mate for himself (Genesis 2:18), which also is ridiculous when you think about it.

In closing, it's hard to believe that the whole Bible is "inspired" when it can be shown that there are hundreds upon hundreds of contradictions such as the ones above.

Any comments?

-R.T., Buffalo, NY

ANSWER: Creation is documented in Genesis 1, while Genesis 2 gives further details of the events that took place in Genesis 1. This type of journalism is practiced even today. Have you ever considered that these alledged "contradictions" only exist because you may be in darkness: "...*the natural man receiveth not the things of the Spirit of God: for they are foolishness unto him: neither can he know them, because they are spiritually discerned*" (1st Corinthians 2:14)?

The Bible is God's full counsel to man. You have a free will to believe it or reject it. This liberty doesn't just apply to religion, but to other areas as well, including politics, where our thoughts and philosophies are based on faith. When the Democrats and Republicans argue, each group believes they are right. They have faith in their own understanding of correct public policy.

It is my prayer that the Lord grants you the faith that will save you for all eternity.

CREATION PROOF

Dear Brother Froese,

This letter is in response to the letter from K. O. and your answer in the May issue of *Midnight Call*.

As you know, when Christians come up against "things" in this world that apparently go against our faith and/or belief, we must remember that the Bible is and must always be the final authority. Second Timothy 3:16-17 tells us, *"...All scripture is given by inspiration of God, and is profitable for doctrine, for reproof, for correction, for instruction in righteousness: That the man of God may be perfect, thoroughly furnished unto all good works."* We are also reminded in Titus 1:2 that *"...God cannot lie."* Therefore we must accept the Bible as the truth, the whole truth and nothing but the truth.

When scientists in the secular world date bones and fossils at over 6,000 years old, many Christians just accept that and would rather adjust the Bible to fit the world than to stand on God's Word. So Christians timidly decide to put a gap between Genesis 1:1 and 1:2. However, if Christians would follow the directions given in 2nd Timothy 2:15 and study their Bibles, not just casually read them, they would find that there is no gap in Genesis. Exodus 20:11 makes it very clear that *"...in six days the LORD made heaven and earth, the sea, and all that in them is, and rested the seventh day: wherefore the LORD blessed the sabbath day, and hallowed it."* We see from this that everything (*"all that in them is"*) was created in six days; part of it was not created at one point and then the rest created some millions of years later.

21

If we follow 2nd Timothy 2:15 and study the Scriptures, then we will be able to *"rightly* [divide] *the word of truth"* and that will help make us *"thoroughly furnished"* (2nd Timothy 3:17), *"and be ready always to give an answer to every man that asketh a reason of the hope that is in* [you] *with meekness and fear"* (1st Peter 3:15).

Once we get back to believing what the Bible teaches, then we can start looking for information that will help us repudiate the information that evolutionists are putting out.

-L. E., Eight Mile, AL

ANSWER: The issue is a vain attempt to scientifically prove creation. Hebrews 11:3 reads, *"Through faith we understand that the worlds were framed by the word of God."* No "scientific" answer would ever prove anything to an evolutionist because access to the understanding of truth comes exclusively through faith.

FAITH UNDERSTANDS CREATION

Dear Mr. Froese,

I would like to respond to K.O.'s question in the May issue regarding dinosaurs and creation. Genesis and creation week was a major stumbling block to my full acceptance of the Bible and, subsequently, Jesus Christ, even though I had been a regular church member for a long time. Once [the issue was] resolved, I was able to totally commit myself to our Lord and accept the Bible as God's true Word to us.

22

I now believe that Genesis 1-11 can be accepted for what it says: Everything was created during creation week, [which was] thousands, not millions, of years ago. That includes dinosaurs, which were created on day 6 along with all other land-dwelling creatures. What has led many people, including Christians, astray is the lie created by man: the "theory of evolution" which cannot be scientifically substantiated at all. The Bible states that there was no death until Adam sinned. Peter says in 2nd Peter 3:4-6 that in the last days people will deliberately forget that long ago "...*by the Word of God the heavens were of old, and the earth standing out of the water and in the water.*" Evolution has only been accepted on a wide scale since Darwin, only a short time ago.

-J. E., Agoura Hills, CA

ANSWER: The Bible says, "...*faith is the substance of things hoped for, the evidence of things not seen*" (Hebrews 11:1). While I consider evolution to be utter nonsense, creation science attempts to prove something that must be grasped by faith, "*Through faith we understand that the worlds were framed by the word of God*" (verse 3). True faith does not need any so-called "scientific evidence" because "...*we walk by faith and not by sight*" (2nd Corinthians 5:7).

MORE EVOLUTION

Dear Friends of Truth,

God bless your efforts to teach the whole counsel of

Scripture. Please recommend an approach and materials for friends of mine who breed and show horses.

They are Baptist Christians. I am a Missouri Synod Lutheran Christian, and we disagree about origins. The LCMS and I believe in the inerrancy of Scripture; the "recent" six-day creation *ex nihilo* [out of nothing] by God's Word; no bloodshed and death before Adam sinned; the world-wide flood of Noah; a different atmosphere and man's reduced longevity after the flood; and the fact that we need a Savior from sin, death and the power of the devil.

They believe that the arrangement of fossils presented by some as the evolution of the horse and the bump inside a horse's legs being presented as a vestigial thumb, "is just the way that horses have evolved, whether I believe it or not."

Although I don't know horses like they do, I know from attending public school, and from taking science classes at the University of Nebraska in Omaha 30 years ago, that only the small fraction of evidence that can be used to support evolution is presented in tax-funded "education."

As my anthropology professor, explained when I'd bring up other evidence: "We don't have time to present all the evidence." This man would move quickly to the other side of the street whenever our paths crossed on campus.

He had previously taught the same godless ideas in a Soviet satellite country. A local newspaper frequently supports requiring belief in evolution in public schools.

Thanks for any recommendations and help you can offer.

-V. C., Omaha, NE

ANSWER: Quite frankly, the evolution theory doesn't deserve our attention because it is utter foolishness. If evolutionists had at the very least one tiny shred of evidence, then they might have a case. Since they do not, it is fruitless to discuss the subject any further.

EARTH DIVIDED?

Dear Mr. Froese,

I am a new subscriber to *Midnight Call* magazine and I really enjoy it.

I have just finished your July issue and have a comment on a reader's question regarding the location of the Garden of Eden.

We all too often forget that the first 6 chapters of Genesis and the rest of the Bible are separated by the flood of Noah, "...*Whereby the world that then was, being overflowed with water, perished*" (2nd Peter 3:6).

I believe the flood rearranged things so dramatically, geographically speaking, that it is impossible to pinpoint the location today. Even the reference to the Euphrates River cannot be the same exact river.

I'm sure that the name of rivers and other places, such as towns, were retained in the memories of the survivors of the flood. Perhaps they simply renamed the new features they saw after the flood just as our ancestors brought the names of their towns in England, Scotland,

and Germany and used them to name towns in the U.S.A.

I also have a question. It is stated in the article, "The Gods of Olympus" [April-July, 1998 MC] that no other major culture in history sanctioned all manner of sexual license as did ancient Greece. Homosexuality and the abuse of young boys was rampant.

Why didn't the Greeks suffer from the social diseases that our society is suffering from today: syphilis, gonorrhea, other STDs and, of course, AIDS?

It certainly seems like they should have switched their lifestyle.

-A. O., Lincoln, NE

ANSWER: Reference to the division of the continents is found in Genesis 10:5,25,32. In verse 25 we read, "...*in his days was the earth divided.*" That occurred before the flood.

Second Peter 3:6 refers to the "living creatures" who have perished because 1st Peter 3:20 confirms that only "...*eight souls were saved by water.*"

I don't know whether or not there were any special diseases during the time of the Greek culture. However, we do know that terrible diseases will come about, as documented in Revelation 9:6, "*And in those days shall men seek death, and shall not find it; and shall not desire to die, and death shall flee from them.*"

PROGRESSIVE CREATION

Dear Brother Arno:

Re: Your anti-evolution article in the August *Midnight Call*.

The credibility of the faith community depends on our honesty and integrity. In fighting atheist versions of how we came to be, it isn't wise or necessary to misrepresent your enemy's best arguments. Your intelligent readers will see you are taking shortcuts where the better strategy is to get to the core of their misrepresentation. Fight propaganda with truth.

To deny the age of the earth and the rest of God's creation is a losing strategy, since every one of the radiometric methods of dating rocks and fossils speaks to an old, old scenario. Let's discard Bishop Usher's misguided attempt to prove a young creation and concentrate on how we may read Genesis 1 in light of science. Evolutionists have their interpretive disputes, and they now generally discount Darwin's insistence on a slow transformation of species by natural selection. We cannot, however, dance over the grave of evolution just because scientists are seeking a revised theory consistent with new evidence. This is, after all, the scientific quest since they are not wedded (or should not be) to any theory that fails to explain reality consistently and comprehensively. The kind of criticism displayed in Deubois', *Evolution, A Theory in Crisis* is fair and shows the effectiveness of using "wise as a serpent" reasons to criticize.

Hugh Ross' ministry, Reasons to Believe, follows a similar attitude. Without denying Psalm 19, it is possible to re-read Genesis without violating our understanding that Holy Scripture is indeed "God breathed." You may prefer literalism as your understanding of inspiration, but I am more flexible if the facts warrant a more allegorical approach. But we give you one or two examples of how traditional fundamentalist readings actually add assumptions to previous assumptions that are not really in the text itself, but come from the theology of simple literalism, based on fear of science.

"*In the beginning*" tells us what? That God began a creative act and put time in motion. John 1:1 tells us there was yet another, "*In the beginning*" when the Word was with God and was God. Here we assume that this beginning was not started, but has always been. Yet even eternity has a "beginning" if we are to take John's words literally. But eternity, by definition, cannot have a beginning. Either John misspoke or we understand this "beginning" as a figure. Now, in Genesis, we assume phrases like, "*God created the heaven and the earth*" were a miraculous work, not a work employing the laws of nature (also created by God). But Genesis does not actually say God acted miraculously. Since Hebrews tells us the worlds were framed by the Word of God, we know that God's will is expressed by His Word set in motion. And once in motion, a chain of being emerged - perhaps even evolved - rather than just jumped miraculously into existence (although this, too, is possible in certain conditions, but not in every case).

"*And the earth was without form, and void*" has caused much speculation. That is because we don't care to accept it for what it says, but wish to speculate based on other information, such as science's theory of how the solar system was founded or a previous age of satanic ruin we draw from other parts of the Bible. But I feel it is related

28

to Jesus' idea in John 6:63 that, "*It is the spirit that quickeneth; the flesh profiteth nothing.*" Until, "*...the spirit of God moved upon the face of the waters,*" the earth was "*...without form, and void.*" God's Spirit gives life. Period.

Now all the "days" of Genesis begin with the words, "*And God said*" and conclude with the words, "*And the evening and morning were the day.*" Not once does it say God (until the command was given) made something without reference to a process: "*And God said let,*" - "*Let there be light,*" "*Let there be a firmament,*" "*let there be* (etc.)*" After the process of letting, it is stated that God was responsible for the making - "*And God made.*"

If you do not wish to read Genesis this way, consider the creation of vegetation, where the text says, "*And God said, Let the earth bring forth grass, the herb yielding seed, and the fruit tree yielding fruit after his kind, whose seed is in itself, upon the earth: and it was so.*" God commanded the earth (using His laws of nature) to bring forth but three typical vegetative growths (not mentioning the thousands of other kinds we know exist). "*And it was so,*" refers to the process, not the completion, thus allowing for evolution (at least within species). Now we know it takes more than a literal day to do all this, so when the text confirms, "*And the earth brought forth grass,*" it ends with God's satisfaction that the earth had followed His will to grow vegetation and judged the result: "*And God saw that it was good.*" Literal days become an anomaly when read this way, and rightly so. "*And the evening and morning*" could better be understood as the time it takes for darkness (non-being) to become light (being), paralleling verse 5, which reads "*And God called the light Day, and the darkness he called Night. And the evening and the morning were the first day.*" That there were six divisions of creation is clear, being called "*days,*" but meaning that by God's Spirit being (light) comes after the non-being (darkness). Day comes after night. "*Though I walk through the valley of the shadow of death,*" portrays a similar understanding: God's light always follows by faith in time, no matter how fearful the darkness. By faith we receive it, if we hear His voice and respond with our heart of flesh. My heart of flesh tells me science is revealing in matter, the ways of God as summarized in Genesis 1, and it is so unique and ingenious that it affirms Psalm 19 in splendid detail not only in the heavens, but in the unseen world of the microcosmos.

What a great and mysterious God we have!

P.S. The argument that entropy (the 2nd law of thermo-dynamics) defeats evolution is not sound. Entropy only applies to closed systems where no extended energy is introduced to sustain the thermodynamic processes. It is obvious that the earth and its life is not a closed system, since the sun introduces new energy daily and the volcanic heat from below alters both the earth's geology and its environment from time to time. Other cosmic rays also influence the balance of the ecosphere, as does the electromagnetic system of the poles. Sorry, this argument against evolution is specious and should be dropped as propaganda. Truth is more powerful and will defeat all that is not of God. Have faith.

-E. O., Calumet City, IL

ANSWER: Innumerable volumes of literature have been written about evolution and creation, none really convincing the other permanently. Your detailed letter reinforces my stand that you cannot scientifically disprove evolution, nor can you scientifically disprove creation science, *"Through faith we understand that the worlds were framed by the word of God, so that things which are seen were not made of things which do appear"* (Hebrews 11:3). Therefore, I reconfirm my statement, "You cannot prove something scientifically that can only be grasped by faith."

CHAPTER 2

SIN

UNCONFESSED SINS

Dear Bro. Froese,

My question concerns the doctrine of forgiveness as related to unconfessed sins. It is my understanding that all sin is forgiven when we accept Christ: past, present, and future. If this is correct, can you provide scriptural documentation for it? Assuming this to be the case, why are we admonished to seek forgiveness for our sins after salvation?

I know that unconfessed sin destroys fellowship, but is that because the unconfessed sin is unforgiven? Also, what happens to unconfessed sin at the death of the believer, and how is it dealt with at the believers' judgment? Thank you for any light you can shed on this matter.

-Mrs. A. L., Clintwood, VA

ANSWER: From the moment God saves us, we are

33

cleansed from all sin. Colossians 2:13 states, *"...having forgiven you all trespasses"* and Hebrews 1:3 confirms, *"...by himself purged our sins...."* When the Holy Spirit calls unconfessed sin to our attention and we refuse to repent, this is classified as unforgiven sin. In 1st John 1:9 we are admonished, *"If we confess our sins, he is faithful and just to forgive us our sins, and to cleanse us from all unrighteousness."* A person with unconfessed sins will be ashamed at His coming (see 1st John 2:28). First Corinthians 3:15 warns, *"If any man's work shall be burned, he shall suffer loss: but he himself shall be saved; yet so as by fire."*

SIN AND SINS

Dear Brother Froese,

In the story, "The Baptism of the Spirit" (May 1999), Hermann Schmalzle writes, "Whoever accepts the accomplished, substitutionary sacrifice of Jesus receives forgiveness of all sins and simultaneously the gift of the Spirit," with which I agree. But two pages back, he says, "A born again Christian who does not let himself be convicted of sins - whether in thought, word or deed, including the sins of omission - and who does not seek cleansing in the blood of the Lamb of God will become lukewarm and sluggish in his spiritual life." That sounds like a contradiction to me. First, he says that my sins are forgiven, then he says that I have sin in my life that I need to be cleansed from. Either the blood cleansed me of sin or it didn't. Well, it did. Jesus preached repentance, which means to think differently. To me, that means to recognize things that are contrary to the holy nature of God and to turn away (first mentally) from those things. But if I make a mistake, then what? Repent! I could ask forgiveness, but the blood of Christ already has been applied and God sees me as righteous because of it regardless of what I do. But all I truly want to do is please Him and live an upright and holy life.

-R. B., Louisville, KY

ANSWER: The forgiveness of sin, which is our very nature, takes place once and for all through the substitutionary sacrifice of Jesus. However, sins that we commit after we have been forgiven are another matter. First John 2:1 says, *"...if any man sin, we have an advocate with the Father, Jesus Christ the righteous."*

LIVING ABOVE SIN

Dear Mr. Froese:

I got as far as reading your editorial and was stopped short by a comment you made, which I have clipped and am enclosing. It's a comment pertaining to suicide. Are you under the impression that people who commit suicide enter heaven? Suicide is self-murder, and murder without repentance is penalized by eternal damnation. If you were to repent of something, you would not do it.

Just because you accept Jesus doesn't necessarily mean that you are born again. If you are born again, you will not commit the sin of murder, or any other sin for that matter. It is the breaking of the commandments that Jesus said we are to keep. This is a very serious and erroneous thought and has no biblical foundation. See the gospel of John, chapter 6, and the epistles of John, which are very strong in denouncing such beliefs, and include Revelation 21:8 too, if you will. I cannot accept such teaching of error.

-T. E., Plevna, MT

ANSWER: I do agree that suicide is self-murder. However, your statement that a born again person will "not commit... sin" is contrary to Scripture. Addressing believers, John says, *"If we confess our sins..."* we do receive forgiveness but, *"If we say that we have not sinned, we make him a liar..."* (1st John 1:9-10). The apostle Paul confessed, *"...the evil which I would not, that I do"* (Romans 7:19). In verse 20 he explains, *"Now if I do that I would not, it is no more I that do it, but sin that dwelleth in me."* However, Scripture admonishes us not to sin, *"...if any man sin, we have an advocate with the Father, Jesus Christ the righteous."*

SIN IN GENES?

Dear Sir:

Midnight Call has exceeded expectations in its scope and quality of articles, especially in covering "old" subjects in fresh and enlightening ways and in the fundamentals of God's truth.

It is this pattern to date (I have been a subscriber for

one year) that leaves me disappointed in Marcel Malgo's article, "When Light Breaks Through the Darkness" (May 1999).

The statement that depression is inherited, [that it is] "in the genes" (along with a listing of stealing, lying, foul language, alcoholism, and homosexuality), reflects the influence of psychological theory. Depression is a state of mind induced by the negatives of either a traumatic event or environmental conditioning. The latter would be the contributing factor in all the examples cited by the author. The genes have nothing to do with the mind-set caused by a negative environment or events.

As believers, we have the high privilege of God's presence and power to get through those times of trial (trauma, negative surroundings that harass and any other stressful situation) in a victorious way. In 1st John 5:4 and 1st Corinthians 15:57, God promises that our faith in His care will give us the victory over the world, even over death. God has promised (1st Corinthians 10:13) that we will not be tempted (tried) beyond our ability (in Him) to bear it.

The condition, the requirement for meeting life without depression (apart from medical problems), is to *"walk in the light as He is in the light,"* in the power of the Holy Spirit. Twentieth-century human philosophies (including godless psychology) have drawn mankind (including God's children) away from Divine provisos.

The sin nature is not genetic. Genetics (DNA) control physical characteristics and probably the propensity to certain personality characteristics such as talents. The sin nature is a "disease of the heart," the spirit of man (Psalm 51:10, John 3:5-8, 16-21).

For your information, a non-Christian (Catholic) friend in Belgium (plus his family) is carefully reading each issue of *Midnight Call*. Any content to help any unbelieving reader (there must be others) to see the light of God's truth would be helpful. Daniel is learning that others believe as I do.

I believe the time is short. May God bless you all.

-L. R., Priest River, ID

ANSWER: The Bible makes it clear that every individual is responsible for his or her own sins. We are genetically sinful because flesh and blood shall not inherit the kingdom of God. However, the tendency to commit certain sins is closely related to our genes. Statistics reveal that parents who lie, steal or cheat will most likely have children who follow in their footsteps. I do agree that Marcel (or the translators) may have confused the proper scientific terminology relating to genetics, but the bottom line is the same: every human being on the face of the earth is in bondage to sin and can only be redeemed through faith in the accomplished work of our Lord Jesus Christ.

CHAPTER 3

ISRAEL

ARABS IN ISRAEL

Mr. Arno Froese, Editor:

Regarding Mr. Kollek's article, "Jerusalem Wisdom," [*News From Israel*] in the February issue: I take issue with his statement that Arabs of Jerusalem are an integral part of the city by right, not by favor.... was that a direct quote? Why the ellipses?

Mr. Kollek must not understand God's covenant with Abraham for all of the land - through the seed of Isaac.

Ishmael's covenant was for another great land (Genesis 17:15-21; 21:9-21; covenant land boundaries, Genesis 15:18-21).

Arabs have no legal or hereditary claim to any part of the land of Israel. But only the return of the Messiah will solve this dispute.

-H. L., Eugene, OR

ANSWER: I wholeheartedly concur with your last

sentence, "But only the return of the Messiah will solve this dispute."

However, if you deny the Arabs the right to live in Israel, you must also deny your right to live in North America because you have no scriptural documentation proving that God covenantally gave this land to European immigrants and African slaves.

The fact that the Jews are the legitimate inheritors of the land isn't up for debate; the Lord will fulfill His intention.

ISRAEL AND THE RAPTURE

Dear Brother Froese,

Examining the *Midnight Call* magazine, I have some serious reservations about your understanding of the present-day nation of Israel. I do NOT believe that the nation we see in the Holy Land today is the prophesied Israel of either the Old or New Testament. The prophetic land of Israel will be filled when God's people come into the land believing that the Lord Jesus Christ is God! God will draw believers—not the Talmudic Jews of this day—into the land. I fail to see the hand of God in the activities in and around the Israel of today. Perhaps you can show me some of the things that lead you to believe that the people presently in the land are following the leading of God.

Also, I have had some serious questions about your position on the pre-tribulation, pre-millennial Rapture of the Church, the Body of Christ. I believe that we, as saints today, have a heavenly hope (1st Thessalonians 4:17, etc.), not a position in the land of Israel. We are *"ever to be with the Lord"* in the air! I am excited about your professing a belief in the Rapture. Most of apostate Christianity gives up on the Rapture first, then on the eternal security of the believer, then on the virgin birth, and then they adopt universal reconciliation of all souls, even Satan.

-S. P., Dresser, WI

ANSWER: Overwhelming evidence in the Scripture indicates that the Jews will come back to the land in unbelief. How else can Zechariah 12:10 be fulfilled? An unbeliever needs *"...the spirit of grace and of supplication."* Carefully read the succession of their return in Ezekiel 36 and 37. God's first concern is the land, then food for Israel, then the people's *"new heart"* and *"new spirit,"* and finally, *"I will put My Spirit within you."* The Bible makes it clear that the Jews in Israel will need conversion.

ZIONISTS OR JEWS?

Arno Froese,

Just finished your book, *How Democracy Will Elect the Antichrist.* Very fitting book for these times. The information helps clear up some questions I had. Gave the second copy to a friend. Up to this point, she hasn't been too interested in discussing the topic. Your book has helped reverse that idea. Thanks for the favor; now I have someone who can enter my discussion.

However, there are a few things you need to clarify that

still have me puzzled:

1) At the bottom of page 39, the last sentence reads, "...so the Church must be removed." [Note: Hold that thought until after the next question.]

2) Are you holding the belief, as so many other ministries, that the Jews have returned to Israel?

3) From your quote, do you believe in the oft-quoted Holocaust figure of 6 million?

Attached are some articles that will back up my contention: Zionists, not Jews, are in control of Israel. Please make that distinction. People are confused as it is, the reason why others are prone to give away the store.

The 6 million Holocaust figure has been refuted by more than one author - they have been criticized for it. So please, don't you maintain the gross error. Why are we spending $28 million in support of a Holocaust museum in Washington? Why one in Miami, Florida? Why are we helping them advertise?

Well, anyway, your book will be read and re-read, and discussed with my friend.

-A.A., Huntsville, AL

ANSWER: Jews, Zionists, Israelis and Hebrews are one and the same.

The twelve tribes of Israel found their identity in the tribe of Judah; thus, they became Jews.

Jesus, the great Jew, came from the tribe of Judah and He proclaimed, *"...salvation is of the Jews"* (John 4:22).

The purpose of Zionism is to bring Jews back to Zion.

I endorse Zionism wholeheartedly, and without reservation.

While there may be "more than one author" who refutes the 6 million Holocaust figure, millions can testify to the fact that the Jews were slaughtered in numbers that approach or succeed 6 million. The Holocaust Museum in Jerusalem clearly documents that number and has been inspected by numerous agencies all over the world.

Bible prophecy tells us that when all the Jews are back in Zion, "...*ten men shall take hold out of all languages of the nations, even shall take hold of the skirt of him that is a Jew, saying, We will go with you: for we have heard that God is with you*" (Zechariah 8:23).

Even if the United States increased its support ten-fold for the Jewish state, we would never be able to repay the contribution that the Jews have made to our country and the world!

MIDEAST FAMILY CONFLICT

Dear Mr. Arno Froese:

In regard to your May article, "Family Conflict in the Mideast," I would like to point out a few simple facts. You state: "...this century also experienced something that is absolutely unique in history: The return of the Jews to the land of their fathers." This may in fact be true, but how can Christians or Jews rejoice in the fact that this return left thousands of Palestinians, who had lived there recently and had legal rights to this land, homeless and unwelcome? Is this what Jesus would really want? Is this what God would want? Surely anyone under the influence of God's Holy Spirit could not believe such complete nonsense. In addition, you might respond by saying that many Palestinians have returned to their homeland. However, not to the same homes. Their rights of ownership were taken without retribution or compassion. Today, yes, many are back; yet they are not considered equal citizens. They are not even given enough water or other necessities for life. It has been proven that Israel has been tapping its water supply for decades. This is not to mention the millions of gallons of water Israel diverts from the Litani River of Lebanon by invading and trying to claim their territory in addition to what they already greedily have taken.

Another fact that Christians tend to forget is that there is a large Christian population in Lebanon–some say as many as 50%. Are we really supporting the endless bombings of our Christian brothers and sisters?

You list Abraham as a role model and more. With the Christian values recently resurging, especially through Promise Keepers, do you think it is really appropriate to list Abraham, who abandoned his own son because of his mistake? Foreign Minister Shimon Peres was wrong to think that the Israeli nation would live in peace with the Arab nation. It is he, after all, who is promoting this Israeli war on Lebanon (which is certainly not new - over 20,000 have been killed since 1982) and what for? His political gain. I was offended by this article more than I could ever describe. You clearly show both your ignorance and lack of understanding of Middle Eastern problems, which rely too highly on swayed perspective and an incorrectly used Bible.

-T.E., Aloha, OR

ANSWER: The land of Israel was given to the descendants of Abraham, Isaac, and Jacob in an unconditional covenant. At this time, there is much Arab-occupied Israeli territory that the Jews will have to take possession of. In the absence of the majority of Jewish people prior to 1948, few Arabs lived on the territory that was deserted, forsaken, and never claimed by any Arab political identity. The so-called Palestinians are a political invention by the British and no such nation, race, or group of people ever existed.

Abraham was very concerned for his son Ishmael, and prayed, *"O that Ishmael might live before thee!"* (Genesis 17:18). Nevertheless, God answered *"...my covenant will I establish with Isaac"* (verse 21).

Incidentally, there is an abundance of literature at your local library that will help you to distinguish fact from fiction. The official religion in Lebanon is 70% Muslim and 30% Christian. The word "Christian" has little, if any, relation to Bible-believing Christianity. Indeed, Lebanon has greatly suffered, and an estimated 60,000 lives were lost during the civil war between Muslims and the Maronite (Catholic) Militia, the Phalange and other "Christians." A number of Arab countries provided political and military support for the Muslims while Israel aided the "Christian" forces. In any event, peace will come to the Middle East when the Prince of Peace has arrived.

THE HOUSE OF ISRAEL

Attention Arno Froese:

In the *Midnight Call* edition, April 1996, page 15, where Arno Froese answers A.O. in the middle of the page, he said, "The Church of Jesus Christ is the Bride." This is an error. The Bride of Christ is a nation, a government, the House of Israel. They were led by the anointed one of Genesis 48: Joseph's son Ephraim and Manasseh. They led the ten-tribe house of Israel, the covenant people. They are the captives that scattered north into Europe. Please look up Matthew 9:15, Isaiah 62:4, Micah 4:8, Luke 12:36 and Revelation 21:2-10.

The Body of Christ is the congregation. It gathered in an ecclesia, not a church, for the word "church" is not in the Holy Bible. (Acts 3:21-26, Ephesians 5:29-30, Ephesians 11:22-23, Colossians 1:18, and Ephesians 1:22-23).

Keep in mind that NO one was called a Jew until 2nd Kings 16:6. It was Solomon and his half-breed son Rehoboam whose mother was an Ammonite (See 1st Kings 14:21). They mixed races and religions and worshiped the heathen Sidonian religions. Rehoboam overtaxed the people, ruled as a dictator, and they created the bad fig Jews mentioned in Jeremiah 24. Deuteronomy 23:1-6 and Deuteronomy 7 demand the separation of these people (Nehemiah 13, Ezra 9:10, Ezekiel 15 & 16, Romans 1:1). Paul said they had reprobate minds.

-N. S., Topeka, KS

ANSWER: Neither Joseph nor Ephraim were chosen:

"*Moreover he refused the tabernacle of Joseph, and chose not the tribe of Ephraim: But chose the tribe of Judah, the mount Zion which he loved*" (Psalm 78:67-68). Who are the Jews? They are the descendants of the twelve tribes of Israel. Judah, Benjamin and Levi are listed on the commandment King Cyrus of Persia gave for the rebuilding of the temple in Jerusalem (Ezra 1:5). Later in Ezra 4:3, "*...the rest of the chief of the fathers of Israel...*" are mentioned. Where did they come from? Read 2nd Chronicles 11:16, 15:9, and 34:9. Thus the remnant of the so-called ten lost tribes of Israel is found in the tribe of Judah. No wonder the apostle Peter addressed the Jews in Jerusalem by saying, "*Ye men of Israel...*" (Acts 2:22); "*...let all the house of Israel know assuredly...*" (verse 36); "*...Ye men of Israel...*" (Acts 3:12); "*Be it known unto you all, and to all the people of Israel...*" (Acts 4:10).

ARE ALL JEWS GOD'S CHOSEN PEOPLE?

Dear Mr. Froese:

I must begin by commending you for looking at today's world affairs through the eyes of God's divinely inspired book, the Bible. You stand among the very few who do. It is for this reason that I eagerly await the arrival of your magazine each month.

Perhaps you can take the time to answer a couple of questions that are weighing on my mind.

To begin with, I have good Christian friends who say the Bible says we are to support all Jews no matter what because they are God's chosen people. I am aware that the

Bible does tell us to do this, but I am also aware that immediately after the Israelites possessed the Promised Land of Canaan, He instructed them to kill all the inhabitants because these people were so sinful that he did not want the Jews living among them.

Because of this, I have classified the Jews into at least two categories:

First, [I see] the Zionist Jews, into which I place the Mossad, as the [Israel's Secret intelligence agency] most brutal terrorist organization in existence today. This group, according to what I have read, is so preoccupied with putting the Jew on top of the world's political "heap" by any means necessary that the true concept of godly religion is the furthest thing from their minds. In fact, they feel justified in slaughtering women and children and, in some cases, their own people and making it look like it is the work of the Arabs to achieve this goal. I find it hard to believe that God would have us protect them.

Second, I see the fundamental Jews, who are God-fearing and doing their best to abide by God's Law and Old Testament Jewish tradition. They are still patiently awaiting the appearance of the Messiah because they do not believe that Jesus was the one.

I value your opinion very highly and would like to know your thoughts on this.

Next question: Isn't the Golan Heights area that the Israelites just gave back to the Arabs [actually, at this writing, no return of the Golan Heights has been made-Ed.] part of the original land of Canaan that God promised to the Jews and that they finally occupied and conquered for their own? If so, what events do you perceive will take place now that they have given it up?

I anxiously await your reply.

-A. E., Bellingham, WA

ANSWER: In all of my contacts with Zionist Jews, I have never heard or perceived in any way, shape, or form the atrocities you describe that were allegedly committed by the Mossad.

It seems unbelievable to me because Israel is the only democracy in the Mideast. Any human rights violations are quickly noticed by the press and various groups whose task it is to investigate brutality.

I do realize that Israel's Jews could be classified as "godless," especially when viewed from the scriptural fact that, *"As concerning the gospel, they are enemies for your sakes: but as touching the election, they are beloved for the fathers' sakes"* (Romans 11:28).

The Golan Heights and other parts of the Promised Land will be given to Arabs because the whole world, particularly the U.S.A., is pressuring Israel to do so.

Nevertheless, these treaties are not the final authority because God has given the land from the river of Egypt to the Euphrates River to the Jews and He will see to it that one day they will take possession of it in His own time.

PEACE FOR ISRAEL: WHEN?

Dear Brother Froese,

I am an ardent student of prophecy and agree with

49

your views.

There is one technical point that you or Bro. Lieth never address: When will Israel ever live in peace and safety? In the December '96 magazine, you say in the first 1/2 of Daniel's 70th week. I have no problem with that and I'm sure it's true. But if that's true, then this will spill over into the millennium. Right?

Please help me understand this.

-T. I., Bryant, AR

ANSWER: The first 3 1/2 years of the Great Tribulation will bring about unprecedented peace, prosperity and success. All the world, including Israel, will have facts and figures to support the claim, "peace, peace." But real peace can never come into existence until the Prince of Peace comes. On one hand, His appearance will mark the end of the Great Tribulation, and will usher in salvation and peace for Israel. On the other hand, it will also mark the beginning of the judgment of the nations.

ISRAEL A SECULAR NATION?

Dear Mr. Froese,

In the department - "This Week in Bible Prophecy" - of the *Midnight Call* magazine of November 1996, Mr. and Mrs. Lalonde reviewed some news articles from *The Jerusalem Report* (July 11, 1996). They mentioned that secularism in Israel is growing: "The recent influx of over 600,000 Russian immigrants, (the most secularized immigrants in the nation's history) has substantially strengthened the large, influential minority that feels little or no sentimental attachment to religion." Some of my acquaintances are supporting, both morally and financially, the immigration movement of Russian Jews to Israel. When these people were confronted with that report of the Lalonde's, their reaction was that it does not make any difference whether those Russian Jews are Christians or not, for with Christ's return to Jerusalem and the resurrection of the dead at that same time, all Jews, born again or not, *"will look on me, the one they have pierced, and they will mourn for Him as one mourns for an only child"* (Zechariah 12:10 NIV). *"On that day a fountain will be opened on the house of David and the inhabitants of Jerusalem, to cleanse them from sin and impurity"* (Zechariah 13:1 NIV); *"And so all Israel will be saved"* (Romans 11:26 NIV).

This sounds like a strange doctrine to me, for if that is so, then it has never been necessary for the Church to preach the Gospel to the Jews or to evangelize Israel. Therefore, I have some questions:

Is it true that repentance and rebirth can also take place after the resurrection of the dead and after the return of Christ? Is this only so for Jewish people, not Gentiles? Are only Jews resurrected and living in Jerusalem at the time of Jesus' return "saved?" What about those still living in Russia, or in New York, or elsewhere in the world?

I am looking forward to your reply.

-No name given

ANSWER: Israel is an overwhelmingly secular nation and

the founding fathers were not motivated by religion either. Theodore Herzl, the accredited father of modern Zionism, envisioned a secular Jewish state, primarily for the sake of security and the continued identity of the Jewish people. When reading Ezekiel 36, we notice that the Jews will come back in unbelief. Your quoted passages in Zechariah 12:10 and 13:1 could not be fulfilled if the Jews of Israel are already believers.

Of course, there will be salvation after the Rapture, (compare Revelation 7:9) but these people do not belong to the Church. Also, during that time, the Comforter will no longer be present on earth and these people will have to lay down their lives for Jesus without the comfort of knowing that He could come back at any moment.

According to Scripture, it is my understanding that all Jews will be in Israel. Ezekiel 39:28 says, *"...but I have gathered them unto their own land, and have left none of them any more there."*

ZIONIST CONTROVERSY

Mr. Arno Froese:

In your May 1999 issue of *Midnight Call*, page 5, "The Resurrection Of Israel," I was shocked by your comparison of our Lord and Savior Jesus Christ's resurrection to that of the resurrection of Israel. Christ's life was a life of love and humility even toward those who persecuted Him. The resurrection of Israel is no miracle at all and is based on hate, warfare, lies, murder and deceit of all kinds. In view of the fact that the German and U.S.

taxpayers have been sacked for hundreds of billions of dollars over the past 50 years or so, it becomes obvious who has financed the great miracle of a productive Israel that you proclaim. This productive land was also taken from the Palestinian people by force with the U.S. blessing. It seems ironic that today we are involved in a war against Serbia for doing the same thing Israel has done and continues to do with our blessing and financial help. The terrorism started in the 40's when the Zionists murdered and terrorized the Palestinian people and thousands had to flee for their lives.

The only miracle I see is how the AIPAC can coordinate approximately 120 Israel lobbies here in the U.S., terrorize our gutless politicians into giving them what they want, and get away with it. It only takes a fraction of the approximately $5 billion gift from the U.S. to buy the elections here in the U.S. All a politician has to do is be labeled "Anti-Semitic" and he is history.

When God promised the Hebrew people the Promised Land, was the promise conditional? Who are the descendants of Abraham? Could it be that most occupants of Palestine are not even true descendants of Abraham?

One more point I would like to make. If you go to Israel, be careful what you say. I understand it is a criminal offense to preach Christianity there. Please correct me if I am wrong.

-R.L., Maineville, OH

ANSWER: In Genesis 15:18 we read that *"...the LORD made a covenant with Abram, saying, Unto thy seed have I* *given this land, from the river of Egypt unto the great river, the river Euphrates.*" To Abraham's son God confirms, "*...I will give all these countries, and I will perform the oath which I sware unto Abraham thy father*" (Genesis 26:3). To Jacob, God said, "*...the land whereon thou liest, to thee will I give it, and to thy seed*" (Genesis 28:13). Notice that it is the Giver who makes the covenant and the promises and He will keep them independent of the receiver. Just before Jacob died, he made this prophecy about Judah, "*...unto him shall the gathering of the people be*" (Genesis 49:10). Judah is the origin of the Jews; thus, all twelve tribes became Jews. The apostle Peter addressed the Jews in Jerusalem with the words, "*ye men of Israel,*" "*let all the house of Israel know assuredly,*" "*to all the people of Israel*" (Acts 2:22,36;4:10). Israel's miracle is described in Ezekiel 34:13, "*...I will bring them out from the people, and gather them from the countries, and will bring them to their own land....*" God even speaks about the topographical land when He says, "*...yield your fruit to my people of Israel; for they are at hand to come*" (Ezekiel 36:8). That has been happening since 1948 and continues until today. What a miracle!

I admit that the Zionists make a great mistake in practicing excessive generosity toward Arab intruders. Americans acted differently; they simply killed the Indians or put them on reservations (concentration camps). Every neighbor of Israel is guilty of occupying Israeli territory: Egypt, Jordan, Syria and Lebanon. Arab settlers live freely in Israel, and the countries you mentioned occupy Israeli territory until now. But just as sure as the Lord brought the Jews back to their land, He will also restore their borders and disperse all foreigners.

Incidentally, you have your figures wrong. America has received an estimated $385 billion of technical know-how from Israel and quite frankly, I don't think the U.S. will ever be able to repay.

Finally, it is illegal to convert anyone to another religion in Israel. That, too, was prophesied, *"As concerning the gospel, they* (Jews) *are enemies for your sakes: but as touching the election, they are beloved for the father's sakes"* (Romans 11:28).

C H A P T E R 4

AUTHORITY OF SCRIPTURE

KEEP TEN COMMANDMENTS?

Dear Mr. Froese,

Even though keeping the Ten Commandments will not save us, when we are saved we should keep them all. So what about the fourth commandment? Even though we who love Jesus always try our best to keep the commandments, we seem to ignore the one about the seventh-day Sabbath. For the last few months this has been disturbing to me. I don't rest on Saturday or keep it any holier than any other day of the week. I worship God on a daily basis and attend church on Sunday.

Last week I heard a man on God's Learning Channel in Midland quote the Bible about the importance of keeping the Sabbath. I don't want to be among those to whom Jesus says *"depart from me...I never knew you."* Not keeping His law seems disobedient. Does that make us a doer of lawlessness? I know we are saved through grace, not the Law, but God does want obedience from His children. I hope you can help me understand this part of His Word. I pray I have made this letter understandable.

-R.R., Abilene, TX

ANSWER: God gave the Ten Commandments to Israel. The Sabbath day in particular was designated as *"...a sign between me and the children of Israel for ever..."* (Exodus 31:17). (Incidentally, governments all over the world are founded upon the principles set forth in the Ten Commandments. Not even the communists reward killing, stealing, dishonoring parents, or coveting other people's property.) In relation to your question, Jesus said, *"Thou shalt love the Lord thy God...Thou shalt love thy neighbour as thyself"* and He concluded, *"On these two commandments hang all the law and the prophets."* As believers in Jesus, salvation is not attained by our trying to keep the Law, but is based only on His accomplished work: we are saved by grace!

KEEP THE LAW

Dear Brother Froese,

Thank you for the *Midnight Call* magazine. I enjoy it very much. I felt that an answer had to be given about the Commandments question. I am a Messianic Gentile who belongs to a Messianic Congregation that consists of believing Jews and Gentiles in Yeshua (Jesus) the Messiah. There is a difference between the Sabbath, the seventh day of the week, and keeping of a day of rest on Sunday. Here's how to explain it.

Yeshua (Jesus), God the Son, gave all the commandments, including the Ten Commandments, to Moses; likewise, He gave the commandment of the day of rest, the Sabbath, to the Jews, as a day of rest and remembrance along with the rest of the commandments.

Yeshua (Jesus), as a Jewish man, kept all the commandments that He had given to Moses on Sinai, setting the best example of one who keeps the commandments and the Sabbath.

So shouldn't we who are believers in Yeshua (Jesus), who love and serve Him and are called Christians, do what He did? Yeshua (Jesus) didn't change the Sabbath. God doesn't renege on His Word. Yeshua's disciples observed the Sabbath and didn't change it. The apostle Paul kept the Sabbath and didn't change it.

-L. N., Hot Springs, MO

ANSWER: The word "Messianic" usually describes a Jew who believes in Jesus, so what are the words, "Messianic Gentile" supposed to mean?

Why do you write "Yeshua" in Roman letters? Is that supposed to be better? Is there something wrong with "Jesus?"

You asked, "Shouldn't we do what He (Jesus) did?" My answer is "No" because He did it for us and He–not you or I–fulfilled the Law. His Word says, *"But after that faith is come, we are no longer under a schoolmaster* [law]." So much for the Law!

TEN COMMANDMENTS TO END?

Dear Brother Arno:

I agree with you that we are justified by faith. Justification by faith alone *(sola fide)* [is] staunchly decreed by Scripture.

As for the Sabbath, the other side of the coin is, Jesus said in John 14:15, *"...keep my commandments"* and he recited enough of them in New Testament Scripture to know that He was referring to the Ten Commandments. Additionally, in Matthew 5:17, He said, *"Think not that I am come to destroy the law, or the prophets: I am not come to destroy, but to fulfill."* Any number of pastors I have questioned about the Ten Commandments all contend that they are as valid today as they were when God gave them to Moses on tablets of stone. He did not say to ignore the fourth commandment, so it is valid also. Just because Rome says the first day of the week is the Sabbath doesn't make it so.

-Name withheld

ANSWER: Galatians 3:24 says, *"...the law was our schoolmaster to bring us unto Christ, that we might be justified by faith."* Verse 25 continues, *"But after that faith is come, we are no longer under a schoolmaster."*

It is interesting that if the tenth commandment were kept, *("Thou shalt not covet...")* the foundation of democracy and free enterprise, which is based on greed, would be destroyed.

Please don't say something that is not true; the Bible, not Rome, tells us that the disciples came together on the first day!

SABBATH OR SUNDAY?

Dear Arno Froese,

Upon study of Revelation, the verse *"Blessed are they that do His commandments..."* (Revelation 22:14 and Revelation 14:12) keeps troubling me. Also, Jesus said, *"If ye love me, keep my commandments"* (John 14:15).

In the latter chapters of the Bible, He is still saying *"Keep my commandments,"* so they can't be of no importance to Him.

Sure, we're saved by grace, not by keeping the Ten Commandments. I know the Mosaic law was done away with, but apparently the Ten Commandments carry as much weight as they originally did.

I've always been a Church of God follower and a Pentecostal. I believe as you do as far as our Lord's near return.

But the Lord is saying, "Remember especially the fourth commandment!" It makes me seriously wonder if we are all worshipping on the correct day.

Saturday worship was changed by the Catholic Church, which it openly admits. Shouldn't we be holding to that day instead of Sunday?

Nowhere does the Bible say we are to keep the day on which the Lord rose.

Why are all of the churches and believers following Sunday, with the Seventh Day Adventists and Seventh Day Baptists being the only exceptions outside of the Jewish faith?

I need your input on this and I pray you will answer this because it is a very important part of my walk with the Lord. I wish to eliminate as many traditions of men from my life and fill them only with the desires of Jesus regarding all things.

Please give me scriptural references concerning the Sabbath issue. You've answered me a previous time and the advice and wisdom you shared wasn't wasted or disregarded.

Praise God, the Holy Spirit helped me to lead my neighbor to Jesus. Join with me in this rejoicing.

-E.I., Lake City, FL

ANSWER: Please read Matthew chapter 5 carefully and notice the words, *"but I say unto you."* His New Covenant law is the real thing. Jesus is the fulfillment of all commandments.

As far as a particular day of worship is concerned, Romans 14:5 states, *"One man esteemeth one day above another: another esteemeth every day alike. Let every man be fully persuaded in his own mind."* Colossians 2:16 adds, *"Let no man therefore judge you in meat, or in drink, or in respect of an holyday, or of the new moon, or of the sabbath days."*

THIS GENERATION

Dear Mr. Froese,

I am struggling with the series of articles written by Mr. Ice regarding Bible prophecy already being fulfilled. Not being a scholar of the Bible, I do not profess any expertise. However, I do know a stumbling block when I see one.

Matthew 16:28 and Matthew 24:34 certainly do give cause
for any layman to stop and look again. In Matthew 24:34,
Jesus is teaching His disciples what signs to look for at the
end of the world (age) in response to their question. The
text of the Bible seems clear to most laymen that Jesus was
talking to His disciples, and not to some future generation, as Mr. Ice supposes. Had these words been written by
men under the influence of the Holy Spirit, then I can
only surmise that they have been poorly translated
through the ages. To follow the reasoning of Mr. Ice, the
text should read, *"that generation shall not pass, till all
these* (or those) *things be fulfilled."* The word "this" always
refers to the person, thing or idea that is present or near
in place, time or thought, or that has just been mentioned.
Any child in grammar school can tell the difference
between "this" and "that." We (the Church) are constantly
advised by our teachers to trust in the plain words of the
Bible and not to read into them unless we are so advised
by the Bible.

In your response to Mr. E.S. you stated, "If 'brother'
doesn't mean 'brother' and 'sister' doesn't mean 'sister,' is
'son of Mary' also invalid? Let's stick to the word of God.
The Bible is not confusing. Man-made doctrines are." I
contend that the interpretation of Matthew 24:34 by Mr.
Ice is "man-made" and contrary to the plain usage of the
word "this." Clearly "this generation" refers to the generation which was present at the time.

One further question please, Mr. Froese. In your
response to Mr. H.T., you agreed with him that the
Antichrist must be a Jew. How then do you reconcile

Daniel 9:26, which clearly identifies the Antichrist as a descendant of the people who destroyed the city and the sanctuary? Israel (Palestine) was never a member of the Roman Empire. It was a conquered region that was forced to pay tribute to Rome and its people were never automatically granted Roman citizenship. Even more specifically, *"the people...shall destroy the city and the sanctuary"* may refer to Titus or a member of his armed forces.

I hope I can look forward to your response.

-E.D., Port Charlotte, FL

ANSWER: Part of the Lord's sayings have been fulfilled, including the destruction of the temple. However, the abomination of desolation has not yet taken place. Old Testament prophecies speak of the physical coming of the Lord to the Mount of Olives, the signal of the end of the Great Tribulation. This has not taken place yet either. I do not see any significant difference between "this" or "that" generation. [This passage] is referring to the generation that sees the fulfillment of those signs.

Whether the Antichrist is Jew or Gentile is open to interpretation. I have concluded that he must be Jewish, probably a Roman Jew; otherwise, the Jews would not receive him.

Israel certainly did belong to the Roman Empire. The Romans installed a king and the religious authorities argued amongst themselves, *"If we let him* [Jesus] *thus alone, all men will believe on him: and the Romans shall come and take away both our place and nation"* (John 11:48). The apostle Paul was born in Tarsus and testified to his Roman citizenship when he said, *"...but I was free born"* (Acts 22:28). That is automatic citizenship.

WILL CHRIST TAKE BACK THE EARTH?

Dear Friend and Brother Froese,

Your messages in the magazine have further focused and blessed me, being very helpful to clear things up, rightly dividing problems that have bothered and side-tracked me.

Now I sense more than ever when something is not quite right with churches or writings that stray from the truth, subtly deceiving the churched and unchurched.

One thing I recently saw does not seem right. This is the idea of "men building the kingdom of God." Words are important, and even though this idea sounds fine and noble, I have read in David Breese's works that Christ the King will be the one to take back, not "build", His earth and re-establish His Kingdom in which all men will bow their knee.

This is still not completely clear. Please further clarify this issue for me, noting the Scripture verses if possible.

Praying for you all and loving you in the name of Jesus Christ.

-A.O., Elbridge, NY

ANSWER: Dave Breese is correct: Christ will "take back His earth." He created all and He owns all. But we must note that the Bible says that *"...he who sins is of the devil."* Because the world sins, Satan legally owns this world.

When will Jesus "take back the earth"? *"...When he shall have put down all rule and all authority and power"* (1st Corinthians 15:24). However, the Church that incorporates the "kingdom within" is in the process of being built. Jesus said, *"I will build my church."*

TEMPLE DESTROYED TWICE?

Dear Mr. Arno Froese,

In reference to the article in the March 1996 edition of *Midnight Call* entitled, "The Future Temple," you stated that the temple has been destroyed two times, and the next temple will have animal sacrifices.

There are many Christians who do not fully understand this teaching. According to history, the temple has been desecrated several times and burned. However, [it has been] destroyed only once. Please correct me if I'm wrong.

The temple was desecrated and burned in 586 B.C. by the Babylonian king. Then in 538 B.C., Cyrus the Great ordered those who were captured to return to Jerusalem and rebuild the temple. In 325 B.C., the temple was desecrated by the Greeks, perhaps Alexander the Great. Then in 175 B.C., the Syrians captured Jerusalem and once again desecrated the temple. The Macabees Revolt of 167/145 B.C. made it possible for the temple to be re-dedicated on December 25th 167/145 B.C.. This date has been celebrated ever since as either, "The Feast of Dedication," "Chanukah," or "Christmas." Then, in 70 A.D., the temple was destroyed in such a way that there weren't two stones left standing from the temple.

-E.N., Vacaville, CA

ANSWER: In Ezra 3:11, we read, *"...the foundation of the house of the LORD was laid."* Foundation stones must be laid before anything else can be built. The first temple must have been destroyed to such an extent that it had to be rebuilt from the ground up. Jesus' prophecy came true when the temple was destroyed for the second time in A.D. 70, when not one single stone was found upon another.

ENDTIME EVENTS

Dear Sir:

I would very much like for you to answer a question for me and some of our church members.

We know that the Rapture is the next thing to happen, and that believers will be judged and rewarded. This will be the seven-year tribulation period on earth. Then the Second Coming of Christ to earth with His saints will take place, followed by the 1000-year reign.

Where will the Christians be? Will they be on the earth during the Millennium? What will the people be doing during the Millennium? Also, where will the wicked be at this time?

Please explain this to me. We would sure appreciate some light on this.

I enjoy your magazines on prophecy. May the Lord continue to bless you. I believe Jesus is coming soon.

-C.U., Littleton, NC

ANSWER: First Thessalonians 4:17 says, "*...and so shall we ever be with the Lord.*" That is our eternal position; wherever the Lord is, that is where we will be. When He rules from Jerusalem, we shall rule with Him. Keep in mind that the Millennium begins after the Great Tribulation, during which most of the world's population will be destroyed. The remnant will enter the Millennium. Sin will not be tolerated, but sinners will be punished instantly.

What will the people be doing? I assume they'll be carrying out the same types of activities as today; going to work, earning money, building homes, having families. Micah 4:3 amplifies this fact, "*...they shall beat their swords into plowshares, and their spears into pruninghooks....*" An industry is needed to accomplish the transformation from military into agricultural machinery.

Only after the 1,000 years have expired will the final judgment of the wicked take place. There will be no more grace at the Great White Throne, nor will the Lamb or the blood be present. The Great White Throne is the light which will unmercifully expose the darkness. Those who have rejected Christ will be "*...judged every man according to their works.*"

HOLY SPIRIT REMOVED?

Dear Bro. Arno,

My best friend insists that there will be no pre-trib Rapture. He cites the martyred saints in Revelation 6 (under the altar) as being Christians martyred during the tribulation. He also says that if the indwelling Holy Spirit in the believers is what is holding back the arrival of the Antichrist, then how can anyone be saved once He leaves the earth? Please clarify these issues for me. I am waiting for the blessed hope and don't think I'll have to face the Antichrist.

-I.C., Russell Springs, KY

ANSWER: The martyred saints in Revelation 6 do not belong to the Church. Revelation 7:15 describes their position to *"...serve him* (God) *day and night in his temple...."* The Church is located in the place where there is no temple (Revelation 21:22).

The Holy Spirit convicts the world of sin. We receive the Holy Spirit, or Comforter, upon repentance. The Comforter will be gone after the Rapture. However, the Holy Spirit is God, who is omnipresent, and the Spirit will continue to convict millions of their sins. At that time there will be no comfort because the Rapture will have already taken place.

EASE MY MIND

Dear Brother Froese,

Thanks for all the good literature I receive from you. I learn things I would never know.

Brother Froese, I am attending a Bible study on the endtimes, but I am so confused. Please answer these questions for me and give me the appropriate Scripture references. I do not want them for arguments, but to ease my mind.

1) The teacher said the Antichrist will be a homosexual. Is this true?

2) [The teacher also said that Antichrist] will not be a full-blooded Jew; that he may be part Jew, part Gentile. Is this true?

3) When will the Marriage Supper take place? During the seven-year tribulation or at the end of the Millennium?

4) Who are the ones Satan will tempt for a short season during the end of the Millennium? Won't we be free from that? Will we have a glorified body like Jesus?

Thank you.

-Mrs. M. C., Calhoun, GA

ANSWER: Daniel 11:37 reads, *"...nor the desire of women...."* This statement apparently led your teacher to believe that the Antichrist will be a homosexual.

Deuteronomy 18:15 says that the great prophet will come from *"thy brethren,"* which is confirmed by Acts 7:37, *"...A prophet shall the Lord your God raise up unto you of your brethren, like unto me...."* The Jews will not accept a Messiah who is not Jewish.

After the Rapture we will stand before the Judgment Seat of Christ (2nd Corinthians 5:10), followed by the Marriage Supper of the Lamb. Our unity with the Lord is pictured as a marriage. First Thessalonians 4:17 says, *"...and so shall we ever be with the Lord."* The bride cannot be in the presence of the bridegroom without being "married;" in other words, you can't postpone the wedding!

The "nations" that will be deceived after the Millennium are the host of fallen angels, not actual human nations. I deal with that subject at length in my book, *How Democracy Will Elect the Antichrist.*

ENOCH AND ELIJAH

Dear Mr. Froese,

I have a doctrinal question about two Old Testament characters: Enoch and Elijah.

The Bible teaches that after Adam's fall in the Garden of Eden, the bridge between God and mankind was separated because of sin. Heaven's gates were closed until the perfect blood sacrifice of Jesus Christ on the cross made us right with our Holy Father.

The Bible says in Genesis 5:24, *"And Enoch walked with God: and he was not: for God took him."*

In 2nd Kings 2:1, the Bible says, *"And it came to pass, when the LORD would take up Elijah into heaven by a whirlwind, that Elijah went with Elisha from Gilgal."*

My question deals with Enoch and Elijah's destination of rest. Did they go to the place referred to in Luke 16:19-31 as Abraham's bosom, or did they go to Abraham's bosom and then were taken into heaven after Jesus' resurrection? If I am wrong, could you please guide me through Scripture to teach this correctly?

-A.N., Cincinnati, OH

ANSWER: Because flesh and blood cannot inherit the kingdom of God, Enoch and Elijah must have experienced this transformation before their Rapture. Since Enoch and Elijah did not experience physical death and

71

are already in their glorified bodies, I must conclude that they are not in "Abraham's bosom" but are in the direct presence of the Lord.

TRIBULATION IN TWO PARTS?

Dear Brother Froese,

Just recently I finished your book, *How Democracy Will Elect the Antichrist.* A job well done and recommendable for every student of eschatology.

I agree with you in seeing a striking similarity between "The Fuhrer" and the coming Antichrist. Hitler was elected by the people through a democratic process, as will a corrupt, demonized, anti-God society voluntarily march under the Antichrist's agenda. When listening to Hitler's speeches, you can almost hear and sense whose control he was under.

However, I have a few questions in regard to your above-mentioned book. On pages 83 and 262, you write: "The first 3 1/2 years (under the Antichrist) will be a time of jubilation. There will be peace and prosperity." I wonder if this will be the case rather than a stormy time occurring right from the beginning of the seven-year period of [the Antichrist's] reign. It is true, according to Revelation 6:2 (the first seal) that he will come under the banner of peace and prosperity, but how will he subdue three kings out of the federation of ten (Daniel 7:24)?

Furthermore, all of the following seal judgments fall under the first 3 1/2 years when billions of people will be killed (Revelation 6:8). In addition, the two witnesses also will be giving him a hard time (Revelation 11:6). Surely this will not be a time of absolute glorious jubilation.

On page 272, you identify the nations of Gog and Magog (Revelation 20:8) as masses of fallen angels who will have originally taken sides with Satan and not literal nations of human beings. I don't know. You are right in saying, "Since we know in part only, we cannot fully recognize the events of the future." Sometimes it is wise not to publish everything we believe in. When war breaks out in heaven and Satan and his angels are thrown down to the earth, nothing is ever mentioned about these fallen angels in the book of Revelation. However, Matthew 25:41 states that a place of eternal fire is prepared for the devil and his angels.

-N.A., CANADA

ANSWER: I see no statement in Revelation 6 indicating that these catastrophes will occur during the first 3 1/2 years of the Great Tribulation. If the Antichrist employs force and destruction, then he will not need deception. Revelation 13:4 indicates that there is no force, *"...and they worshipped the beast, saying, Who is like unto the beast? who is able to make war with him?"* Because of the acceptance of deception, we read in 2nd Thessalonians 2:11, *"And for this cause God shall send them strong delusion, that they should believe a lie."*

How will the two witnesses *"torment them that dwell on the earth?"* Besides having the power to stop the rain and turn water into blood, their prophecy will probably be the greatest torment, and that is preaching the truth. They will tell the world that they are being deceived. They will preach that salvation can only be obtained through the shed blood of Christ. Their death will cause jubilation and rejoicing among the nations.

During the Millennium, sinners will be eliminated and the earth will be filled with the knowledge of the Lord. Additionally, man shall learn war no more. Furthermore, these *"nations"* come *"up on the breadth of the earth,"* which indicates that they are coming from below. When they are finally destroyed, there is no mention of any remnant such as bodies or weapons of war, which is usually the case with all other wars mentioned in the Bible.

TEMPLE RESTORATION

Dear Mr. Froese,

I've enjoyed the *Midnight Call* very much for many years and I feel you have great insight and discernment in spiritual matters.

My question concerns the restoration of the new temple in Ezekiel chapter 40. According to Ezekiel 43:18, the future temple altar is to be for the purpose of burnt offerings and the sprinkling of blood upon it. Why would sacrificing animals be repeated in the future since Christ died once and for all? Also, at Christ's Second Coming, Israel will look upon Him as the one they pierced (Zechariah 12:10). Revelation 21:22 states no temple will be found in the city.

Ezekiel 44:3 and 46 contain many references about the

prince. Ezekiel 46:16 states the prince may give land to his sons or servants. Is this prince Christ, and if so, who are the sons?

Lastly, Ezekiel 48:16 describes the future city as being 1 1/2 miles square and verse 35 gives the circumference of the city as 6 miles. Revelation 21:16 describes the new city as 1,500 miles each way.

Are these two different times, events and cities? Please explain. I'm confused. Thank you and God bless.

-A.N., Yukon, OK

ANSWER: Ezekiel's list of measurements for the temple do not correspond with Solomon's temple, so we can assume that he is speaking about the Millennial temple.

Until this day, we follow the Lord's instruction, "...*This is my body which is given for you: this do in remembrance of me*" (Luke 22:19). That constitutes a memorial service on earth, while in heaven He lives forevermore. Both the Millennial temple and the sacrifices serve as a memorial to what transpired in the past.

Revelation 21:22 reveals the new Jerusalem, a different identity from the temple in Jerusalem. The Jews will experience salvation in Jerusalem, while the Church dwells in the heavenly Jerusalem.

The "prince" mentioned in Ezekiel 44 and 46 cannot be the Lord Jesus Christ because He completed His work on Calvary's cross when He exclaimed, *"It is finished!"*

Dr. J. Vernon McGee speculates that this prince could be David.

FUTURE DATES

Dear Editor,

THE SECOND COMING OF CHRIST

These are the possible dates and order of biblical events:

May 31, 1998
Removal from earth of all spiritually born Christians (the Rapture).

May 28, 2001
A. Beginning 7 years of the biblical tribulation period (you don't want to be here).

B. Animal sacrifice is reinstituted in the new temple in Jerusalem.

September 13, 2007
A. Removal of all tribulation Christians from throughout the world, including newly-born Jewish Christians (Rapture II).

B. Judgment day for God's children.

C. The end of the "shortened" tribulation, for the sake of the tribulation Christians.

D. There are exactly 7 more months until the Second Coming of Jesus Christ. During this time, Israel cleanses the land of the dead from wars.

E. The nations of the east and north reorganize to destroy Israel.

F. Coronation of Jesus Christ.

April 6, 2008
A. Jesus Christ will return this day as Lord of lords and King of kings.

B. Battle of Armageddon begins and ends.

May 20, 2008

The new Millennium of peace begins with Jesus Christ as King and ruler of the world.

We must make a solemn agreement with God the Father by sacrifice. His only acceptable sacrifice for our sins is His Son, Jesus Christ. We receive Him as our personal Savior by accepting the blood sacrifice of Jesus Christ's death on the cross for our sin. The proof of our being accepted by Jesus Christ is our being spiritually born into God's family. Only then can God show Himself to us.

-R.E., Victorville, CA

ANSWER: To "...make a solemn agreement with God the Father by sacrifice" was already done when God, in Christ, reconciled the world to Himself. You cannot add anything to it! Salvation is a finished fact. Judging by the way you word your letter, you are making the Lord's return dependent upon your actions.

THE LAST GENERATION

Dear Mr. Froese,

When Jesus mentioned the fig tree and summer being near, He spoke of a generation that would not pass until certain things were done. It was at this mention that He cautioned an alert for a watch because the day and hour are unknown (Mark 13:28-37). Mark records that His discourse about the tribulation was preceded by the importance of not setting a day or hour.

We do not need to know many things – including the day and the hour of Christ's return – in order to be on the alert for His arrival. However, we can see that the generation and the fig tree indicate that His coming is not too far in the distance.

A teacher in the Methodist church cautioned me not to pay attention to those who suggest that "Christ will return in this generation." I had not said anything to her so I just thought: "Oh well...." I heard another one say, "Israel may leave again and it may be thousands of years yet." I think the teacher, being 88 or 89, just wanted me to comment.

I really feel that to say "He will not" is date-setting, although I made no comment. I don't think that I am so ignorant that I can't see the day nearing. If it is not nearing, He would not have said *"...when you see...."*

Whether He has chosen the fall [season] or a feast day, I do not know, but I'll watch on those days also because I can see Sodom and peril all around me and it vexes me, and I cry, "Lord have mercy on this generation."

-N.L., Bixby, OK

ANSWER: I wholeheartedly agree with your statement regarding the imminence of the Lord's coming, regardless of how we interpret "this generation." The apostle Paul clearly admonished us, *"So that ye come behind in no gift; waiting for the coming of our Lord Jesus Christ"* (1st Corinthians 1:7). Also read Philippians 3:20; 1st Thessalonians 1:9-10; Titus 2:13; Hebrews 9:28; and Luke 12:36 (just to mention a few).

If the Church was admonished to wait for the Lord almost 2,000 years ago, then how much more expectantly should we be waiting today? A description of those who do not wait is provided in 2nd Peter 3:3-4.

TWO WITNESSES

Dear Mr. Froese,

I just received my October *News From Israel*. I always enjoy reading this one and my *Midnight Call*, and then sharing them with my loved ones.

I certainly am no authority on the subject of the two witnesses who will come in these last days, but I don't think they are Moses and Elijah, because Moses died and God buried him.

Elijah went up in a whirlwind and Enoch was translated. These two, I believe, will be the two witnesses because they didn't die, and they will have to die as humans. It will be so sad that they will return to earth to die after they have been with God, but after three days they, of course, like Jesus, will come back to life to return to heaven.

We know that false peace is approaching, and at some point, Jesus will appear and send His angels to gather His elect (His Church).

The signs are all around us now and while we cannot know THE time, we are in the signs of the time today.

It would be really scary if one didn't have Jesus, but He said He would protect his own. This is my own belief and has been for many years.

I believe the twelve tribes of Israel will be restored to their own land, which is a vast territory. I would like to get your opinion on my thoughts.

-I.L., Stockton Springs, ME

ANSWER: There are two reasons I believe that the two witnesses are Moses and Elijah:

1) Moses turned water into blood and Elijah shut the heavens so that it wouldn't rain.

2) Jesus said, *"...it cannot be that a prophet perish out of Jerusalem"* (Luke 13:33).

Moses' life was taken by God and he died on the other side of the Jordan River. Elijah didn't die, but was raptured into heaven, not from Israel but from the other side of the Jordan.

Both of Israel's great prophets will have to die in Jerusalem.

DIE TWICE?

Dear Mr. Froese,

I have questioned the response you gave for some time and it has come up again.

You believe (and so do I) that Moses is one of the two witnesses spoken of in Revelation. It makes a lot of sense but the part I can't understand is this: The Scripture says, *"...as it is appointed unto men once to die but after this the judgment"* (Hebrews 9:27), so regardless of where Moses died, he still died. If all Scripture is truth, how do we explain to others, assuming that we are correct, that

Moses is indeed one of the witnesses? There is another man, Enoch, who did not die, and who therefore might be that witness.

I am eagerly awaiting your reply, as so many of us take your views seriously.

-E.R., Niobrara, NE

ANSWER: Since the two witnesses are not named, their identity is open for speculation. The phrase *"once to die"* does not mean they can't die twice. Eight people recorded in the Bible were resurrected, so they obviously had to die twice.

TRIBULATION SAINTS

Midnight Call Ministries,

I enjoy your ministry: Thank you. Please have someone respond to this question when they can.

What is the status of the tribulation saints (those who become believers after the Rapture and don't die during the Great Tribulation)? When will they become glorified?

When will they become eternal beings (as those believers both before and during the tribulation)? What will be their status during the Millennium?

In all my years of study, I haven't read anything that specifically deals with this issue. Please help if you can.

-N.G., Wabash, IN

ANSWER: The martyrs of Jesus who have not received their glorified bodies but who are waiting in *"white robes"* are mentioned in Revelation 6:10-11. Revelation 7:9 speaks about a great number of believers from *"all nations"* who *"came out of great tribulation"* (verse 14). They are in heaven. There is no record indicating "live tribulation saints" on earth.

SPECIAL REVELATION

Dear Editors:

The Bible is full of mystery and secret meanings. Revelation may be the most mysterious of all its books.

The tenth chapter, one of the most important, cites two references to the mystery that Christians need to know. There surely is this need, because those who take it upon themselves to "enlighten" others are apparently unenlightened about the biblical mystery that is brought to light in my work.

Because of this failure of theologians to recognize and reveal vital biblical mysteries, Christians and the whole of Christianity remain in a stupor, lacking great truth, and falling prey to anti-Christians whose goal is its extinction.

The secret purpose of Christianity remains a secret and is of no value until Christians heed the works of this artist/author.

Their ignorance of this matter will continue to keep Christianity at a dangerous disadvantage, when, on the other hand, knowing the secret could be a powerful blessing and give new life to the great work of Christ.

-E.H., Rahway, NJ

ANSWER: Indeed there are mysteries contained in the Bible that we may not fully comprehend. However, the assumption that you have the answer is no mystery at all; it is called pride.

LAMB AND LION

Dear Brother Arno,

Many thanks for the tapes on the Atlantic Coast Prophecy Conference. They are just wonderful.

One thing I would like to ask you: No one (generally) ever says anything about the two witnesses in Revelation 11. I am curious as to why.

Also, in Dr. Thomas Ice's message on Revelation, he doesn't mention the Lion of the tribe of Judah (Revelation 5), but dwells at great length on the Lamb (the two are one and the same as I understand it - in different functions, but still the same).

However, it isn't the Lamb by name that opens the seven-sealed book in chapter 5, it is *"...the Lion of the tribe of Judah, the Root of David, hath prevailed to open the book, and to loose the seven seals thereof"* (verse 5). After the Lion opens the book, we see the Lamb in all of His marvelous glory (praise His name), Jesus our Lord, the King and Creator God, the Word and the Light of the world.

-Mrs. Y.T., Lexington, KY

ANSWER: The Lion presents royal power, for He shall rule with a rod of iron, *"...the Lion...has prevailed...."*

However, it is the Lamb, not the lion, who opens the seals: *"...the Lamb opened one of the seals..."* (Revelation 6:1).

We speak so much about the Lamb because He has *"...redeemed us to God by thou blood."*

The two witnesses are dealt with at length in my new book, *The Great Mystery of the Rapture.*

INTEGRATION

Dear Editor Arno Froese:

I have been receiving *Midnight Call* for six months. I thoroughly enjoy and eagerly look forward to your next issue because I have always found you to follow God's holy Word to the letter.

In regard to your article entitled, "The Eight-Fold Resurrection," please don't take offense, but I must take issue with part of that article. I'm certain that it was merely an oversight, but I must raise the issue.

At the end of the seventh resurrection (on page 13 of the February issue) you say, "During the Babylonian, Medo-Persian and Grecian Empire the nations were clearly separated, but under the Roman Empire, they were integrated."

A large portion of Scripture, in fact, virtually the entire book of Ezra, is devoted to the rebuilding of the temple in Jerusalem. There is also mention elsewhere in the Bible of this rebuilding, but for the sake of this letter, I will stay in the book of Ezra.

Beginning with Ezra 1:1, we find that it was King Cyrus of Persia who issued a proclamation throughout the land which began this rebuilding process in the first place. By the time we get over to Ezra 4:5-6, we discover that the process of rebuilding the temple spans the entire reign of King Cyrus, Darius, Xerxes and Artaxeres, all of whom are of Persian descent. When we come to Ezra 5:12, we learn that the reason for the Diaspora to begin with was that the forefathers of the Israelites had angered God. Thus He handed them over to the Babylonians, whereby the temple was destroyed and the people were deported to Babylon. The fact that their fathers did in fact anger God alludes to my point.

Then we read in Ezra 9:1 through the end of the chapter the cause for God's anger (Ezra prays about intermarriage). This, of course, stems from God's instruction back in Leviticus 18:24-30. (Note verses 27, 28, and 30).

For all who missed the point of chapter 9, there is Ezra 10:3, which says it all, *"...let us send away all these women and their children...according to the law."*

Hence, the integration of people prior to the Roman Empire. As I said at the beginning, I'm certain that it was merely an oversight. Please, also know that I am eagerly looking forward to your next issue.

-V.E., Warren, MI

ANSWER: I suggest that you re-read the article and you will notice that I am speaking about a "national" separation and integration, not an individual one . Even when Israel moved out from under the bondage of the Egyptians, an unspecified number of "strangers," or foreigners, were among them. However, on the national scene, it is specifically emphasized that *"...the LORD doth put a difference between the Egyptians and Israel"* (Exodus 11:7).

During the Babylonian, Medo-Persian, and Grecian Empires, political integration was an exception. Under the Roman Empire it was the rule. The apostle Paul was born under Roman rule in the city of Tarsus, in today's southern Turkey, as he stated, *"...I was free born"* (Acts 22:28). The chief captain who arrested him was not born under Roman rule but was a nationalized citizen. He said, *"...With a great sum obtained I this freedom..."* (Acts 22:28). In other words, the Roman Empire mirrors our society's best. For example, anyone born in the U.S. is automatically a U.S. citizen; integration is active today on all levels, even religion.

RESURRECTION

Dear Arno,

Please help us understand the part of Scripture that deals with the resurrection. As we understand it, there are two resurrections: the first resurrection to eternal life and the second resurrection to eternal punishment. These two resurrections are separated by 1,000 years, the period known as the Millennium, during which Christ rules in righteousness.

The first resurrection occurs in three parts: the firstfruits, the harvest proper and the gleaning. Christ is called the firstfruits and as I understand (whether this is correct or not) the bodies that were raised after His resurrection mentioned in Matthew 27:52-53 are included in the firstfruits (firstfruits being plural). The harvest would next include those at the Rapture (1st Thessalonians 4:16-17).

Then the gleanings would include those who were martyred during the tribulation and will be raised just before He comes to set up His Millennial kingdom (Revelation 20:4-5). (This would include the Old Testament saints, but depending on how you interpret Scripture this could be debated).

The people saved during the tribulation, yet experience no physical death, will be alive when He comes. They will be judged at His Second Coming, as stated in Matthew 25:31-34; and they will inherit the kingdom (Millennium). If the first resurrection is complete at the end of the tribulation and just before His Millennial reign, when will the people who enter the Millennium as born again believers in their natural bodies, or those born during the Millennium who have become born again, receive their resurrected bodies?

The people who have not been born again during the Millennium and are tested when Satan is released to deceive the nations after the Millennium will be included in the second resurrection.

If you can recommend any books to help answer this question about the Millennium saints, it would be appreciated. Maybe your answer in itself will enlighten us.

Thank you very much.

-E.U., Nordlun, Anoka, MN

ANSWER: The first resurrection includes all believers of all times. Salvation is based on the shed blood of the Lamb. The resurrection of Jesus marks the beginning of the firstfruit (Colossians 1:18). The resurrection/Rapture signals the completion of the Church of the firstborn

(Hebrews 12:23). Death will be swallowed up in victory at the last trump of God (1st Corinthians 15:54).

Neither the saints of the Old Testament who were resurrected after Jesus' resurrection nor the tribulation saints belong to the Church of the firstfruit. Death is swallowed up in victory only for the Church of the firstborn. Many of the tribulation saints will die and those who remain will become part of the Millennial Reign of Christ. During that time, the world will be filled with the knowledge of the Lord and sin will not be tolerated. The Lord shall rule with a rod of iron, which means that all sinners will be eliminated in the process of the 1,000-year kingdom of peace. According to my knowledge, the translation of the Millennium saints is not described in the Bible, but obviously they will be changed in order to fit into the new heaven and earth that will be created.

My new book, *How Democracy Will Elect the Antichrist*, discusses the "nations" that are to be deceived by Satan in length. It is my understanding that they are not nations of people, but nations of fallen angels.

FALLEN ANGELS DECEIVED?

Dear Mr. Froese,

I'm writing in regard to your June (1997) "Letters To The Editor" column in which Mrs. M. A. wrote asking about the Antichrist and what would take place after the Millennium. She asked who would be deceived by Satan when he is loosed for a while.

I certainly disagree with your answer – saying the ones

to be tempted were the fallen angels. This is wrong – it will be the people who are to be born during the Millennium even if they are professing Christians, since they will not have been tested as we have because Jesus will rule with a rod of iron. Why would the fallen angels be tempted? They are lost already. Please write. I will be looking forward to your explanation. Am I wrong?

-T.E., Cincinnati, OH

ANSWER: There are a number of reasons why I believe Revelation 20:8-9 deals with the nations of fallen angels.

One of them is found in Isaiah 14, where the *"...son of the morning..."* (KJV adds the word "Lucifer") is cast into the pit, *"...it stirreth up the dead for thee...all the kings of the nations"* (verse 9). Verse 12 adds *"...which didst weaken the nations."* Who are these *"nations?"* In this case, it is clear that they are the powerful underworld that will rule all the nations of the world. These *"nations"* are the ones in which Satan weakens. They are subject to his authority because they have left their original habitation with God and followed Satan.

The Bible also tells us that the physical nations of the world will learn *"war no more."* Nations can't gather themselves to battle if they learn *"war no more."*

Furthermore, Revelation 20:9 indicates that these nations came *"up,"* meaning from the depths.

Of course, my interpretation is not the final authority; we may have to wait for the fulfillment.

CHAPTER 5

SPIRITUAL FUNDAMENTALS

MESSIAH AND SAVIOR

Dear Mr. Froese,

I am a subscriber to your magazine, *Midnight Call*. I am very eager to know the answer to the following question: The Jews are looking forward to the coming of their Messiah. Christians are looking forward to the Second Coming of their Messiah. Are they one and the same?

Your answer will be very much appreciated. Also, could you please quote the source to your answer.

-E.T., CANADA

ANSWER: Jesus, the Messiah of Israel and Savior of the world, is not yet *"...the glory of thy people Israel"* (Luke 2:32). At the birth of John the Baptist, Zacharias prophesied, *"...That we should be saved from our enemies, and from the hand of all that hate us"* (Luke 1:71). That has not been fulfilled yet either. Israel has plenty of enemies and a great number of people who hate her. John testified, *"He came unto his own, and his own received him not"* (John 1:11). The Messiah whom the Jews await, and the Savior whom the Christians await to come again are the same person; however, He must come twice in order to fulfill these Scriptures (Read Isaiah 51).

JESUS IN THE OLD TESTAMENT

Dear Sir:

In the *New Unger's Bible Dictionary*, page 682, under the subheading (other titles) it says Jesus was the Jehovah in the Old Testament.

This confuses me, since everything I read about this name for God (i.e. the meaning of) known to the Hebrews has been entirely lost.

The first chapter of John tells me that Jesus, the man, was in a glorified state before He was born by the will of the Father to Mary without divine and human nature.

He ascended bodily and in his original glorified state now returns to us as the Holy Spirit. Right?

Was He actively working in the lives of the people in the Old Testament in His glorified state before coming into the world as Jesus?

-I.O., Richmond, TX

ANSWER: First Timothy 3:16 states, *"And without controversy great is the mystery of godliness: God was manifest in the flesh, justified in the Spirit, seen of angels, preached unto*

the Gentiles, believed on in the world, received up into glory."
I for one, admit to being incapable of intellectually explaining this *"great mystery of godliness."* However, we do know that before Jesus became a man, He was not limited in the form of flesh and blood. I understand the word "glorified" as meaning change. God's plan of salvation was not yet accomplished in the Old Testament, so there was no need for "change" or "glorification" because He is, was, and always will be eternal. First Corinthians 10:4 identifies Christ in the Old Testament, *"...that spiritual Rock that followed them (Israel): and that Rock was Christ."* Jesus did not return as the Holy Spirit. In Acts 7:55, we read that Stephen, being full of the Holy Ghost, said, *"...[he] saw the glory of God, and Jesus standing on the right hand of God."*

DIVINE BLOOD

Dear Mr. Froese:

I attended a prophecy conference in Ontario some years back. I subsequently have been on the mailing lists of Dave Breese and Dave Hunt, and a subscriber to the *Midnight Call.*

I love the magazine; so far haven't disagreed with you on any doctrinal point. I love...Dave Breese and admire the forthright opinions of Dave Hunt; but I have a question regarding a controversy in Dave's [newsletter] *The Berean Call,* pertaining to the precious blood.

A woman wrote that Jesus' blood had to be divine. It struck a cord. How could that blood that runs as a red stream through the Word of God not be special? I feel the pressure of the precious Holy Spirit as I write and a sense

93

of awe, yet Dave said that as Jesus was wholly God and wholly man; that the blood shed was of a man, the Son of Man, and that is correct. But is that all? I searched for a book by Andrew Murray, who wrote that the eternal life of the Godhead was carried in that blood. He uses Acts 20:28 as a reference. Can you comment?

-N.E., CANADA

ANSWER: The blood that was shed was the blood of a man: Jesus Christ, who was and is the Son of God. He is the Word that became flesh and the Bible states that the blood is the life of the flesh.

Biology shows that the bloodline runs through the father. Since the father is the Holy Spirit, "divine blood" sounds correct. However, 1st Timothy 3:16 reads, "...*great is the mystery of godliness: God was manifest in the flesh...*"

When Acts 20:28 says, ..."*he hath purchased with his own blood*" it means the blood of Jesus, not of the Holy Ghost. Many verses state that He [Jesus] shed His blood, "*...the blood of Jesus Christ his Son cleanseth us from all sin*" (1st John 1:7). (See also Ephesians 1:7; 2:13; Hebrews 10:19; 12:24; 13:12; 13:20; and 1st Peter 1:2).

PRAY TO THE HOLY SPIRIT?

Pastor Arno Froese,

The Holy Spirit has about it the difficulty that belongs to that of the Trinity or the existence of God as a purely spiritual being - this difficulty arises from the narrow limits of my human understanding. It is true; nevertheless, many churches pray to the Holy Spirit, or ask the Holy Spirit for help. Nowhere in the Scriptures can I find direction from God to pray to the Holy Spirit or call on the Holy Spirit for help. I, in my prayer life, talk to God and to Jesus and they answer my prayers, utilizing the Holy Spirit of God to intervene and to help me.

I believe, in accordance with the Scriptures, that the Holy Spirit is a person distinct from the Father and the Son, though united to both in the mysterious oneness of the Godhead.

He is an intelligent agent, possessed of self-consciousness and freedom. The relation of the Holy Spirit to the Father and to the Son is that He moves upon the hearts and consciences of all men, attending revealed truth.

His power, by gracious influence, convicts men of sin, graciously aids them in repentance and faith, regenerates, comforts, sanctifies believers, bears witness to their acceptance with God and adoption as God's children and dwells in them as the principle of a new and divine life. Please, if I am wrong, point out to me where in the Bible it tells me to pray to the Holy Spirit.

-R.T., New Port Richey, FL

ANSWER: Our Lord Jesus described the work of the Holy Spirit in John 16:13-14. The Holy Spirit *"...will shew you things to come. He shall glorify me...."* In other words, the Holy Spirit reveals to us the Word that became flesh. The Bible does not teach that we should address the Holy Spirit in our prayer.

IN JESUS' NAME

Dear Rev. Froese:

I am a subscriber to the *Midnight Call*. I thoroughly enjoy MC, as it challenges me to think, and I have always appreciated communication from and with those who can present a challenge to my opinions. I have a question for you that has been troubling my peace of mind for many years now.

As I read your June issue of MC, particularly a letter from A.I. in which she touched on the subject of the water baptismal formula in reading St. Matthew 28, I found a very interesting point to consider. In verses 7-10 we are given to understand that the disciples were sent for by Jesus. The only one excluded was Judas, as he had hanged himself. Now if all of the disciples were present when Jesus gave the command of Matthew 28:19, if they understood His command, why didn't they obey that command? In the book of Acts, we find Peter preaching repentance and water baptism in the name of Jesus Christ for the remission of sins. If Peter was in error in using this baptismal formula, why didn't at least one of the disciples who also heard Jesus (Matthew 28:19) step forth and correct Peter? Yet I find no record in the New Testament where the baptismal formula was ever used as stated in Matthew 28:19. Can you explain this to me, giving me the proper Scriptures to support your explanation? This seems like an important issue to me.

Further doubts have been raised in my mind by the fact that the Father, Son and Holy Ghost have never been used as names, but appear to be titles of position to me. I have never (in the natural) heard of a person named "Father J. Smith," "Son L. Jones" or "Holy Ghost C. Williams." Also [note] the fact that the word "name" is in the singular in that verse of Scripture.

If Father, Son and Holy Ghost were names, verse 9 tells us that the name of Jesus is still exalted above all others!

Ephesians 1:21 tells us the same thing, *"Far above all principality, and power, and might, and dominion, and every name that is named, not only in this world, but also in that which is to come."*

Ephesians 3:14-15, *"For this cause I bow my knees unto the Father of our Lord Jesus Christ; Of whom the whole family in heaven and earth is named."*

In light of these Scriptures, Rev. Froese, set me straight if I am wrong. I am not concerned about WHO is right, but rather, WHAT is right. Please also take into consideration that I did not take time to relate historical documentation of the fact that over 300 years after the death, burial and resurrection of Jesus Christ, people were baptized in the name of Jesus, the Lord Jesus, or the Lord Jesus Christ.

-A. O. in Desoto, TX

ANSWER: In Matthew 28:19 Jesus gave the commandment to His disciples regarding the "nations." Who are they? Ephesians 2:12 answers, *"That at that time ye were without Christ, being aliens from the commonwealth of Israel, and strangers from the covenants of promise, having no hope, and without God in the world."* In contrast, Israel was already under the Law for 2,000 years and familiar with the covenants of promise. Moses said, *"Did ever people hear the voice of God speaking out of the midst of the fire, as thou hast heard, and live?"* (Deuteronomy 4:33). And 1st Corinthians 10:2 reports they *"...were all baptized unto Moses in the cloud and in the sea."*

Peter did not disobey when he baptized the Jews in the name of Jesus because they had the knowledge of the Father and the Holy Spirit. This was also the case with the half-Jews, or Samaritans in Acts 8:16.

In Acts 10:48 the Gentiles were baptized *"in the name of the Lord."* What is the name of the Lord? The Father, the Son, and the Holy Spirit. Additionally, Cornelius, *"feared God with all his house"* and undoubtedly was familiar with the God of the Jews.

Acts 19:1 also concerns the Jews because they are called *"certain disciples."* I believe Matthew 28:19 still applies to Gentiles. Remember that water baptism is an act of obedience and is a demonstration of our saying "yes" to Jesus. An answer to the baptism of the Holy Spirit is God's "yes" to us.

TRINITY

Dear Arno:

It would be interesting to have this letter printed in your paper to see what others think about the points I am about to make.

You state that Trinity doctrine is beyond our capacity to intellectually analyze. Perhaps that is true, because as we will see, it is man's doctrine. God's truth only needs to be *"rightly divided."* Let us look at the facts and the truth, and let the rest disappear.

Mark 1:10-11, *"And straightway coming up out of the water, he saw the heavens opened, and the Spirit like a dove descending upon him: And there came a voice from heaven, saying, Thou art my beloved Son, in whom I am well pleased."* Your statement that Jesus is true God has a problem here. God is speaking to God? God is receiving the Spirit?

You see, God has not only given me an understanding of His Word, but [He also has given me] the questions to ask as well. Your statement about the Trinity doctrine above simply proves to me that you cannot answer the question regarding Mark's gospel.

This is not the only place; there are many others as well. For instance, Jesus does not know the day or hour He is to return for the saints? Jesus is true God and does not know that? Your intellectual analysis cannot be true. Why? First, let us look at 1st Timothy 2:5, *"For there is one God, and one mediator between God and men, the man Christ Jesus."*

What is a mediator? To be a true mediator, one cannot be partial to one of the parties for which he is a mediator." Therefore, in order for Jesus to be a true mediator between God and man, He can be neither.

Now about your statement that Jesus is true man. Really? If so, then any of us could have died on the cross. No? Of course not. Jesus cannot be true man. Jesus first was born of a virgin, but more importantly, He had no sin. Every true man has sin; therefore Jesus cannot be true man, but a man nonetheless.

More verses could be used; however, you will either see the error from these verses about Trinity doctrine or else you will not.

This is as simple as I could possibly make this letter, at least at this time. Truth will always be known because nowhere in the Bible will it conflict with other verses.

If we honestly seek truth there should be no question we cannot answer – you especially should understand that – if the Spirit is the one teaching us.

There is just no other way. Jesus answered even tougher questions than these. Jesus received it in power. God did not. Amen. Just give truth a chance and do not be afraid; it is all in the Bible.

-N.E., Germany

ANSWER: The first three verses of our Bible reveal the doctrine of the Trinity. Verse 1: God the Father; Verse 2: God the Spirit; Verse 3: God the Word. Jesus said to Philip, *"...he that hath seen me hath seen the Father..."* (John 14:9). Thomas confessed, *"My Lord and my God"* (John 20:28). First John 5:7 testifies, *"For there are three that bear record in heaven, the Father, the Word, and the Holy Ghost: and these three are one."* Does this intellectually explain the Trinity? I say "no." Why not? Because, *"...the natural man receiveth not the things of the Spirit of God: for they are foolishness unto him: neither can he know them, because they are spiritually discerned"* (1st Corinthians 2:14).

JESUS' RETURN AND TRINITY

Dear Mr. Froese,

I'm very fortunate enough to have received your *Midnight Call* publication and other material like *News From Israel* continuously for more than three years now.

In fact, the information is very helpful. [These publications have]opened up my eyes to see the reality – news about the coming King Jesus and the endtime events.

[Please consider] a question in the Scripture [that] confuses me so much. The Bible reports that the Son of man – Jesus, in fact, is one of the Trinity (God) Himself. Then how come He didn't know the date of the coming of Himself to this earth? Jesus answered, *"But of that day and that hour knoweth no man, no, not the angels which are in heaven, neither the Son, but the Father"* (Mark 13:32) to one of the worrying apostles.

-H.A. in New Guinea

ANSWER: I do not believe that any mortal man can fully comprehend the mystery of the Trinity with his limited, sin-tainted intellectual mind.

As the "Son of man," Jesus did not know of His return. His human limitations are repeatedly described in Scripture. He felt hunger and thirst, and He also got upset. Hebrews 2:17-18 reveals His humanity. As another example, the "Son of man" didn't know that He would not have to die in the Garden of Gethsemane. At that point, He prayed, *"O my Father, if it be possible, let this cup pass from me"* (Matthew 26:39). Which cup? The cup of death right in the Garden of Gethsemane. Jesus knew He would die on Calvary's cross, outside the walls of Jerusalem. He knew the Scripture and He came to fulfill it. But when death came upon Him at Gethsemane, He prayed for His life. Later, we read the testimony in Hebrews 5:7, *"Who in the days of his flesh, when he had offered up prayers and supplications with strong crying and tears unto him that was able to save him from death, and was heard in that he feared."*

GENEALOGY

Dear Arno:

I greet you in the name of our Lord and Savior Jesus Christ. I love the *Midnight Call* magazine.

I am in a quandary over the genealogy of the line through to Joseph. Joseph had nothing to do with conception of Jesus. Thus, through this line, Jesus is only a legal representative of the line of David.

Now, in Luke 3:23, we see another line which gives a totally different genealogy and goes all the way to Adam. My Bible has a caption that states, "Genealogy of Jesus through Mary." It starts with Joseph and says that he was the son of Heli. I understand that the custom of the time was to present the father's name; however, if the father's name is presented twice, how do we know which line went through Mary?

I can't find anything in all of my Bibles or concordances to help me. The only reference to Heli in my concordance is Luke 3:23.

My Sunday school instructor says that Jesus has a legal representation of the line of David. Could you please help? I need to know I can prove conclusively that Jesus was a blood descendant of David. Thanks.

-O. E. in Richmond, VA

ANSWER: Matthew 1:1-16 lists the genealogy of Joseph as a descendent of King David. Notice verse 16: *"And Jacob begat Joseph the husband of Mary, of whom was born Jesus, who is called Christ."* Clearly, Joseph did not "begat" Jesus, thus, he is not His biological father.

Luke 3 provides the genealogy of Mary, which is counted through Joseph's father-in-law, Heli. Because only males were counted, we read the following in Luke 3:23, *"And Jesus himself began to be about thirty years of age, being (as was supposed) the son of Joseph, which was the son of Heli."* The genealogy of Mary had to be listed through her father, Heli.

RESURRECTION TIME

Gentlemen:

How can the New Testament be divinely inspired and therefore infallible when it is full of contradictions?

A literal translation of Matthew said the discovery of the empty tomb was late on the Sabbath, but Mark said after sunrise on the first day of the week and John said while it was still dark on the first day of the week.

How could it be late on the Sabbath as the first day of the week approached, before sunrise Sunday morning and after sunrise Sunday morning?

If they saw the tomb was empty on Saturday, why would they go back two more times [on] Sunday morning?

Also, John 3 plainly says if you are born again, you are an invisible spirit being, but other places say you're born again if you are a believer.

If we have an immortal soul, what is the need for a resurrection?

-L.O., Madison, WI

ANSWER: Matthew 28:1, *"...toward the first day of the week...."*

Mark 16:2, *"...very early in the morning the first day of the week."*

Luke 24:1, *"Now upon the first day of the week, very early in the morning."*

John 20:1, *"The first day of the week...when it was yet dark...."*

Four authors describe the same event; none contradict the others.

The apostle Peter testified to the rebirth here and now, *"Being born again, not of corruptible seed, but of incorruptible, by the word of God, which liveth and abideth for ever"* (1st Peter 1:23).

Please notice that the word "soul" is often used to describe life. Man consists of spirit, soul and body. When we are born again, the spirit and soul go to heaven at death and remain in the presence of the Lord.

Not until the Rapture will born again believers receive a glorified body as unto the Lord.

According to Revelation 20:15, the person who is not saved will be cast into the lake of fire and will remain in that position *"for ever and ever"* (verse 10).

DOCTRINE

Dear Midnight Call Friends,

I'm glad to find yours one of the few publications that stands on Bible truths; it seems many are leaning toward watered-down religion.

I recently heard of a minister who is telling those in his church that doctrine is no longer important. How would man explain 2nd Timothy 4:1-4? Could this be what Paul was speaking of – the perilous times to come (2nd Timothy 3:1)? *"Having a form of godliness, but denying the power thereof: from such turn away"* (verse 5). This was the verse that directed me out of a very liberal church years ago.

Although I've read through my Bible many times, I still have much to learn, so [I] continue to search the Scriptures for God's leading.

How good He has been to give us His Word and daily guidance.

-H.L., Pocahontas, IA

ANSWER: It is indeed shocking to hear that a minister would make such a statement. Without doctrine, we have no faith! Doctrine must be taught in order to instruct the Body of Christ. We believe that Scripture is our only authority for the Christian life. Keep the faith, sister!

PREDESTINATION

Dear Arno Froese,

Something has bothered me for a long time that maybe

you can help me understand.

I was brought up in the Presbyterian faith, whose doctrine leans toward predestination and an elect chosen of God as stated by Paul in Ephesians 1:4-5, *"According as he hath chosen us in him before the foundation of the world, that we should be holy and without blame before him in love: Having predestinated us unto the adoption of children by Jesus Christ to himself, according to the good pleasure of his will."* How can we reconcile man's free will if it is God who chose us?

I recently read an article by an evangelical theologian that brings up this whole problem, or at least what I don't seem to be able to reconcile. He, of course, states the God whom the Bible talks about and whom Jesus Christ incarnates is a God of love, and this entails that He is a God of freedom, for you cannot have love without freedom.

Humanity, thus, was created with the ability to choose love but also with the ability to choose its opposite-evil. Humans are therefore not robots who simply act out divine pre-planned programs.

He further states that although God in His omniscience knows everything there is to know, He has voluntarily limited His omniscience so man can truly have free will and this, to a large extent, is irrevocable.

If this is true, then humanity has been given freedom to create the reality of our decisions by making them-and until we make them, they don't exist.

Even by the more traditional view, God's action of foreknowledge is based on the people's future action and not people's action based on God's future knowledge. If aspects of the future are already determined either by present circumstances or by God's own will, then God would foreknow, for they are presently there to be known-but not all free will acts.

How are we to understand predestination and man's free will?

We also know the Bible states that God isn't willing that any should perish but that all should come to repentance; God takes no delight in the destruction of the wicked; whosoever should come, etc.– [these passages] seem to indicate free will choice.

But a real problem is [that] man in his fallen state isn't capable of reconciling with God by his efforts, and he needs a Savior.

But how can man use his free will if sin has corrupted his every decision? He can't. So it comes back to God choosing, but when, and how and on what basis?

Remember, God has given us freedom to create the reality of our decisions by making them and until we make them, they don't exist.

Does God choose the people He chooses to save in the foreknowledge of the world which is independent of the actual world? God judges, I thought by the heart and the light we know and understand, so when does He select?

Why did God select to change the heart of one and not another? Why a Peter and not a Judas? Both were betrayers.

So many questions! I, of course, am a believer who puts such questions on hold in hopes there may be an answer some day.

-O.H, St. Petersburg, FL

ANSWER: Many great theologians have tried to rationalize their attempts to reconcile man's free will with God's predestination. A wonderful explanation I once heard went as follows: "In my lost and hopeless condition, I stood before the narrow gate over which was written, `Come unto me all ye that labor and are heavy laden and I will give you rest.' Burdened under the load of sin, I squeezed through the narrow gate and then looked back. From the inside over the gate was written, "Chosen before the foundation of the world!'"

Based on the summarizing message of the Scripture, man has a free will and the capacity to choose to believe in Jesus or reject Him.

Paul clearly stated that his choice to preach the Gospel "might save some of them," meaning his fellow Jew. God's predestination is based on His foreknowledge. In other words, He knows how a person will decide even before birth. To assume that He deliberately causes some to be saved and others to be lost is contrary to the Holy Word.

NAME OF GOD

Dear Brother Arno Froese,

I have a question for your publication. It concerns God's original name. Could it be distorted and derogated [modified, diminished]?

I recently came across a publication based on the doctrine of Jehovah Witness[es]. It contains an issue about God's name.

Basically, I believe that the Creator, the governor of the

universe, our merciful heavenly Father, has His own peculiar, honored, beloved and unchangeable name: "Jehovah." That name remains eternally in heaven and will never pass away, although the world will. True Christians know His true name, which "Jehovah" verbally expresses (Psalm 91:13-15, Isaiah 12:4-6).

"God" or "Lord" is not His personal name in word, letters, or full meaning. You and I have personal names with a meaning, voice, letters, even history – am I wrong? So what is the name of our heavenly Father? Is it possible to translate anyone's name that is given in Hebrew, English, Arabic, or Latin? Really, we know it is impossible.

Our Holy Father, Jehovah, the God of Abraham, Yitzhak Israel, has a great and holy name that He expressed for Moses in Exodus 34:5-8 and for many other olden-day prophets in Hebrew, not in Latin, Greek, or Arabic!

Didn't David sing and call for his glorified name by his language? (Psalm 145:1-5). So our righteous Father has one - only one - holy and honorable name, which is "Jehovah" in Hebrew. It is written not only on old scrolls or Holy Scripture but also in the clean hearts of true Christians. It is written in our time by the blood of our Lord and Savior Yeshua (John 12:26-33).

It is really satanic or blasphemous if we do not use the correct Hebrew name (Romans 10:9-12).

Dear Mr. Froese, what do you suspect about it from the Holy Scripture's point of view?

Send me your answer.

-H.A., Harrar, Ethiopia

ANSWER: Please read Acts chapter 2 and you will notice that Jews from no less than sixteen different countries were present at the first Gospel meeting where the apostle Peter preached. They testified, we *"...hear...every man in our own tongue (language)."*

The name of the Son of God in English is "Jesus." That name is written and pronounced differently in other languages. The Lord doesn't have a problem with languages. He has heard the cry of millions of people throughout the centuries who have called upon His name in their own language and He has saved their souls and added them to His Church. The teaching that we must learn the original Hebrew in order to honor the Lord must be rejected because it is contrary to the Holy Scriptures.

THE NAME OF JESUS

Dear Mr. Froese:

Your article, "Mystery Babylon Exposed," is excellent. The testimony of Yahchonan (John) states, *"In the beginning was the Word."*

The Word said:

1) that He came in His Father's name
2) that He is the "light" of this world
3) that He is the "bread" of life
4) that He is the "truth" and in Him is no darkness
5) that He is "Eternal Life"
6) that He is our provider
7) that He is the Savior and beside Him there is no other

These are basic foundational truths. Yet the first is totally ignored. The King James translation says that the holy name of our Father is "Yahweh," which is a transliteration of the Hebrew symbol YHWH (Tetragrammation). This has been translated over 6,823 times as "Lord" and "God," which are titles, not names. First Corinthians 8:5 is inspired to correct us.

John 5:43-44 clearly speaks to His people that the name "Jesus" is false. Jesus was never called this name when He came in the flesh. He was a "Yehudi" not a "Jew." He said salvation is of the "Yehudi" (John 4:22). Verses 23-24, *"...true worshippers shall worship the Father in spirit and in truth: for the Father seeketh such to worship him."* God (Yah) is a spirit: and they that worship him must worship him in spirit and in truth. Hallelujah! (Praise ye Yah, Psalm 68:4).

Also, so many ministers are talking about the Rapture of the Church, when the Messiah returns for a "Bride" that has made herself ready (Revelation 19:7-9). But we are not ready.

What about Revelation 6:9-11, *"that they should rest yet a little season until their fellow servants also and their brethren should be killed as they were, should be fulfilled"* (Mark 13:13); *"...hated of all for my name's sake* (1st Timothy 1:12-16; 2nd Timothy 2:12; 3:12-17). That he was chief of sinners and received grace and mercy that he might show forth the pattern of them that believe. All that live godly shall suffer persecution. (Isaiah 57:1, these are blessed ones).

Finally, back to the letter "J," which is spurious. It

came into the language with the invention of the printing press during the 15th century. It takes its value from the letter "I" by adding a "tail." The Messiah said He was Aleph and Tau (Hebrew) the beginning and the end, the first and the last, He is "the Word."

If you have read this to this point, with all your knowledge concerning Babylon, I'm sure the Father has opened your eyes and ears to this truth (see Proverbs 30:4).

-no name given

ANSWER: Regardless of the language or translation, millions of precious souls have been added to the Church through the name of Jesus for the last 2,000 years.

The Word of God has been translated in over 4,500 dialects. Many languages have multiple translations in which the names quite often differ from one another, yet thousands come to the Lord through the translated Word by His wonderful grace.

He does not require us to call upon Him through the arrangement of certain alphabetical letters or proper pronunciation. We can call on Him in Spirit and in truth by whatever name our translation may list.

I disagree with your statement that the Bride of Christ is not ready. The true Church of Jesus Christ, consisting of born again believers, is ready and waiting today.

SPIRIT AND SOUL

Dear Mr. Froese,

First, let me thank you for your excellent publication, *Midnight Call*. I read it cover to cover. The articles are first rate and the news of the world shows how close we are to the glorious appearing of our Lord. "Come quickly, Lord Jesus!"

I do have a question. On page 16 in the October [issue] of *Midnight Call*, [where an article] mentioned the dividing of soul and spirit. Sorry for my ignorance, but what is the difference between soul and spirit?

-B.P.S. in Norcross, GA

ANSWER: Man consists of a trinity: spirit, soul and body. When we are born again, the spirit connects to God, and the soul to the body. The spirit leads to the cross, the soul attempts to pamper the body.

There is only one remedy: the Word of God, which is sharper than any two-edged sword, *"...piercing even to the dividing asunder of soul and spirit..."* (Hebrews 4:12).

CHAPTER 6

PRAYER AND SALVATION

MORE PRAYER MAKES IT WORSE

Dear Brothers and Sisters in Christ,

I received your letter the other day and was touched. In our fast-paced world we seem to overlook the most important things. Your magazine has always been a blessing to me.

Unfortunately, sometimes when subscription renewals come due, [I] don't always have the money.

I would love to be able to support your ministry more, but most of the time, all I can offer is prayer.

I've never had anyone to offer something like you have. I shall never forget it. May God bless you always.

Can you offer any advice on how to overcome recurring thoughts the devil brings to your mind during sleep, when you know you would not or have not done these things since your rebirth, and then you pray for forgiveness as soon as you awake? This seems to be worse the more I pray, study and witness.

-R.E., Alabama

115

ANSWER: In regards to the devil disturbing your sleep, may I say one word? Rejoice! Why should you rejoice? Because you are a child of God, therefore, you are a target of the enemy.

The devil does not need to bother those who are dead in their sins and trespasses; they belong to him in the first place. However, those who are alive in Christ are his prime targets.

He desperately wants you to come to the conclusion that "This (whatever the situation may be) seems to be worse the more I pray..." You must practice James 4:7, *"Resist the devil,"* and as a result, *"he will flee from you."* Also read 1st Peter 1:6-7.

WRITTEN PRAYERS

Dear Pastor Froese;

In Luke 11:1-4, the disciples asked Jesus to teach them to pray, and He instructed them to pray this way: *"Our Father..."*. My question is this: Is it necessary to recite formal prayers out loud or is it acceptable to communicate with Jesus in our minds, in our own words, anywhere [and] anytime as the need arises? Learned or written prayers seem artificial to me because they are someone else's words.

I praise and worship our Lord deep in my thoughts but not in words, for many different reasons, throughout the day. Or I pray in my own words for my family, others and myself. Is this proper?

-H.K., Genoa City, WI

ANSWER: Jesus gave His disciples an outline to prayer in Luke 11 revealing the eternal God the Father, and then the fulfillment of the prophetic Word and our relationship to it. You may indeed pray any time, any place and for any reason. I agree that pre-written prayers are superficial. For one thing, we address the eternal God with the words, *"Our Father."* Imagine a child pulling out a piece of paper and reading a request to his/her own father!

The Lord warns of repetitive prayer in Matthew 6:7, *"...use not vain repetitions, as the heathen do: for they think that they shall be heard for their much speaking."* However, your prayer life should also include fellowship with like-minded believers where you pray audibly so others can hear and add their own "amen." (See 1st Corinthians 14:16).

PRAYER CHANGES GOD?

Dear Sirs:

Grace and peace to you from God our Father and the Lord Jesus Christ.

I got the chance to read your *Midnight Call* magazine of November from my Christian friend and brother in Christ. I found it very inspiring and helpful in the understanding of endtime prophecy. Therefore, I kindly request you to send me a copy of your magazine.

I would like to take this opportunity to ask a question on the article, "Called to Pray" by Dr. Wim Malgo on page 38 and 39 of the magazine. The article says, "Does God change His mind in a certain matter because of prayers?

No! We can never change God and His intentions. The opposite is the case. Through earnest prayer we are changed. We come to that inner state of mind through which God can bless us and through us others and the world." When God blesses us and our world doesn't it mean that God changed His mind because of prayer? I am not clear on this idea. Therefore, could you please make it clear to me?

May the grace of the Lord Jesus Christ, and the love of God, and the fellowship of the Holy Spirit be with you all.

-A.B., ERITREA

ANSWER: God is the same yesterday, today and forever. When He blesses us, He does not change His way or plans because His original intention was to bless mankind. First Timothy 2:4 says, "[He] *will have all men to be saved, and to come unto the knowledge of the truth."*

We need to be changed and conformed more and more into His image. Prayer is the avenue toward that change.

SATAN HINDERS MY PRAYERS

Dear Brother Arno,

I enjoy *Midnight Call* from cover to cover, but I guess one of my favorite sections is "Letters to the Editor." There always seems to be a selection of good quality questions from your readership, plus top-notch answers. The January issue's letter section prompts me to write the following:

Mr. V's letter [entitled] "Save Our Nation" also put my

mind to thought. I have felt for some time that I was going through some sort of tribulation period here on earth. I think God requires believing Christians to go through this to further test their faith before the Rapture. After the Rapture, the only unpleasant event I can think of will be the "believer's judgment" when we have to face Jesus and account for all the things we didn't do in His Name on earth when we had the chance. I don't look forward to that at all because I have been such a failure no matter how hard I think I've tried. The tears will flow from millions of believers who have fallen so far short of what we should have done in God's name.

This brings me to my question: I have a problem with my prayer life. I really feel it is a flop! And you don't have to recommend [the book] *Called to Pray* by Dr. Wim Malgo because I already got it and read it twice. It was a big help and informative but I am still very unhappy with my prayer life.

I know God answers all prayers. It isn't always the answer I want, but it is His answer which is the right answer. And I try not to question His answers when I don't understand. An example is I constantly pray (first thing at 5:00 a.m.) that God keep Satan out of my prayer life and not let him control my mind when I pray. But it gets worse each week. The devil is really dealing me a fit. You would think that if God would be going to answer "yes" to any prayer, it would be prayers of this type. So I just tell myself, "The devil is upset with my being a believing Christian and doesn't want me to pray to God. And God is testing my faith. That's why He lets the devil run rampant through my prayer life."

Any suggestions? Don't tell me to pray harder. I'm about green in the face from praying harder! I'm very frustrated and upset over this. I do need help. Is this tribulation? I used to sleep like a baby, now I have 3-4 nights a month with no sleep. It's Satan, I'm sure.

-C.T., New Franklin, MO

ANSWER: You should look forward to the Judgment Seat of Christ with great joy. Please read Colossians 4:3 and 1st Peter 5:4. Martin Luther translates the words with, *"...judgment seat of reward."*

When James says, *"Resist the devil, and he will flee from you"* (James 4:7), he does not mean to fight or, as some say, "rebuke" the devil. You must stand on the solid rock of salvation—consciously acknowledging that you have been saved by the blood of the Lamb—with an unconditional "no" to any and all sins; then the devil will depart. Read Ephesians 6:11-14 carefully and notice the word "stand." Keep in mind that it is more difficult for your mind to wander when you pray aloud. Also, instead of asking God to keep Satan out of your life, why not thank Him that He has already defeated the powers of Satan? Concern yourself less with the defeated foe, and occupy yourself more with the victor, Jesus. After successfully resisting Satan, he not only will *"flee from you,"* but then you may draw nigh to God and He will draw nigh to you.

DATE OF SALVATION

Dear Brother Froese,

Thank you for your ministry. I appreciate that you don't just sit around and "talk and argue" fine points of prophecy while forgetting about being doers of the Word also! If Bible prophecy doesn't spur us on to holier living (2nd Peter 3:10), something is wrong with us!

I have a question that I suppose isn't all that important, but one about which I'd love to hear your input.

Some say we must know when and where we were saved if our salvation experience is valid. Others say that the really important matter is how are we living now.

Belief in Christ must be present tense! I put myself in group #2. I'd appreciate your opinion (Bible-based, of course). Thank you and God bless you.

-I.T., Polkton, NC

ANSWER: First John 5:20 reveals, *"...we know that the Son of God is come, and hath given us an understanding, that we may know him that is true, and we are in him that is true, even in his Son Jesus Christ. This is the true God, and eternal life."* To know Jesus is to have eternal life. This has nothing to do with knowing the exact date and time of our conversion. Some vividly remember the year, day and hour, while others have no recollection of such. Only the assurance of salvation is decisive.

121

LOSING YOUR SALVATION?

Dear Brother Froese,

I love *Midnight Call* magazine and look forward to receiving it each month.

My question is, how can a true, born again Christian lose his or her salvation after our Lord and Savior died in our place and God now sees us in Christ, His righteousness?

After we have been born again, how can we be unborn? God's Spirit, the Holy Spirit, cannot undo His work because His Spirit makes us new creatures in Christ. John 10:27-30 gives believers assurance. I'd like you to explain this because of so much misunderstanding.

Also, please comment on the fact that some Christians will be left behind after the Rapture of the Church.

[I] Thank God for you and this ministry and all the saints.

-N.P., Branchville, SC

ANSWER: I see no evidence in Scripture that suggests a born again person can be lost. However, those who are born again and don't follow the Lord *"shall suffer loss"* based on 1st Corinthians 3:15. What this *"loss"* actually entails is not revealed in the Bible. However, that verse does go on to say, *"...but he himself shall be saved, yet so as by fire."*

Only those who are born again will be raptured; all others will be left behind.

The Body of Christ on earth is the light of this world. After the removal of the Body of Christ, darkness will set in and the Antichrist and his works will flourish.

DOUBTING SALVATION

Dear Mr. Froese,

I can't thank you enough for your timely response to my letter; it was helpful. I happened to get the May copy of *Midnight Call* just a couple of days before I received your letter, and the article on *"Mystery Babylon"* was also very enlightening.

I guess the one question I still would like for you to help me with is the one concerning Revelation 18:4, where God says to His people to come out of her. What are we supposed to understand from this passage? Is it that we are just not to be a part of the world's system? Or is this speaking just to the Jews?

I would like to ask you one more question, and then I will try to not bother you again for a while, as I know your time is very valuable. I feel that you are the one I can ask [who will offer] a straight answer. This is probably the first question I should ever have asked: "How do I know for certain if I am a born again believer?"

I believe in Jesus Christ. I know that I am a sinner and that He came to pay the price for my sins on the cross. I believe He arose on the third day and is now seated at the right hand of God and will come again some day to claim those who are His own.

I do my best to live a life worthy of being called a Christian, but all too often I find myself doing as Romans 7:15-25 says, the things I wish I didn't do, and [I find myself] not doing the things I know I should. Does this mean that I have not been born again? I have a terrible struggle with my temper and at its worst, I use bad language. I also struggle with the sin of gluttony. I went on a diet a year ago and lost 100 lbs., but now have started gaining weight again.

I've reasoned that since we are born very selfish creatures, to be born again is to die to self and live an unselfish life, which I try to do. But I know that of myself I cannot do this. Since I am still struggling, does this mean the Holy Spirit has not been given to me yet? And if that is the case, is there anything other than prayer that I can do about this?

I love Jesus, and I don't want to miss out on going in the Rapture, as I know this is going to be a very terrible place during the tribulation. I want to be certain and have complete assurance of this, and would like to be able to know how to help others be assured of this as well.

I thank you in advance for being in His service for my sake as well as others.

-Name Withheld, Topeka, KS.

ANSWER: Revelation 18:4 is addressed to the Church and applies to both the tribulation saints and the Jews. It shows that we shouldn't take part in the mixture of holy and unholy activity such as political/religious work. Unfortunately, many Christian leaders try to lead us in that direction.

From your letter, it is obvious that you are a child of God, specifically because of your confession about the tendencies you have to sin. That is the work of the enemy who wants to extinguish your light. What must you do now? *"Draw nigh unto God, and He will draw nigh unto you."* In practical terms, that means to spend more time talking to Him (prayer) and let Him speak to you (reading your Bible). That may not eliminate your tendency to sin, which produces habits you wish you could rid yourself of. However, by coming closer to the Lord, you'll learn that the priority of your life is the Lord. Other things will become of lesser importance.

I've prayed that the Lord will give you the needed courage to hold on to Him in faith.

SAVED IN THE GREAT TRIBULATION

Dear Arno,

My brother-in-law said anyone who rejects the Lord Jesus, or doesn't accept Him after hearing the words, is left behind when the Rapture takes place. He said that [those who are left behind] cannot be saved. Is this true?

I told him that I believe that the people who are left behind still can be saved. Can you explain this? Are there any verses [to support] this? Please let me know.

-A.O., Westover, MD

ANSWER: The Bible does not identify a category of people who cannot be saved during the Great Tribulation. John saw those saved ones in heaven, *"...I beheld, and, lo, a great multitude, which no man could number, of all nations, and kindreds, and people, and tongues..."* (Revelation 7:9).

There is no indication that people from certain geographical areas of planet Earth will not belong to that group. However, it is important to emphasize that the [category of people to whom John refers] do *not* belong to the Church of Jesus Christ, which is His Bride, the recipient of His highest glory.

REBIRTH VERSUS CONVERSION

Dear Editor,

What is the difference between "rebirth" and "conversion?" Aren't they the same? (I am referring to pg. 41 of the September magazine).

Aren't you referring to mind conversion as to spirit conversion? I just don't get what you mean.

How can a person live the Christian life without the rebirth? The word "conversion" indicates to me "a changed life." Therefore, the new birth.

Is it possible for a person to say the "sinner's prayer" and not get saved? If not, what about Jesus saying *"All who come unto me I will by no means cast out?"*

I do street witnessing every Friday for my church and I like to tell people they are saved after the sinner's prayer. Please address this, too. I'll share your info with my group. Thanks much.

C. E., Minneapolis, MN

ANSWER: There are religious conversions from Christianity to Buddhism. There are political conversions from Democrat to Republican. Such conversions have no relationship to the rebirth. Unfortunately, conversions also take place within the Church that do not lead to a rebirth.

For example: A person who experiences great distress, emotional problems, or a tragedy in the family often grasps at anything that seems promising. Our Lord explains this in the parable of the sower and the seed (Luke 8). Your responsibility is to sow the seed. I am very happy to read about your street witnessing, which is leading some people to recite the "sinner's prayer." You have done what you can do; the Lord will do the rest. Indeed, *"...him that cometh to me; I will in no wise cast out"* (John 6:37); however, if there is no visible manifestation in this person's life, which there should be, then one can only assume that this person may have had only an "experience."

SAVED BY WATER?

Dear Mr. Froese,

I am inspired and encouraged by the booklet, *Seven Signs of A Born Again Person* that I received in the mail today. But one crucial step is missing from the "How Can I Obtain The New Birth?" section. You refer to John 3:7 but skip over verse 5, which says, *"...Except a man be born of water and of the Spirit, he cannot enter into the kingdom of God."* What about baptism? I would like to think this was a printing error or an innocent oversight, but somehow I doubt it. I'm not talking about infant baptism or sprinkling, I mean baptism for the forgiveness of sins (Acts 2:38). Jesus said in Matthew 7:21, *"Not every one that saith unto me, Lord, Lord, shall enter into the kingdom of heaven; but he that doeth the will of my Father which is in heaven."* In the story of Jesus healing the blind man in John 9, would the blind man have been healed if he refused to *"...wash in the pool of Siloam..."* (verse 7)? Of course not. So then, how can we expect to be saved by simply quoting a prayer and not being "born of water?" The only example we have of someone being saved without [baptism] is the thief on the cross.

-F.U., Covington, KY

ANSWER: Jesus is *"...the author and finisher of our faith..."* (Hebrews 12:2). If we attempt to add anything to our salvation then it is no longer exclusively of faith but becomes faith plus works. We *"...have attained to righteousness, even the righteousness which is of faith"* (Romans 9:30). The word "faith" appears 245 times in the New Testament, clearly establishing in unmistakable terms that faith in Jesus is our salvation, not baptism.

REDEEMED OR SAVED?

Dear Sir,

I am a supporter of *Midnight Call* and have always enjoyed the magazine. I just want to mention one phrase in your recent article, "Euphrates River in Bible Prophecy." I think it is excellent, but I take exception to one sentence, "...Every unredeemed person in the entire world..." I believe that through Christ's death on the cross, all are redeemed. If this is not true, then Christ's sacrifice is not complete. I think the word should be "every unsaved person." All are redeemed, but not all are saved. Salvation is the free acceptance of the gift of redemption.

-D.H., Farmington, MO

ANSWER: Thank you for that correction.

UNSURE OF SALVATION

Dear Arno,

Bless you in the name of our Lord and Savior, Jesus Christ. I just had to write to you, especially for the birthday card and for all the other kindnesses you have shown me.

I just finished your book, *How Democracy Will Elect the Antichrist*. It was one of the best-written books I have ever read. I gained a lot of valuable insight into the Bible that I never knew before. In fact, all the books I receive from your company are the best I receive from anyone.

I was added to our Lord's religion several years ago after [having followed] the Roman Catholic Church since I was born. I would like to consider myself saved. I hope I am, and my wife also. We follow the New Testament to the letter. I consider myself and my wife saved and Christians.

Again, thank you and your staff for all the love and kindness you have shown us.

-O.D., Lake Alfred, FL

ANSWER: I am glad to hear about the helpful information

you have received from my book. However, in your letter, you clearly expressed an uncertainty regarding your salvation. Salvation is the most important thing in the life of everyone on earth. For that purpose, I am enclosing Dr. Wim Malgo's booklet, *Seven Signs of a Born Again Person*, which will help you to determine your position in Christ. By all means, make sure of your salvation today.

CAN SIN CANCEL SALVATION?

Dear Mr. Froese,

I am writing to ask whether eternal security is a biblical doctrine. Hebrews 6:4-6, Hebrews 10:14 and other verses in the Bible seem to say one's salvation is forever guaranteed once he accepts Christ. Can any sin cancel one's salvation (like later selling one's soul to Satan)? Presently, I believe I am saved through Jesus Christ and deeply care to continue serving Him. However, I am scared that later I might fall away, die, and be condemned to everlasting punishment. I would be very grateful for any answer to this question. Thank you very much for your time.

-C.I., Cincinnati, OH

ANSWER: Your knowledge of the wonderful passages of Scripture you quoted contradicts your statement expressing doubt. Please do not insult the already perfected work of salvation by permitting the devil to put disbelief in your mind. If your salvation is kept by your not sinning, then Christ did not accomplish complete salvation. Don't let the enemy rob you of the wonderful assurance given to you in Scripture, *"...I know whom I have believed, and am persuaded that he is able to keep that which I have committed unto him against that day"* (2nd Timothy 1:12).

EXACT BIBLE WORDS

Dear Pastor Froese,

When using some Bible texts to strengthen our faith, or [when using them] in prayer, are we required to quote the passages exactly as they are given in the Bible, [although they] vary in wording many times?

Philippians 4:13 is one I am now concentrating on, *"I can do all things through Christ which strengtheneth me."* I prefer, "I can do all things through Christ who empowers me." Is this wrong and does it really change the meaning of the text? I would appreciate your reply. Thank you very much.

-S.W., Bolivar, MO

ANSWER: Claiming promises in the Bible must be done in Spirit and in truth. In other words, the ability to claim God's promises isn't dependent upon your ability to remember exactly how your particular translation renders the text. After all, our languages are primarily pagan-based. It would probably shock the Old Testament Hebrews to hear the holy and exalted name of the Creator of the universe expressed with the words "Lord God." However, that is the best that our English translation can offer.

Martin Luther translated Philippians 4:13, "...*I can do all things through Him who makes me powerful in Christ.*" To use the "exact words," you would need to recite Scripture in its original language: Hebrew.

I am of the opinion that both the Old and New Testaments were originally written in Hebrew.

DISCIPLES CONVERTED?

Dear Brother Froese:

When were Christ's disciples converted, especially those in the inner circle such as Peter, John, and James? Were they converted before Judas betrayed Christ that night in the garden? I believe that they were. Also, did they all receive the Holy Spirit on the Day of Pentecost, or had they been influenced by the Holy Spirit ahead of time?

Again, I appreciate your keen insight into Scripture.

-R. E. in Burlington, IA

ANSWER: According to Acts 2, the disciples were converted when they were called, but they were born again on the Day of Pentecost.

CHAPTER 7

CHRISTIAN PRACTICES?

CHRISTIAN ASTROLOGY?

Dear Mr. Froese,

Re: August issue, World Focus article about witchcraft. Although I am not a regular subscriber of *Midnight Call*, I found your complimentary issue very fascinating.

I am puzzled by the astrological zodiac picture used in the witchcraft article. As a scholar of astrological history and its influence in our Western Judeo-Christian culture, this seems very inappropriate to me.

To the biblical Hebrews, astrology was literally how God communicated with his chosen people. Much of our Christian morality evolved from astrological morality.

I know that certain fundamentalist Christians make up Scripture and ignore historical facts to keep their under-educated flocks in submission.

For some reason, astrology is often a target of these people. To me, this shows an unethical, non-Christian attitude that is strictly self-serving.

Your magazine shows unequaled quality in your very informative articles and I would hate to see you lose credibility with a small oversight such as what I have brought to your attention.

-H.E., Watertown, NY

ANSWER: Where in the Scripture do you read that "Christ...was familiar with astrology?" Or, "...astrology was literally how God communicated with His chosen people?" The Bible says, "*...holy men of God spake as they were moved by the Holy Ghost*" (2nd Peter 1:21). There is no mention of stars.

Second Timothy 3:16 reads, "*All scripture is given by inspiration of God, and is profitable for doctrine, for reproof, for correction, for instruction in righteousness.*" Again, no mention of stars.

God warned Israel, "*...lest thou lift up thine eyes unto heaven, and when thou seest the sun, and the moon, and the stars, even all the host of heaven, shouldest be driven to worship them, and serve them, which the LORD thy God hath divided unto all nations under the whole heaven*" (Deuteronomy 4:19). Astronomy is the science of the stars. Astrology, on the other hand, is defined as "the divination of the supposed influences of the stars and planets on human affairs."

KARATE
Dear Brethren,

Greetings in Christ's name. I was wondering if you had

any insight into the subject of Christians and martial arts? A Christian follows Jesus in his heart, and as long as he doesn't get involved in other religions, I think it [the martial arts are] O.K.

Is a Christian [who is participating in] martial arts giving a place to the devil just by performing the physical part of the activity? No more than a Christian who uses the Roman calendar. Although the names of months and weekdays have their origins in the occult , a Christian isn't using the calendar that way, so it is only what is in the heart that counts.

Christians in military service and Christians in law enforcement may be in situations where they have to defend themselves. They might possibly have to kill someone in the line of duty. Is that a sin? No. Murder is a sin, but having to defend yourself is not, I believe. Please correct me if I'm wrong.

-C.R., Nashua, NH

ANSWER: According to the Scriptures, each government is ordained by God (Romans 13). However, in martial arts, religions are hidden behind sports. Practicing a martial art requires a person to stand at attention in a prescribed way, bow down, shout certain words and perform other rituals which all have a religious meaning tied to them. I do not doubt that martial arts produces a self-induced superiority over an imagined enemy, but it has little, if any, worthwhile effects. The Bible says, "...*bodily exercise profiteth little...*" (1st Timothy 4:8). Furthermore, all martial arts employ varying degrees of "mind-over-matter" philosophies, clearly a form of occult mysticism.

HEAD COVERING

Dear Friends in Christ,

In your December issue, there appeared a question (and your answer) entitled "Head Covering."

I cut it out, since your answer puzzles me; three months later I am still puzzled.

I would beg to differ with you that women were instructed to keep silent in the church because of their talkativeness. I believe it is because women are not supposed to "lord it over men," and I am sure you know the Scripture passages supporting that. But this is not my purpose in writing. This letter is not meant to open an argument.

My purpose in writing regards the answer you gave that "...her hair is given for a covering." I have heard that argument many times. You, along with many others, are implying that a woman need not wear a hat or similar covering in church because her hair is her covering. However, men must not wear a hat or similar covering in church or while praying, says Paul.

Now my question: If a woman's hair is her covering, then a man's hair is his covering. Nowhere are we told that men must shave their heads (bless the baldies) when they pray. This being so, then there is no distinction when both men and women have their hair for a covering. So, then, what does Scripture mean when it says that women should have their head covered when praying, if it doesn't mean a hat or scarf?

This has puzzled me for many years. I hope you can shed some light on it.

-J.V.B. Tillsonburg, On.

ANSWER: Please re-read the first sixteen verses of 1st Corinthians 11 and you will notice that the key point is not the hair itself; the distinction lies in the length of the hair. Short hair for a man designates uncovering and long hair for a woman *"is given her for a covering."*

HOMOSEXUAL BY BIRTH?

Dear Mr. Froese,

My father and I had a discussion about homosexuals the other day. We are both Christians and do not support the homosexual way, though we did have an argument.

I say that a person is not born homosexual; that is, no one is born to become attracted to the same sex in a sexual manner.

Based on the book of Romans and Leviticus, I don't believe that God could condemn these people for their acts if they were created this way and could not make a choice.

I believe that homosexuality is a choice each individual makes due to various circumstances in their lives.

My father believes that homosexuals are born with a genetic imbalance. He does not support their ways and believes that God expects them to resist this nature and overcome it because it is sin in God's eyes.

Would you please respond in a letter with your views concerning the truth of God?

-R.E., Washington, NJ

ANSWER: All people are born sinners and are equally guilty before God. However, the Bible says, *"Whom the son makes free, he shall be free indeed."*

No one is born a sodomite, a drug addict, an alcoholic or a criminal. These lifestyles are all a matter of choice. Sodomites reveal this truth themselves when they request protection because of their sexual "preference."

HOMOSEXUALITY

Dear Brother Froese,

First I want to commend you for the grace you show in answering the questions you are asked. Many letters seem to start by telling you how great *Midnight Call* is, and how blessed they are by your response to their questions. But in the next paragraph they tell you in no uncertain terms how wrong you were in the last issue. Your answers are worded with biblical wisdom and are very gracious.

I am enclosing an article from our local newspaper about a "Gay Fundamentalist Bible School." In the last paragraph, [the writer of the article quotes] John 3:16, including gays in the *"whosoever."*

If a man who drinks continues to drink after he accepts Christ as his personal Savior, will he go to heaven when he dies if he is truly born again? This gay man seems to apply the same logic to homosexuals.

I do not agree with him, but would like to hear your answer.

-O.E., Sask, Canada

ANSWER: *"Whosoever"* does indeed include sodomites. However, the practice of sodomy is an abomination to God. Romans 1:24 actually says, *"...God also gave them up to uncleanness through the lusts of their own hearts, to dishonour their own bodies between themselves."* First Corinthians 6:18 identifies the sin of sexuality as the most serious one, *"Every sin that a man doeth is without the body; but he that committeth fornication sinneth against his own body."* Then Scripture asks, *"What? know ye not that your body is the temple of the Holy Ghost which is in you, which ye have of God, and ye are not your own?"* (verse 19).

As far as eating, drinking, and holidays are concerned, the Bible says, *"Let no man therefore judge you in meat, or in drink, or in respect of an holyday, or of the new moon, or of the sabbath days"* (Colossians 2:16). We are saved and kept by grace and not of ourselves.

ORGAN DONOR

Dear Arno,

I have considered signing an organ donor card in view of my death, but am hesitant to do so because I don't know if God approves of that practice. I can't find a verse that addresses it. Can you help me?

I eagerly await each copy of *Midnight Call*. It is the best magazine I have found on Bible prophecy and world events leading up to our blessed Savior's soon return.

-E.E., Everett, WA

ANSWER: *"...whatsoever is not of faith is sin"* (Romans 14:23). The fact that you are hesitant is a sufficient reason not to proceed. Many physicians murder unborn children in cold blood by the millions and I, for one, will not trust myself into their hands. Who would be in charge in the case of an accident? However, the major reason for my refusal is 1st Thessalonians 5:23, *"And the very God of peace sanctify you wholly; and I pray God your whole spirit and soul and body be preserved blameless unto the coming of our Lord Jesus Christ."*

CARVED FIGURES OF JESUS

Dear Mr. Froese,

Thank you for all your fine work on *Midnight Call* magazine and your other ministries.

I have a question about sculptures I am making; namely, small carved wooden figures of Jesus crucified. I believed at one time that this was God's leading, but am having doubts lately. What do you think? Can good (the Lord's glory) come of this, or am I being deceived, and engaging in making Nehushtan ("brazen trifles")? My pastor seems to think it's all right, that these sculptures are a work of art, and that art should show all of Jesus' earthly work.

Your opinion in this matter would be greatly appreciated.

-E.O., Dennis, MA

ANSWER: The fact that you are having "doubts" about

these sculptures is a sufficient reason to cease this practice: *"...for whatsoever is not of faith is sin"* (Romans 14:23). Although in this context Paul is speaking of food, this verse can also apply to our daily actions.

OLD TESTAMENT DANCING

Dear Mr. Arno:

I wholeheartedly agree with the article, "The Baptism of the Spirit." I am happy that the writer allowed the Holy Spirit to use him in such a manner. I have been longing to hear a word like this for quite some time. Thank you.

I have an issue with a statement in the article that I think needs further clarification. Spirit of truth... "Inappropriate behavior such as dancing...." Do you mean this inappropriate dancing replaces the sermon or dancing any at all is forbidden/inappropriate?

I do realize that Jesus sent His disciples out to make disciples and to spread the Gospel; He did not say to dance. However, it can't be all that wrong to dance if the Scripture approves of it. Even though I don't dance, my concern is what the Scripture says.

The following passages suggest that the saints should dance: Psalm 149:1-3; Psalm 150:4; Luke 10:21; and others such as [those concerning] David and Miriam. I don't have a lexicon; however, the dictionary I use states that the word "rejoice" used in Luke means to dance. Please clarify, as the article states there is no mention of this in Scripture.

-R.L., New York

ANSWER: In the Old Testament, the expression of joy, even worship, through dance was a totally different story [than it is today]. The people of that time had the temple, a visible manifestation of God's instruction to man completed in stone, wood, gold, and other materials. They were not born again of the Spirit of God, but they rejoiced that God had provided a place for sacrifice so that the blood of animals could be shed for the covering of sin. Notice that this blood did not take away their sin, it only acted as a covering. In the New Testament, we *"worship God in truth and spirit;"* no bodily exercise is necessary.

DANCING IN CHURCH

Dear Brother Froese:

A new song leader is constantly encouraging the church to dance before the Lord like David.

Could you tell me if the Jews ever danced in the temple? I'm having a problem with this!

David is not our example. Could you please send some information?

-N.H. in LA

ANSWER: Nowhere in Scripture are we instructed to imitate David. We are to follow the Lord Jesus Christ. The apostle Paul shows us the way in Philippians 3:10, *"That I may know him, and the power of his resurrection, and the fellowship of his sufferings, being made conformable unto his death."* There is no room for dancing.

DANCING IS PRAISING

To the Editor,

In a recent issue of the *Midnight Call* magazine, there was an article about dancing in the church. In the article, the biblical support of dancing in church was not given.

Many passages in the Bible support dancing in church.

Psalm 149:3 says, *"Let them praise his name in the dance: let them sing praises unto him with the timbrel and harp."*

And Psalm 150:4 says, *"Praise him with the timbrel and dance: praise him with stringed instruments and organs."*

There are many other passages that support dancing in church. Most of these passages are found in the Old Testament, but the ways to praise Jehovah did not change in the New Testament.

When the ark of the covenant was bought back to Israel, David danced before Jehovah.

When David's wife, Michal, saw this she despised him. Because she despised him, she was barren for the rest of her life.

Churches that criticize other churches for dancing before Jehovah should take Michal as an example. If they continue to criticize their brothers and sisters, they too may be barren (or stagnant) for the rest of the time the church remains on earth!

Thank you for your time.

-O.J.B.

ANSWER: Through the temple and priestly services, the worship of God was visibly manifested in Israel.

The people literally had to sacrifice an animal to cover their sins. That was the past!

The expressions of worship and joy you listed in your letter were the result of that visible manifestation.

But then came Jesus, who died on Calvary's cross, causing the veil in the temple to be torn from top to bottom, fulfilling the old way of worship and creating something new: the pouring out of the Spirit of God abiding with man forever.

Man became *"...a new creature: old things are passed away; behold, all things are become new"* (2nd Corinthians 5:17).

Jesus said, *"...the hour cometh, and now is, when the true worshippers shall worship the Father in spirit and in truth: for the Father seeketh such to worship him"* (John 4:23).

This prophecy clearly speaks about a change in worship.

Hebrews 13 speaks of Jesus who *"suffered without* [outside] *the gate,"* and we are invited to *"[bear] his reproach"* (verse 13) and in verse 15, *"...let us offer the sacrifice of praise to God continually, that is, the fruit of our lips giving thanks to his name."*

In our walk following the Lamb, the New Testament gives no encouragement to visibly manifest His praise in dance as it was in Old Testament days.

Neither do I see the Lord or the apostles instructing the Church to *"Praise him...with dance."*

The great apostle Paul testified, *"I will not glory, but in my infirmities."*

CHRISTIAN NUDIST?

Dear Arno Froese,

A member of my family has become interested in a group that calls themselves "Christian Nudists." How can a person be a Christian and a nudist at the same time? According to this person, these people are only being the way God intended people to be. This doesn't sound right to me. What does God say about it?

-E.E., Everett, WA

ANSWER: In Genesis 3:21, it says, *"...the LORD God make coats of skins, and clothed them."* That is exactly how God intends for His people to be...clothed!

ATTENDING RELIGIOUS FUNCTIONS

Dear Mr. Froese:

For years now, my husband and I haven't been able to come to a good strong conclusion on a particular matter. Do you think that as Christians we ought to be attending such functions as Catholic weddings, christenings, or funerals where a mass is performed?

When we were first saved, we went to all of these [types of events]. We began to question others as to whether or not it was something the Lord would want us to be doing. No one could give us a biblical answer, [they would] only tell us that we should go because "we need to love them to Christ" and other comments such as that. That answer doesn't quite seem to satisfy. After all, godly love is sometimes accompanied with rebuke, right?

Recently, my sister-in-law's father passed away. We decided to attend the wake, as we saw no harm in this; however, when it came to the funeral where a mass was to be performed, once again we began to wonder. My husband was asked to read at the mass and agreed, provided he could read his choice of the Scriptures (John 14:1-6 and 1st John 5:11-14). He did this in hopes that the Lord would use this opportunity to touch someone's heart or [to prompt someone] to question his or her own beliefs. Still we don't know if he should even have done that.

Please give us some sound biblical counsel on this matter. Are there any exceptions to attending any of the mentioned functions, such as being a family member or only attending the portion of the event that doesn't pertain to religion? What would the Lord do in the case of a funeral, christening, or wedding where a false religion is involved?

-O.N., Buchanan, NY

ANSWER: I urge you to meet the Lord in prayer before you attend any function so that you receive the inner joy, liberty, and assurance to go wherever He leads you. I would not hesitate to attend such gatherings. Based on your description, I cannot see where you have violated the Lord's command. Christians should always act in a normal manner, especially when relating to family and friends.

GUNS

Dear Editor,

The *Midnight Call* is wonderful! You are doing a great

work. However, I can't help but wonder if the excerpt from *The Kansas City Star* published in the April edition had so many redeeming features that you had to print it, or if you really believe that eliminating handguns would certainly lower the life-threatening consequences of such things as street disputes.

It seems certain that guns will always be available on the black market no matter how well regulated they are, so eliminating them by law will succeed in taking them away from law-abiding citizens.

If that happens, outlaws will be all the more bold, knowing that those who respect the law will not be carrying any protection for their person or property but will be easy marks for their exploitation. No one would even be as safe as they are now. Think about it.

-U.S., NY

ANSWER: The United States has the most liberal gun laws in the developed world; thus, the death-by-gun body count is the highest. The chances of using a firearm "for protection" are extremely slim because the perpetrators are prepared; it is the victims who are surprised.

Incidentally, I own firearms myself. However, that should not make any of us turn a blind eye to the undeniable statistical facts. The bottom line still stands: "*...they that take the sword shall perish with the sword*" (Matthew 26:52).

MORE GUNS

Dear Mr. Froese,

This is your not-so-rest-assured-about Y2K friend and I am writing in response to your editorial about guns in the July issue of *Midnight Call*. I have included several articles about facts from books by experts on this subject that I hope you will peruse. I would also add several comments to your editorial as follows:

1) Your comment that "the perpetrator is prepared and the victim is surprised" is assuming that an attack situation is static. In reality, most attacks are perpetrated by drunk, drugged or unbalanced people who are not surprising victims (i.e., they are following someone or trying to break into a home). About 2 million times a year, legal possession of a gun stops a crime cold without a shot being fired.

2) Your comment on "the most liberal gun laws in the industrial world, thus the death-by-gun body count is the result," is fallacious in the fact that 80% of homes in Switzerland and Israel have full automatic weapons and handguns and they have nowhere near our murder rate.

What really surprises me is that you attribute murder to guns and not SIN. Are these not more signs of the end-times, *"...without self control, brutal, not lovers of the good"* (2nd Timothy 3:3)?

3) Your use of Matthew 26:52 is translated *"live by the sword"* in the KJV, which I would assume is to place your faith in weapons, or else why would Jesus say *"If you don't have a sword sell your cloak and buy one"* in Luke 22:36? I believe Jesus is saying in effect, "If it's a dangerous place,

go prepared to protect yourself."

4) I haven't seen any undeniable statistical facts and I hope you will do some more research on how distorted the media has portrayed gun ownership for the advancement of their agendas.

-E.A., Indianapolis, IN

ANSWER: Sorry, but you picked the wrong two countries (Switzerland and Israel) for your example. Only under the strictest rules can a Swiss or Israeli citizen purchase a private firearm. A police background check is required and a license must be obtained. In the 80% of the homes that have weapons, the weapons are stored and maintained by qualified military personnel, and belong exclusively to the state. Misuse, even in "home-self-defense" is punishable by law. However, because of such an abundance of guns, Switzerland ranges high–with 5.31, and Israel with 2.91–in the number of gun-related deaths per 100,000 population. Please compare this to other gun-control countries:

NETHERLANDS	.70
SCOTLAND	.54
ENGLAND AND WALES	.41
JAPAN	.05
U.S.A.	14.24

-Source: Center for Disease Control and Prevention (The Kansas City Star, 4/17/98. p. A-3)

Matthew 26:52, *"...for all they that take the sword shall perish with the sword,"* is right on target.

ACUPUNCTURE

Dear Mr. Froese,

I grew up with your magazine in Holland in the 60's when my father used to read *Middernachtsroep*. I am a regular reader now and 99% in agreement. I have never been a letter writer, but there are a few things that I have to react to:

First: In the February issue, page 30, there was a news item about acupuncture and your reaction to "the religion of acupuncture." While this is all true in many cases, there is a serious side to the story. Please let me explain, and please make that clear in your column, too.

I work with a Christian doctor of Chinese origin who is Western-qualified.

He has developed a successful treatment for the very painful disease of shingles. This treatment, apart from medicine and herbs, uses needles and "cupping." However, the reason is purely scientific. The needles are used to stimulate/irritate certain nerve points in the skin near the shingles so that the body's natural immune system/defenses will rush the natural antibodies to these sites.

These areas are then punctured, and a vacuum cup is used to draw off blood locally in these areas. This, combined with injections, gets rid of the herpes zoster virus which causes the shingles and which is a dormant leftover from chicken pox in youth.

As this doctor says, "I perform the treatment but glory to God who affects the cure." So yes, acupuncture–[with] no funny religion, yin and yang, good and evil–[is] a purely logical medical use of needles to stimulate the body.

Secondly: I find that as in the above there is another area [in which] you tend to generalize: Roman Catholicism.

Again, I agree with everything you say, but there are many Christian-reborn Catholics.

I work with a local priest who, after the ritual of last rites, asks the patient, "Now [brother/sister,] do you know Jesus Christ as your personal Savior? Because if you don't, no amount of ritual will save you." If the answer is "no," he spends hours teaching the patient about Christ and a personal faith. I asked him once why he stayed in the Roman Catholic Church. He answered: "How else will they ever hear the truth if it is not for the likes of us?"

So please don't generalize: Teach the Word in truth and with love – not by hitting people over the head with a heavy Bible.

-Rev. D. E., Ontario

ANSWER: To claim that acupuncture is scientific, and to actually prove it, are two different things. Medical science does not accept acupuncture as scientific.

You are correct; I do generalize about Roman Catholicism, but not about individual Catholics. I am very happy to hear about the Catholic priest who preaches the Gospel. May the Lord grant that through his work many souls will be added to the Church.

SUICIDE

Dear Brother Froese,

A question on suicide: I have a friend who believes when it is your appointed time to die, it will happen even if you commit suicide. I understand that if a person commits suicide, it may not be God's will but He allows it to happen. Can you answer?

-No Name

ANSWER: The assumption that suicide is fulfilling God's predestined plan is incorrect. For example, Judah expresses the option between the life and death he had in his hand when he said, *"Send the lad with me, and we will arise and go; that we may live, and not die..."* (Genesis 43:8). God gives life and takes life; interference with that is against His will.

WINE

Dear Brother Froese,

I love *Midnight Call* magazine, thank you. Please help me with this problem.

My husband is a wine-drinking alcoholic. He and his alcoholic friends tell me, a born again Christian, that Jesus drank wine and all of His followers drank wine. Jesus even turned water into wine for everyone to drink, so it must be good.

My response has been, the wine of the Bible was not fermented, and do you think for a minute that Jesus would put alcohol in His holy body?

The Bible does not explain the drinking of wine. I hope you can. Thank you.

-D.E.A., Brewer, ME

ANSWER: If your husband is an alcoholic, arguing will not help. Instead, you must pray that the Lord will open his eyes so he may be freed from the bondage of alcoholism.

Regarding wine, we read in John 2:10 that the men were *"well drunk."* You can't get drunk on grape juice. When Jesus testified of John the Baptist, who did not drink wine, He said, *"The Son of man is come eating and drinking; and ye say, Behold a gluttonous man, and a winebibber..."* (Luke 7:34).

MORE WINE

Dear Brother Froese,

We thoroughly enjoy your *Midnight Call* magazine. I especially like to read the question and answer section. I usually agree with your answers given to the questions. However, I got the distinct impression that you feel Jesus made "intoxicating" wine at the wedding at Cana. Sorry, but I beg to differ with you. Enclosed is a short article on the subject. Question: If the men were so "well drunk," how would they even be able to tell that the good wine (grape juice) was saved for last? Anyway, the Bible says, *"the men had drank freely,"* meaning they drank all they wanted, not that they were all intoxicated or drunk.

So you see, as the article states, the word "wine" in the Bible might simply mean grape juice. Then there are verses that surely mean intoxicating wine. The word "wine" in the Bible is the same word for grape juice, and then the juice after it is fermented. The Bible often speaks of *"new wine."* Proverbs 3:10 says, *"...thy presses shall burst out with new wine."* And even the grapes collected from the field are called wine in some places in the Bible. A mixed wine would have been a mixture of fruit juices or the adding of water and perhaps spices to the wine. They made pomegranate wine as well as grape wine.

This is an extremely informative article. Hope it's been helpful.

-R. O. in Heber Springs, AR

ANSWER: In view of the misuse of alcohol and the often tragic results, I wish you were right. The Bible absolutely does warn against drunkenness. In fact, Luther translated Ephesians 5:18 in the following way, *"Do not gulb yourself full with wine which results in disorderly conduct..."* However, we must not falsify the Scripture. It was the governor, not the guests who said, *"...at the beginning doth set forth good wine; and when men have well drink, then that which is worse..."* This statement alone identifies the wine as an alcoholic beverage. A hungry person will eat almost anything. When he is full, he desires something delicate like a dessert because hunger no longer overrides his sense of taste. Consuming alcohol causes the opposite to happen. A person who is "well drunk" will drink virtually anything.

Luke 1 records that John the Baptist *"...shall drink neither wine nor strong drink..."* and Jesus testified, *"The*

Son of man is come eating and drinking; and ye say, Behold a gluttonous man, and a winebibber, a friend of publicans and sinners!" (Luke 7:34). Drinking grape juice is obviously not the issue here.

STRAIGHT EDGE

Dear Brother Arno,

I am a life subscriber to *Midnight Call* and *News From Israel*. I have never made a better investment in a learning tool before. You and your team have really helped me to understand a lot. Brother Malgo, who has passed on to his glorious reward, as you know, was instrumental through his books and writings in leading me closer to the Lord and a re-dedication of my life to Him. God bless you as you continue His work.

Here is an excerpt from our local newspaper on "Straight Edge" teens:

Mr. Benningfield, a finance and philosophy senior at the University of Louisville, doesn't smoke. He doesn't do drugs. He doesn't have casual sex. And he doesn't drink.

"I am proud that I have been able to stay true to my beliefs, which I believe is very important and a big part of your character as a person," he said.

Mr. Benningfield is one of the thousands of young people across the country who call themselves "straight-edge."

They shun illegal drugs, alcohol, cigarettes - even meat - in favor of a life that's vice-free, respects health and promotes individuality.

The movement was kick-started in Washington, D.C. by singer Ian MacKaye and his band, Minor Threat, in the early 1980's with the song "Straight Edge." It trumpeted the benefits of shedding alcohol and drug use, and ushered in the small but passionate new sect of punk rock culture.

The hybrid of heavy metal riffs, punk rock rhythms and evangelical lyrics that form the straight-edge musical style are forever linked to the movement.

Would you please comment on this for me? When I first heard about this, I thought it was great for our teens. Now I have decided it is just another trick of the devil against our youth. God keep you.

-A.G., Seneca, SC

ANSWER: This new belief has no relation to the Gospel. Therefore, it can be classified with all other movements, good or bad, which aim to build a better person through a self-induced faith outside of faith in Christ.

It is not surprising that "evangelical lyrics" are included in these "punk rock rhythms" because the fundamentals of rock-and-roll music have already united the world. Rock-based evangelical lyrics can be heard 24 hours a day in virtually every country on planet Earth. Ultimately, these and other groups will not lead to the promised freedom in Christ, but rather into bondage.

CHRISTIAN POLITICS

Dear Arno,

Perhaps you can help me with my understanding of a very important issue: Christians getting involved in activism to accomplish their agenda. About two years ago, I was listening to the "Grace to You" radio show with John

MacArthur, and he was making quite a convincing case to not get involved in the affairs of the world by using the "tools" of the world to accomplish our goals. His point was that as Christians, our citizenship is in heaven; we should be concerned about a lost and unsaved world and go about doing the work God placed us here to do. Also, [he said] that we should pay our taxes–not complain about our circumstances and the burdens the government places on us– and be good Christian witnesses. I couldn't agree more...but I have one problem.

Clearly, the founding of this country seems to [have been] established with God's blessing. I realize that not all the founding fathers were fundamental Bible-believers, but in all of the "accurate" history I read, God's intervention seems clearly exemplified.

Also, if you look forward through history to 1962 when prayer was removed from school, almost all vital statistics seem to have recorded a decay in morality, whether it be divorce, out-of-wedlock pregnancy, murder, violent crime, and even a decline in academic standings.

Even though I would agree that you shouldn't force spiritual values on a pagan society (i.e., prayer in schools), the absence of prayer in school clearly seems to be God saying, "All right then, have it your way and reap the consequences!"

I read your short answers to complex questions in *Midnight Call* and am looking forward to you answering this one. Should we force implementation of our beliefs on our society? History seems to support its success in some areas.

Don't misunderstand, I'm not looking to make heaven

on earth like my amillennial brothers. I realize things are going to get worse until Christ comes to take us in the Rapture. I just wanted your opinion on this matter.

-T.T., Scenery Hill, PA

ANSWER: Christ never delegated political authority to His Church. We are the little flock who is often despised, frequently persecuted and sometimes even killed. We're pilgrims on earth just passing through. To our shame, there are billions of people who don't know the way of salvation through the Lord Jesus Christ. The Great Commission is clear and straight-forward, *"Go ye into all the world, and preach the gospel to every creature."* The moment we fulfill that task, I'll be a candidate for political office.

The hidden but extreme danger in mixing church with politics is revealed in a statement Pope Leo XIII made: "And if society is to be healed now, in no other way can it be healed save by a return to Christian life and Christian institutions. When a society is perishing, the wholesome advice to give to those who would restore it is to recall it to the principles from which it sprang" (Beziger Brothers, *Encyclical Letters of Pope Leo XIII;* New York: 1903; ISBN 0-89555-529-8). This sounds almost identical to many of the statements from our Freemason founding fathers. Fundamentally speaking, this is anti-Christian because the Church does not have a political or geographic calling.

I surely agree with some of the statistics showing a decay of morality, murder and violent crime, but I wonder about "academic standings." The children who have graduated since 1962 are now successfully running the most sophisticated and prosperous society in our history.

CARNAL CHRISTIANS

Dear Arno Froese,

I realize that the Bible in no way encourages being carnal, but both the Old and New Testament says that there is such a thing as a carnal Christian. Please explain to me how a Christian, who will stand at the Judgment Seat of Christ, will be burned up. The Bible says that if you give a cup of water to someone in Jesus' name, you will receive a reward for it. How could they have ever turned from their sins in order to be saved? Also, please explain how turning from your sins is not works on your part.

The 1st Corinthians' carnal Christians were practicing all kinds of sin and the Bible said many of them were sick, and many of them "slept" because of living that way. Please explain how they could live this way, if they had to turn from their sins in order to be saved.

-L.R.A., Lake City, FL

ANSWER: Even Paul said, *"I am carnal, sold under sin"* (Romans 7:14). He was referring to his flesh and blood. Additionally, the law is considered to be *"carnal ordinances"* (see Hebrews 9:10). First Corinthians 3:15 describes the carnal Christian; his *"work shall be burned."* This has no relation to a lost person giving a *"cup of water"* because upon a person without Christ *"the wrath of God abideth on him."* First Corinthians 11:28-31 describes the result of a Christian who fails to heed verse 22, "*Let a man examine himself.*"

LOTTERY

Dear Mr. Froese:

I would like to ask you a question. Should Christians play the lottery? I was saved 21 years ago and have not played it since then because I do not believe in it, but a couple of Christians I know drove from Ohio to Indiana a few weeks ago to play the big powerball.

I'm not going to say anything to them, but I would like to hear what you have to say.

-W. M., Dayton, OH

ANSWER: What someone does with the money he earns is his decision. However, the question each one of us must answer is: "Are we taking care of our household and our church, and do we follow the Scripture's admonition to, "*...Owe no man any thing?*"

ENDORSE GAMBLING?

Dear Brother Froese,

I love *Midnight Call* and *News From Israel,* and have been receiving them both for a couple of years. They are a great blessing to me.

Brother, I am, however, very concerned regarding your response to a letter headed "Lottery" on page 52 of the October issue of *Midnight Call.* The writer is obviously concerned regarding the right or wrong of gambling for Christians.

I believe the lottery is gambling. The writer of the letter would like your Christian opinion on this matter. I think she should be commended and encouraged for abstaining from gambling for twenty-one years, because she loves Christ. This is implied in her letter.

You didn't give her a straight answer, brother. Rather, you gave her three questions you said we all must answer, and you stated that what we do with our own money is our own decision. Doesn't all we own belong to God?

My question is: If a Christian fulfills the three requirements you mentioned and has money left over, is he then free to gamble, party, womanize, purchase pornographic material, or whatever? It's his money. I need to hear from you, brother.

I would love to know where you stand on this issue.

-N.E., Apopka, FL

ANSWER: The moment we start categorizing certain activities by "do's" and "don'ts," we are re-establishing laws from which we have already been redeemed through the blood of Christ.

For that reason, the lottery, casinos, the stock exchange, investments, mortgages and credit cards are non-issues to me.

The distinction that must be kept is a two-fold identity which Paul reveals in 1st Corinthians 3:21,23, *"For all things are yours; ...And ye are Christ's; and Christ is God's."*

Incidentally, does the last paragraph you wrote ("...free

to gamble, party, womanize, purchase pornographic material...") apply to you or to others? You see, dear brother, our own corrupt sinful nature is always concerned about others but rarely about ourselves. That fact also contributed to my answer to the previous letter writer regarding the lottery.

MORE ON GAMBLING

Dear Brother Froese,

I'm writing in reference to the letter titled "Lottery" in the October issue of *Midnight Call* and in the January issue, the letter titled "Gambling."

The answer you gave on the lottery was the same answer I gave myself when I was gambling and playing the lottery. As long as my bills were paid, and my tithes and donations were taken care of, I was free to do whatever I wanted with the money left over.

One Sunday morning, as I was teaching Sunday School (teenage) class, a young girl asked me if it was wrong to gamble. I told her I would see what the Bible had to say on the subject and give her the answer along with Scripture to back it up.

Early the next morning, sitting at my desk, I no sooner opened the Bible when the Spirit spoke these words with emphasis, "God isn't a God of chance, God is a God of blessing" (Proverbs 10:22). This isn't for everyone, only for those who have an ear to hear.

-I.A., Larence, MI

ANSWER: Your letter seems to indicate that I endorse gambling, which I don't. It isn't my task to identify and, subsequently, recommend which methods of entertainment are acceptable and which are to be rejected. I have no intention of establishing new laws; my exclusive aim is to point people to Jesus, who forgives sins.

You mentioned Proverbs 10:22, which in the King James translation reads, *"The blessing of the LORD, it maketh rich, and he addeth no sorrow with it."*

The NIV reads, *"The blessing of the Lord brings health and he adds no trouble to it."*

My Hebrew Bible reads, *"It is a blessing of the Lord that enriches and no toil can increase it."*

I don't see where this verse has any relation to gambling.

CHAPTER 8

END OF LIFE

DO DECEASED SEE THE LIVING?

Dear Brother Froese,

Recently at a funeral, I overheard someone say that the deceased, being a born again Christian, was in heaven looking down at his loved ones here on earth and smiling down on them.

I haven't been able to find anything in the Bible to back up this statement.

I would appreciate your response to this. Also, we really enjoy your magazine. It helps in our study of the Bible.

Thank you in advance. May the Lord bless your ministry.

-Mrs. R.O., LaSalle, CO

ANSWER: The Bible says, "...*absent from the body...present with the Lord*" (2nd Corinthians 5:8). To look down from heaven and witness the chaos, disappointment and tragedies on

165

earth would certainly not be considered "heaven."

However, heaven rejoices when a sinner repents, and I believe that the saints who went before us participate in the victory of believers based on Hebrews 12:1, *"...seeing we also are compassed about with so great a cloud of witnesses...."*

LAST WILL

Dear Brother Froese,

For years, I have been troubled by a situation that will hopefully occur soon, but certainly in the not-too-distant future. I have spoken to other Christians and even to a Christian lawyer about this matter, but I have the feeling that nobody took me seriously! Hopefully you will advise me and the Christian community as to what we should do about the following:

Since we expect the Rapture to occur soon, what will happen to all the financial and material assets of those who are raptured?

Many Christians who have no close relatives will their assets to any of the many Christian organizations and ministries. However, after the Rapture, there will be no genuine Christian ministry in operation anymore!

When we consider the combined assets of all Christians, some having substantial assets, of all those ministries around the world, should the godless governments be the beneficiaries of this?

After considerable meditation about this, I feel God gave me the only sensible solution from a Christian point of view, which would also be pleasing to our Creator, Redeemer, and Sustainer. We should make the state of Israel the beneficiary of our financial and material assets after the Rapture!

When God promised Abraham, *"I will bless those who will bless you,"* does this not include his seed also? The 144,000 who will proclaim the Gospel after the Rapture, will they not come from Abraham's seed?

Since we have a responsibility before God for what we do with what He has entrusted to us, I would appreciate your advise for this situation.

-E.C., Manlius, NY

ANSWER: To *will* assets to Israel after the Rapture sounds like a simple solution, but it would be a legal nightmare. I would gladly support the 144,000, but how can we legally identify these people? We need their names and addresses. Furthermore, how would a court recognize our departure? Remember that Israel, in conjunction with Rome, will be the headquarters of the Antichrist who will send forth his deceptive gospel around the world.

The only answer I have at this moment is that we are not responsible for those we cannot reach. However, it is our duty to preach now, while we have the opportunity to do so. Anyone who has the means today should make sure that it is being used for the Gospel *now*, while the opportunity presents itself. Don't wait for tomorrow.

WILLS AND ESTATES

Dear Brother Arno,

I am writing to you today to see if you have had any specific knowledge given or made available to you about a very interesting but disturbing problem regarding the Rapture. Naturally, as Christians, we are joyfully looking forward to that wonderful day. Unfortunately, most of us have relatives and friends who do not know the Lord or who reject the message of salvation. This leads directly to the problem: What happens after we are gone with regard to our wills and estates? The government will certainly know that we are gone, but where does that leave the situation legally? If we cannot be legally and officially declared dead, then theoretically, nothing can be done with our wills or estates for a considerable time. That, in turn, could create even more problems. It would certainly be helpful to those who are left behind to be able to benefit from some of the inheritances to which they are entitled.

I am also wondering if Canadian and U.S. legislation may differ on this matter.

Your comments and advice would be appreciated.

May God continue to bless your ministry in the days ahead.

R.A. in Ontario, CANADA

ANSWER: All things will be left behind when the Rapture takes place. Who will benefit? Probably the government of the Antichrist. Since the Church is global, I would presume that international law would apply.

I have urged believers for years to unburden them-selves of excess assets they have accumulated throughout the years. Most important is for us to be totally saturated with the truth of the Scripture so that our testimony will not be misread by our loved ones and that many will still come to Jesus before it is too late.

Of course, this situation would be a legal nightmare, as I mentioned previously, but that's a job for the attorneys. Our local telephone book advertises 65 pages of attorneys and only 18 pages of churches. They will have their work cut out for them.

CREMATION

Mr. Malgo,

I would like to ask what happens to people who are cremated in house fires, car fires, ship fires, etc.

As I look on any kind of leaving this sin-cursed world, we are told we will turn back to ashes. After our spirit leaves our bodies, they are nothing but clay. (Like what we were formed of and made of in the image of God, which was breath, His spirit that each one of us has). When the spirit leaves the body, it is either in God's care or the devil's. [For example,]just as when Jesus arose from the grave, He was no longer in His earthly body, but in the body that Father God gave Him after the awful debt He paid for us, to choose whom we will serve.

So to think of this earthly body, regardless of how it becomes dust, I'm sure does not count as long as we are ready to meet our Lord and Savior Jesus Christ when He returns. I don't want to be cremated, but if I am, I'm going to be with the Lord in my new body like Jesus had when He arose. This is how I feel and see things.

I wrote this letter to also ask you what happens to bodies that are eaten by alligators, sharks, or other animals? I know that the soul lives forever, and that this body will return to what it was made from. The Bible is in no way privately interpreted.

E.O. in Estecada, OR

ANSWER: Brother Malgo went home to be with the Lord on August 8, 1992; therefore, I will answer your question regarding cremation.

Cremation, accidental burnings, or being "eaten by crocodiles" has absolutely no relation to salvation. We do advise the burial of the body because Scripture illustrates how the saints were buried, not burned. As much as it is in our power, we should heed 1st Thessalonians 5:23, *"And the very God of peace sanctify you wholly; and I pray God your whole spirit and soul and body be preserved blameless unto the coming of our Lord Jesus Christ."* You should also note that verse 22 says, *"Abstain from all appearance of evil."* Cremation is a heathen custom popularized by Hinduism.

MORE ON CREMATION

Dear Mr. Froese,

In one of your *Midnight Call* magazines I received a while ago, you answered a question from one of your readers concerning cremation. I always share your magazine with my friends so I do not have the magazine available. It seems that you warned this person against cremation because he could not go to be with the Lord at death. In my understanding of what you said, every Christian who died in some other way, his soul would be with the Lord at death, except suicide.

My question is that if the soul of every Christian goes to the Lord at death, how can cremation have anything to do with his soul when it has already gone to heaven?

I also have a problem with a Christian who dies in a fire, certainly his soul would go to be with the Lord the instant he suffocated.

E. N. in Coon Rapids, MN

ANSWER: According to my understanding of Scripture, the disposal of the body has no relation to salvation. We warn against cremation because it is a pagan practice. The Scripture teaches burial, not burning.

For example, if Lazarus had been burned, the prophetic statement that Jesus made, *"...Take ye away the stone..."*(John 11:39), and *"...Loose him, and let him go..."* (verse 44) would never have been uttered.

If you search the Scripture from Genesis to Revelation, you will discover that burning is always a type of judgment rendered upon objects of God's wrath. It hardly seems right that a Christian would resort to a practice used by pagan cultures for thousands of years. The body of the Christian is placed in the ground at death with the assurance of the resurrection.

ETERNAL FIRE?

Dear Arno,

Refer to *Midnight Call* January, page 36, "Letters to the Editor."

I would like to comment on your answer to the letter entitled, "Is eternal really temporal?"

The words, *"eternal fire"* in Jude 1:7 refer to the incineration of the sinners and their cities of Sodom and Gomorrah. Obviously the charred bodies expired quickly and the flames died out when there was nothing left to burn. As you stated, the eternal God can strike the flint to ignite a burning anytime He feels it's necessary. Hence, eternal fire, although not continual in one area. I don't see the idea of "eternal punishment," (i.e. flames licking at the posteriors of sinners trying not to step on hot coals with their charred feet in an eternal environment).

-H. O. in Ripton, VT

ANSWER: Truth does not change whether you believe in the existence of eternal punishment or not. Revelation 20:15 states, *"And whosoever was not found written in the book of life was cast in the lake of fire."* Verse 10 makes the certainty of eternal punishment very clear, *"...and shall be tormented day and night for ever and ever."*

RESURRECTION OF SATAN?

Dear Sir:

I realize this is an odd argument, but I feel this may be a new angle that may either create more controversy or create new insight into Satan.

Genesis chapter 6:2 says the sons of God saw the daughters of men and married them. Verse 3 is just a prediction that they only had 120 years before the flood. In verse 4, there were giants, and when the sons of God married these women, they had mighty children.

There are two schools of thought here: 1) the children of Shem married into the children of Cain; and 2)angels were marrying women and having children. The only argument against this is that it's believed that angels can't reproduce or "know" a woman in the biblical sense. I agreed with this assessment but I noticed something very strange in Genesis 3 that seems to say angels can reproduce or "know" women in the biblical sense. Notice verse 15, *"...And I will put enmity between thee* (Satan) *and the woman, and between thy seed* (Satan's) *and her seed; it shall bruise thy head* (Satan's), *and thou* (Satan) *shalt bruise his* (Jesus) *heel."* Notice it says Satan's seed. Now in the Gospel, we have the family tree of Jesus listed back to Adam and Eve. This leaves the door open, as Satan is a copycat of Jesus. So can we assume Satan has a family tree that is going to run to the Antichrist of Revelation? And just as Jesus was killed and arose three days later (Matthew 12:40 proves Jesus was killed on Wednesday, was buried as Thursday began [sunset Wednesday], and sometime between sunset on Saturday and sunrise Sunday, He arose. This is the only way you can fit in three days and three nights).

So shall the Antichrist suffer a head wound, die and arise three days later, being indwelt by Satan, at the middle of the tribulation. I know you will argue that all men are the seed of their father, Satan. But this is general, whereas this prophecy is talking about two, the one who is the enemy (Satan) of Jesus (God). The book of Revelation is the story of Satan (angel) and his future in dealing with mankind, and his final defeat by Jesus, God the Son, not Jesus the Son of God.

-E.L. in Barrington, NH

ANSWER: That fallen angels married the children of men and apparently were able to procreate before the judgment of the flood is the theory I follow, and it remains an open question.

Satan's seed are the children of disobedience. Jesus said to His enemies, *"Ye are of your father the devil"* (John 8:44).

I believe in the Friday crucifixion and Sunday resurrection. Why? Because Jesus died the day before the Sabbath and rose on the third day – not *after* the third day. Even if Jesus spent only a split second of one day in the grave, it is counted to Him as 24 hours. Consider the following verse, *"For whosoever shall keep the whole law, and yet offend in one point, he is guilty of all"* (James 2:10). You don't need to break all the laws, [breaking] one breaks them all. Therefore in the reverse direction, there is no requirement for a 24-hour day. The disciples on their way to Emmaus testified, *"...today is the third day since these things were done"* (Luke 24:21). That clearly reveals that Jesus was not in the grave for the duration of the "third day," which according to verse 13 was *"that same day,"* being Sunday, the first day of the week.

"And I saw one of his heads as it were wounded to death; and his deadly wound was healed: and all the world wondered after the beast," does not signify his death but simply states that one of his seven heads receives a wound that is deadly but does not result in death. The fact that he does not die and this wound is healed causes the world to wonder after the beast.

SATAN IN HEAVEN?

Dear Brother Froese:

Just a few words to express my appreciation for this prophetic magazine, *Midnight Call.* I love to read your cover story each month. And the "Marks of a Cult" by Dave Breese is very good and informative.

But I do have a question: You state that Satan and his angels will be cast out of heaven in the future. The way I understand it is that he already has been cast out (Luke 10:18). Jesus said that He saw Satan fall from heaven. Revelation 12:7 says *"...there was war in heaven."* This was an event that had happened in the past. Some people believe that everything mentioned in Revelation is future. But I believe that Revelation 12 describes the rebellion when angels *"...kept not their first estate, but left their own habitation"* (Jude 6). This is what I believe to be the invasion of heaven in an effort to dethrone God - when Lucifer desired to become God. I know that there is much mystery here, that perhaps we will never know all that we desire to know in this life.

Jack Van Impe also teaches that this is all future. So you

perhaps know things that I have not seen as yet.

-I.E. in Atlanta, GA

ANSWER: Revelation 12 is prophecy of the past, present and future. In Egypt, 3,500 years ago, Satan persecuted the woman (Israel) and he continues to persecute her today. This persecution will culminate during the Great Tribulation.

No doubt Satan has access before the throne of God because it is there that he accuses the brethren.

Who are the brethren? Believers. For that reason we have an advocate, a lawyer, in heaven – One who stands in our defense.

Only when the Rapture takes place will Satan be cast out of heaven to earth, *"Therefore rejoice, ye heavens, and ye that dwell in them. Woe to the inhabiters of the earth and of the sea! for the devil is come down unto you, having great wrath, because he knoweth that he hath but a short time"* (Revelation 12:12).

C H A P T E R   9

SCRIPTURE EXPLANATION

UNPARDONABLE SIN AND JUDAS

Dear Mr. Froese,

My sister informed me that she sent a letter asking you to explain the "unpardonable sin." Although I did not read your response to her letter, I agree the "unpardonable sin" appears to be total rejection of Christ, and because of this rejection–it becomes blasphemous to the Holy Spirit! But NOT ALL of those who receive the Holy Spirit are instantly sealed, as is clarified in Hebrews 6:4-6, *"For it is impossible for those who were once enlightened, and have tasted of the heavenly gift, and were made partakers of the Holy Ghost, And have tasted the good word of God, and the powers of the world to come, If they shall fall away, to renew them again unto repentance; seeing they crucify to themselves the Son of God afresh, and put him to an open shame."*

Also, my sister and I have had many discussions in

reference to Judas–she feels that Judas was forgiven, but he could not be forgiven until after Christ arose from the dead! She cited Matthew 27:3, which states that *"Judas repented himself."* This sounds good on the surface, but there are no Scriptures verifying that Judas was forgiven. In fact, in Acts 1:25, we find, *"...Judas by transgression fell, that he might go to his own place."*

-A.D. in Harrisburg, PA

ANSWER: Hebrews 6 states that a person cannot be saved twice. He who deliberately sins is *"...nigh unto cursing."* Such a person's work is *"...to be burned"* (1st Corinthians 3:15). The sealing of the Holy Spirit, also known as the baptism of the Holy Spirit, is one and the same. It takes place at the moment of our rebirth (see Ephesians 1:13 and 1st Corinthians 12:13). You are certainly correct regarding Judas. Jesus plainly testifies in John 17:12 that none were lost except *"the son of perdition."*

ADOPTION

Dear Brother Froese,

Could you tell me in a few sentences exactly what adoption means, as found in Romans 8:23, Ephesians 1:5, and Galatians 4:5? I understand it's the placing of a son, but how and when? Since we are born into the family of God, why do we need adoption? Can you help?

-H.O. in Ontario, Canada

ANSWER: The word "adoption" can also mean "sonship."

Martin Luther translated it as "kindschaft," identifying a parent-child relationship. The word "adoption" seems to be a good translation because we are added to an already existing family: Israel (read Ephesians 2:12-13 and 3:6).

SAVED BY GRACE

Dear Mr. Froese:

I am writing as a Bible-believing Christian to say that I enjoy the *Midnight Call* magazine. There are some questions I would like answered so that I can share the Word of God more fully and truthfully. Hope you can help.

1) Are there any Scriptures or any prophecy pertaining to cloning?

2) Would you explain the process of dividing by lot as to inheritance, etc.?

3) How do you explain Luke 9:62, which says, *"No man, having put his hand to the plough, and looking back, is fit for the kingdom of God?"*

4) What is the explanation about Lot's wife, who looked back and became a pillar of salt? Was she saved or not?

5) Do you believe once saved, always saved? I don't.

I would like to be enlightened on this. It seems like Catholics are going to their priest each week for forgiveness and then doing whatever they wish the rest of the week. Please explain and thanks so very much. May God add his richest blessing to your ministry.

-L. N. in Philippi, WV

ANSWER: I will answer your questions according to the numbers you listed:

1) I have not found a reference to cloning in the Scripture, other than the fact that the Antichrist will perform lying signs and wonders.

2) There is much disagreement regarding the actual process of casting the lot. However, the meaning is simple: it was a lottery by which an election was made.

3) Luke 9:26 tells us that once we have made a decision to follow the Lord, we should never look back.

4) Lot's wife certainly was saved from the destruction of Sodom and Gomorrah. Old Testament saints are saved on the basis of their "looking ahead" to the Messiah-Redeemer, the one who would be the ultimate sacrifice for their sins.

5) John 3:15 says, *"...whosoever believeth in him should not perish, but have eternal life,"* and is reinforced by verse 16, *"...whosoever believeth in him should not perish, but have everlasting life..."* This is settled eternally in heaven once and for all.

You are confusing the rebirth with the "conversion" which takes place quite often, but does not produce the rebirth. If salvation is not eternal, then I must work for my salvation. If I have to work for my salvation, then it is no longer received through grace, but through works.

6000 YEARS?

Dear Mr. Froese:

First, I think your *Midnight Call* magazine is the best

publication around and I am also glad to be a supporter of your ministry.

I have a question that I hope you can explain to me in a letter. I have been taught that it has been approximately 6000 years since Adam and Eve. Approximately 2000 years until Abraham, 2000 years until the first coming of Christ and then 2000 years to the present. How do we know how many years there were from Adam to Abraham and so on? Are times and dates indicated in the Old Testament Scriptures or historical writings that tell us?

-R. E. in Washington, NJ

ANSWER: There are a number of ways to calculate the years back to Adam, but the simplest is to read Genesis 5 and 11.

Abraham was born in 2212 B.C. and died in 2037 B.C. The ages from Jacob through David are listed. The captivity, the return to Jerusalem and the conclusion of Old Testament prophecies by Jeremiah and Malachi are dated at approximately 400 B.C. Most of the biblical figures are substantiated by archaeology and historical sources.

INFANT BAPTISM

Dear Reverend Froese,

I have been a Christian for several years. Reading *Midnight Call* has helped me in many ways to strengthen my faith in Jesus Christ our Savior!

I recently came across an article in one of your previous issues that dealt with the subject of baptism. I hold a

Bible study group with some friends. The day we came across this article, we got into a discussion on baptism. The discussion brought up questions that left us all stumped. We are hoping you will be able to answer them for us.

Why do churches baptize infants? Mark 16:15-16 says, *"And he said unto them, Go ye into all the world, and preach the gospel to every creature. He that believeth and is baptized shall be saved; but he that believeth not shall be damned."*

Does this mean that if you are too young, or have not been introduced to the Gospel, you will not be saved?

Another question is when a person is baptized, should he or she be completely submerged or should water just be sprinkled on the head?

Thank you for all your input. Your information will be very helpful to the other members of my Bible study and me.

There are a couple other things I was wondering if you could answer for me. Do you know the location of the Garden of Eden spoken of in the Old Testament? Do you know where and when the "new Jerusalem" will be built? Do you believe in life after death?

-E. E. in Fergus Falls, MN

ANSWER: According to Romans 6:4-5 and Colossians 2:12, baptism demonstrates the burial and resurrection of Christ. We preach the message "believe and be baptized," not vice versa. Thus, the biblical way is by immersion. Baptism does not determine salvation. Salvation is only obtained through faith in Jesus. The last part of your quoted verse continues, *"...but he that believeth shall not be* *damned."*

Based on Genesis 2:10-14, the only geographical reference to the Garden of Eden is the Euphrates River.

Scripture does not tell us "where" or "when" the "new Jerusalem" will be built, but it clearly shows its existence in Revelation 21:26.

Indeed, I believe in life after death.

GEOGRAPHICAL AND POLITICAL PROMISE?

Dear Mr. Froese,

Regarding "Replacing Israel" (June). You replied, "The Church does not have a geographical and political promise, but the Jews do!"

What about Romans 11:17, *"And if some of the branches be broken off, and thou, being a wild olive tree, wert graffed in among them, and with them partakest of the root and fatness of the olive tree."*

Grafted into what? The Abrahamic Covenant! If not, then to whom is Christ speaking about judging the twelve tribes of Israel in the regeneration (millennium) (Matthew 19:28, Luke 22:30)? The apostles are part of the Body of Christ.

I am confident the "Bride" will be with Christ after "Armageddon," and from then on, upon the "old" and "new" earth.

-D. A. in Blavisville, GA

ANSWER: You are confusing the spiritual with the carnal. Indeed, we have become partakers of the Abrahamic

Covenant by faith in spiritual matters. But the Church does not have the promise of a geographical area such as was given to the Jews. Nor do we have a political promise as some suppose (that we are to establish a Christian government). The fact that Jesus will return with the Church on earth has no relationship to any geographical or political promise here and now.

EGYPT'S 40-YEAR DESOLATION

Mr. Froese,

In your October "Letters to the Editor," you responded to a question concerning Egypt's desolation, prophesied by Ezekiel (29:8-16; 30:10-12, 20-26; 32:11-15). You correctly stated that, "Egypt was never desolate for forty years and thereafter gathered back to the land of Egypt." You then indicated that, "this is yet to come."

My follow-up question is this: How can Ezekiel's prophecy possibly be fulfilled in the future? Nebuchadnezzar has been dead for 2,557 years, and Babylon lost its sovereignty 2,534 years ago. Isn't it too late to fulfill Ezekiel 30:10?

Furthermore, Ezekiel prophesied that every prophecy would be fulfilled in the lifetime of his contemporaries (Ezekiel 12:21-28). Is it correct to suppose that Ezekiel 12:21-28 applies only to chapters 6-12? Notice the phrases "...*every vision*" (verse 23), "...*saith the Lord God*" (verse 25), and "...*none of my words*" (verse 28). Also, notice the future tense of verse 25, "...*I will speak.*" It seems that Ezekiel was telling his contemporaries that from that time forward, every prophecy would be fulfilled in "...*days are at hand*" (verse 23), "...*in your days*" (verse 25) not "...*many days to come*" (verse 27), not "...*that are far off*" (verse 27), and not "...*be prolonged any more*" (verse 28). It appears to be 2 1/2 millennia too late.

Was Ezekiel a false prophet? Or is there another explanation?

-L. M., Spring City, TN

ANSWER: Egypt did in fact become a "base kingdom" during the reign of Babylon. It never amounted to anything of significance even until this very day. Egypt is presently one of the poorest Arab countries, with an $800 gross national product per capita per year. "How could Babylon destroy Egypt if it has disappeared from the world scene for two and a half millennia?" is a valid question. Ezekiel 28 documents the judgment of the king of Tyrus. The prophet is speaking about the king, but Satan is clearly revealed as he continues to write. How do we know? Because King Tyrus was never the "*anointed cherub,*" nor had he ever walked "...*up and down in the midst of the stones of fire.*" It also cannot be said that he "...*was perfect in all thy ways.*" Through the king of Tyrus, we are provided with a prophetic glimpse back to the origin of Satan.

My interpretation is that the power structure that implements final judgment on Egypt will be the last Nebuchadnezzar: Mystery Babylon, which is Rome. Don't confuse God's words with man's. God's Word is eternal and not limited to time, ours are. God fulfills His Word in His time.

185

RULE WITH HIM

Dear Mr. Arno Froese:

I would like to take this opportunity to say, "Thank you" to your staff for an excellent job on keeping *Midnight Call* up-to-date with the news. Christians and non-Christians need this knowledge on world events along with the truth of the Scriptures. It is one of the finest magazines I have had the privilege to read. Each month, I look forward to my copy and get excited to see what topic you will write about. Your articles on Abraham were great.

I do have a question concerning your article on Abraham. I find Abraham was the grandfather of Sheba and Dedan, yet I find Ham's son Raamah also had 2 sons, Sheba & Dedan. How do we know in Ezekiel 38 which Sheba and Dedan it is referring to? Ham's grandson or Abraham's grandsons? Genesis 10:7 (Seba) or Genesis 25:3 (Sheba)?

The second question addresses the Church saints and the saints during the tribulation. When Jesus returns with His saints and sets up His kingdom for a thousand years, what will the Church saints be doing (our duties) and what about the tribulation saints? What will be their duties? Will we all be doing the same duties or work? This part isn't too clear to me. Thank you again for your help and teachings on the Scriptures. God bless all of you.

-E. E. in Stephenville, TX

ANSWER: Seba is mentioned in Genesis 10:7 while Sheba is mentioned in Genesis 25:3. Ezekiel 38 speaks of groups of people expressed in the words, *"all of them."* Verse 13 reads, *"Sheba, and Dedan, and the merchants of Tarshish, with all the young lions thereof...."* These are primarily Arab people.

The Church shall rule with Him as kings and priests (Revelation 5:10) and the tribulation saints shall rule with Him as priests (Revelation 20:6). What will be our duty? I don't know. One thing we can be sure of, whatever we will be doing will be indescribable glory.

REIGN WITH HIM

Dear Brother Froese,

Recently in a Bible study, I was told that after the Rapture, Great Tribulation and Millenniall reign, Satan will be loosed for a season.

Now here's the problem: The teacher said that there were people who wouldn't give into Satan's temptation and that these people would stay on earth, coming into the new Jerusalem once a year. The raptured ones and all who were ever saved would live in heaven, but these people would live on earth.

I read in 2nd Peter 3:10 that the earth shall be destroyed by fire.

I am looking for a new heaven and a new earth. Maybe you can help shed some light on this.

-A.T. in Pelham, AL

ANSWER: The Church, also known as the spiritual temple, is the body of Christ. She will be raptured to meet the Lord in the air and *"...so shall we ever be with the Lord"*

187

(1st Thessalonians 4:16).

The Lord shall rule in Jerusalem for a thousand years and quite naturally, "...*we shall reign on earth...*" with Him. Wherever He is, there we shall be also.

However, the saints who come out of the Great Tribulation "...*lived and reigned with Christ a thousand years*" (Revelation 20:4). They don't belong to the Church, but are saved on the merits of the shed blood of Christ for all eternity.

Second Peter 3:10 will be fulfilled after the thousand-year kingdom is over.

LUCIFER

Dear Editor:

I was reading your article on Satanology. You call Lucifer "**daystar**" in Isaiah 14:12 but the King James says "*son of the morning.*" Also, the King James Version of 2nd Peter 1:19, the "daystar" clearly refers to Jesus. I do not understand why you use "daystar" for Lucifer.

The Revised Standard Version of Isaiah 14:12 leaves out Lucifer; it has "*O Day Star, son of dawn,*" so it really calls Lucifer Jesus. I understand all new versions leave Lucifer out of Isaiah 14:12.

These new versions are corrupt, confusing and deceitful. God is not the author of confusion; I don't know why so many Christian leaders promote and use them. This is why our morals are getting worse and worse and why we have no spiritual power in this country anymore.

I heard a man call in on a talk show discussing

Christianity and Islam. The caller said he was thinking about becoming a Muslim because it really sounded good, and then he said, "The Christians can't even agree on a Bible; I've read several of their (Bibles) but they don't agree and are confusing." So much for the new versions–they do more harm than good, and bring in many false doctrines.

-Mrs. W.K. in Crosby, MN

ANSWER: Because it is virtually impossible to precisely translate from one language to another, the word "Lucifer" has been added to the KJV translation to emphasize that this "morning star," or, as the Hebrew translation says, *"O shining One, Son of dawn,"* must not be confused with the *"bright and morning star,"* the Lord Jesus, as revealed in the book of Revelation. Please keep in mind that the Word of God is perfect, without error, and is never in need of revision, alteration, or correction. However, our translations do need to be revised because languages change, and they did so particularly during the Middle Ages. For that reason, the King James translation of 1611 has been revised 11 times; these revisions were deemed necessary by the original King James scholars.

GOD FORSAKEN

Dear Sir:

I am always encouraged by your magazine and its unwavering stand for the truth at any cost. I was alarmed, however, to read Marcel Malgo's interpretation of Matthew

27:46, "...*My God, my God why hast thou forsaken me?*"

Mr. Malgo has read this text to mean that God must have looked away from His only Son. Jesus was quoting from Psalm 22:1 to bring direct attention to the fulfillment of Messianic prophecy. If Mr. Malgo continued through the Psalm, he would have read the following in verse 24: "*For he hath not despised nor abhorred the affliction of the afflicted; neither hath he hid his face from him; but when he cried unto him, he heard...*". Also, Ephesians 5:1 can assure us that Christ's sacrifice was a fragrant offering, pleasing to His Father. Jesus might have felt forsaken as David did in Psalm 31:22, but God never forsook Him.

-T. L. in Kitchener, Ontario

ANSWER: I certainly wouldn't interpret Jesus' cry, "*Why hast thou forsaken me?*" with your words that He "might have felt forsaken." God the Father had to forsake His Son. Jesus died on Calvary's cross. As the Son of God, He is eternally one with the Father and the Holy Spirit, but as the Son of man, He became sin for us and had to be God-forsaken.

BAPTISM FOR THE DEAD

Dear Mr. Froese:

What does 1st Corinthians 15:29 mean by being baptized for the dead? Why would someone want to be baptized for the dead since there's no chance to repent after one dies?

I often wondered what Isaiah 66:24 and Mark 9:45-48 meant when they spoke of hell as being a place, "...*where their worm dieth not."* However, I recently read a book called, *A Divine Revelation of Hell* by Mary K. Baxter, where she is taken to hell in the spirit by Jesus Christ so that she can warn others that the torment of hell is real, as the dead are conscious of their surroundings and they can actually feel the worms crawling around in their decaying bodies while they are in the pits of fire pleading for a chance to repent; and there is no forgiveness after death. Their pain and torment never ends.

-N. N. in Wingdale, NY

ANSWER: Since there's no further detail in the Scripture regarding "baptism for the dead," I must use an explanation a Russian believer gave to us during communist persecution. "When a brother was taken to prison because of his faith, the church would pray for a new convert and that person would be baptized 'for the dead' meaning to take his place in the church for the one who was taken away."

Isaiah 66:24 and Mark 9:45-48 simply describe eternal damnation. Those who are saved will experience indescribable glory and those who are lost will experience indescribable torment. For that reason, I must reject the book, *A Divine Revelation of Hell* by Mary K. Baxter.

Absolutely no verse in Scripture that tells us that the Lord would, in latter days, inspire a woman to describe hell. God's full counsel, which is all-sufficient for salvation, sanctification and knowledge, is found from Genesis to Revelation.

WILL WE BECOME GODS?

Dear Brother Froese:

This is the most important question I will ever ask, so I am trusting in your wisdom to set this straight in my mind. Please don't misunderstand: I am not on the devils' side, but the Bible says what it says. Help!

In the Garden of Eden, one of the claims made by Satan was that if Adam and Eve disobeyed their Creator and ate the forbidden fruit, they would be as gods (Genesis 3:5). As soon as this happened, *"And the LORD God said, Behold, the man is become as one of us, to know good and evil"* (Genesis 3:22). Doesn't this mean that Satan was right?

-M. L. in Williamsport, PA

ANSWER: It should come as no surprise that Satan camouflages the truth with lies. Satan lied to Eve by saying, *"You shall surely not die."* To reinforce that lie he used some truth, *"Ye shall be as gods knowing good and evil."* That old saying "once a liar, always a liar" applies in this case.

IN THE WORLD, BUT NOT OF IT

Dear Arno Froese,

I thank you and your staff for the fine magazine you put forth, along with all the helpful information [about living] a Christian life in the top layer of a human septic tank that is getting nearer to the overflow; then Jesus will intervene.

In the December 1997 issue on page 34, your answer to Mrs. B said, "My advice, learn what it means to be 'in the world but not of the world.'"

Please, Mr. Froese, let me know where I can find that verse. We discussed that three weeks ago in church and no one could find it. As I said that also, I just knew it was true.

Thank you very much.

-M. R. in Marion, NC

ANSWER: John 17:11, *"...now I am no more in the world, but these (us) are in the world..."* Verse 16, *"they (us) are not of the world, even as I am not of the world."* As born again believers, our true citizenship is in heaven, as clearly demonstrated in Philippians 3:20 and Ephesians 2:6.

THE THIEF ON THE CROSS AND ADAM

Dear Brethren,

Greetings in Christ Jesus our Lord. I am greatly blessed the way you answer questions. Please answer me regarding the following verses in the Bible:

1) Matthew 27:44 and Mark 15:32 indicate that the thieves crucified with Jesus reviled Him. But in Luke 23:39-43, one of them believed on the Lord Jesus Christ. Please explain why Matthew and Mark do not seem to agree with Luke.

2) Adam and Eve had three sons: Cain in Genesis 4:1, Abel in verse 2 and Seth in verse 25. Where did Cain get his wife? Even Seth? Did Adam and Eve have daughters, too?

God bless you all.

-L. O. in Las Vegas, NV

ANSWER: Luke does not contradict Matthew or Mark, but rather goes into greater detail by showing that one of the "thieves" did, in fact, repent.

Genesis 5:4 reads, *"...and he (Adam) begat sons and daughters."* Adam was 130 years old when Seth was born. Of Noah we read, *"...Noah was five hundred years old: and Noah begat Shem, Ham and Japeth"* (Genesis 5:32). One estimate indicates that by the time Adam died, more than a million people were already counted as his descendants.

FALSE CHRISTS

Dear Friends in Christ,

I would like very much like to see an answer to the following in your "Letters to the Editor" section of *Midnight Call,* or by return mail.

1) Page 33 March issue: "Between these two comings there are 2000 years"–then mention of Acts 7:13 is made. I have a tract that infers the same but in different words, such as 6000 years plus the 1000-year Millennium for a total of 7,000 years. Now we are near the end of the 6,000 years, thus, the Millennium must be near. Is Acts 7:13 the answer? If so, please explain, or give another Scripture that does. Thank you.

2) Page 27 March issue: Having read somewhere in the past about some figure alive now who would reveal himself as the Christ, but I never saw the news report, a

full-page advertisement on that subject. Can you shed more light on who this new age "Christ" is? Thank you.

-L.T. in Park Rapids, MN

ANSWER: Acts 7:13 is certainly a fitting analogy of Jesus' Second Coming in which He will reveal Himself to his brethren (the Jews). Midnight Call founder, Dr. Wim Malgo used to say "Man lived 2,000 years without the law, then 2,000 years under the law, and finally, 2,000 years under grace. The coming 1,000 years will be the Millennium of peace."

Benjamin Creme has been announcing the hidden existence of a messiah that he claims in due time will be revealed. Such prophecies of false messiahs will continue. Jesus warned, *"And then if any man shall say to you, Lo, here is Christ; or, lo, he is there; believe him not"* (Mark 13:21).

FIRST BORN: MALE OR FEMALE?

Dear Mr. Froese:

Would you please help me and answer my question? I was reading my Bible and came to Numbers 3:12. My question is who is the first born? Is it the first son in a family? For example, if the first child born to a couple is a daughter and the second is a son, is the son considered the first born male in a family or not? I will wait for your reply.

-N. A. in Tumwafer, WA

ANSWER: The priesthood is limited to males and it is my understanding that the reason is found in 1st Timothy

195

2:14, *"And Adam was not deceived, but the woman being deceived was in the transgression."* That is why the governing of the church is placed into the hands of brothers, not sisters. However, it is important to remember that this has no relation to our position in Christ, where everyone is equal.

NO DAUGHTERS OF GOD?

Dear Editor Froese,

Men and women make up the "Church" on earth. The Church is called the "Bride" of Christ.

When a person believes the Gospel of Jesus, he or she becomes a "son" of God. (Children of God are often mentioned in the Bible). Sons are mentioned many, many times, but "daughters" of God are never mentioned. As a consequence of becoming sons, they became "heirs" of God, and "joint-heirs" with Jesus Christ. That means [they have the privilege of]reigning in the millennium and eternity with Jesus Christ.

I am a woman. Will God transform me into a "man" in eternity so I can be called His "son"?

-No Name

ANSWER: Galatians 3:28 says, *"There is neither Jew nor Greek, there is neither bond or free, there is neither male nor female: for ye are all one in Christ Jesus."* This is our spiritual and heavenly position. In Matthew 22:30, Jesus confirmed that the believers are *"...as the angels of God in heaven."* The reason sons, not daughters, are mentioned in this relationship is that the priestly office was given to men. Why? *"...Adam was not deceived, but the woman being deceived was in the transgression"* (1st Timothy 2:14). Therefore, the administrative structure of the church and implementation of its doctrine is placed in man's care. However, I emphasize that this has absolutely no relation to eternal salvation, reward or inheritance because then we will be perfectly *"one in Christ Jesus."*

DEVIL NOT THE ENEMY OF GOD?

Dear Reverend Froese:

I take this time to say thank you for the *Midnight Call* and all the information you offer.

There is one thing I have to ask. I have read in your magazine that the devil is an enemy of God. I state that the Bible says: God created an angel called Lucifer and for a time he was very beautiful. When the time was right, he became the dragon we know as the devil.

Now I have four questions: 1) Who created the devil? 2) Who controls the devil? 3) How many beings were created perfect? 4) Don't you think the devil is doing God's bidding and can only do as much as God allows, therefore is not an enemy, but an aid of God?

God, being perfect, must have two sides: the God who sent his Son and the God who sent the devil.

-E. A. in N. Chicago, IL

ANSWER: 1) God created the devil (John 1:1-3). Originally, Satan was considered the *"son of morning"* (Isaiah 14:12) who was perfectly created (Ezekiel 28:15).

197

Through pride, sin was born in his heart and this glorious creature became *"the great dragon...that old serpent, called the Devil and Satan..."* (Revelation 12:9).

2) God has reserved ultimate control for Himself as stated in Amos 3:6, *"...shall there be evil in a city, and the LORD hath not done it?"* God permits the devil to act, but not beyond the limits He sets (Job 38:11).

3) All! *"...God saw every thing that he had made, and, behold, it was very good"* (Genesis 1:31).

4) Jesus said, *"The enemy that sowed them (bad seed) is the devil"* (Matthew 13:39). First Corinthians 15:26 states, *"The last enemy that shall be destroyed is death."* And James warns, *"...whosoever therefore will be a friend of the world is the enemy of God"* (James 4:4).

CHURCH-BRIDE

Dear Sir:

Please tell me which Scripture says that the Church is to be Jesus' Bride? Revelation 21:9-10 states that the great city, the holy Jerusalem, is to be the Bride of the Lamb. Verse 24 says the nations of them which are saved shall walk in the light of the great city.

-T.O. in Baton Rouge

ANSWER: *"For I am jealous over you with godly jealousy: for I have espoused you to one husband, that I may present you as a chaste virgin to Christ"* (2nd Corinthians 11:2).

In Revelation 21, *"The Lamb's wife"* is veiled with the glory of the heavenly Jerusalem, so John cannot describe it for us.

Please read Genesis 24 where the bride is presented to the bridegroom: "...*she took a veil, and covered herself...*" (verse 65).

WIFE OR BRIDE?

Dear Mr. Froese:

Thank you for your outstanding publication, *Midnight Call*. Some of the information is new to me, some is comforting and some is challenging.

For instance, the Bride and the letter in the April 1998 issue, page 37, with which I agree for two reasons: 1) Paul was bold, not bashful, and if we are the Bride, he would have told us outright; and 2)Revelation 21:9 refers to the Bride, the Lamb's wife, and I have not heard any Christian claim to being the Lamb's wife.

In Jewish tradition, the betrothed woman was the wife for a year and then became the bride. Even Mary was Joseph's wife before she became his bride.

-S.K. in Satellite Beach, FL

ANSWER: Paul addressed the Church with the following words, "...*for I have espoused you to one husband, that I may present you as a chaste virgin to Christ*" (2nd Corinthians 11:2). In Revelation 19:7, "...*the marriage of the Lamb is come, and his wife hath made herself ready.*" In chapter 21, the bride is "...*prepared as a bride adorned for her husband*" and in verse 9, John is invited to "...*Come hither, I will shew thee the bride, the Lamb's wife.*" The Church is both the

Bride and the wife.

It's important to add that our understanding of the words "bride," "wife" or "bridegroom" have no direct relation to our earthly understanding of these things. The husband/wife relationship will cease to exist; but this relationship serves to show the most intimate relationship between God and man. The Bible says, *"God shall dwell with man."*

TRIBULATION SAINTS

Dear Mr. Froese,

If the Holy Spirit is taken out of the way during the Great Tribulation, according to 2nd Thessalonians 2:7, then how do the martyrs during the Great Tribulation get saved without the presence of the Holy Spirit? Revelation 7:14 reads, *"And I said to him, Sir, thou knowest. And he said to me, These are they which came out of great tribulation, and have washed their robes, and made them white in the blood of the Lamb."*

Isn't the Spirit with all those who accept Christ?

-C. K. in Frontsville, WI

ANSWER: As the third person of the Godhead, the Holy Spirit is omnipresent. In His office as the Comforter, the Holy Spirit will depart with the Church. Therefore, the tribulation saints will not have the comfort of *"the blessed hope."*

GENTILE DOGS?

Dear Mr. Froese:

I am deeply troubled by a passage in the Bible (Matthew 15:21-28). In this passage, a woman is asking Jesus to cast a demon out of her daughter. What troubles me is the response from Jesus. Specifically in Matthew 15:26, *"But he answered and said, It is not meet to take the children's bread, and cast it to dogs."* Undoubtedly, Jesus was testing the woman's faith.

However, what troubles me is His choice of words. I assume the woman was a Gentile. I believe He meant that it wasn't right for him to give blessings and miracles to Gentiles and take them away from the Jews. I believe that when He said "dogs," He was referring to Gentiles.

Aren't Christians the Body of Christ and the Church? What do you make of the response Jesus gave to the woman? I understand *"...to the Jew first, then to the Gentile."* But was He really referring to us when he said "dogs?" I guess one could say that this was a metaphor, and that I'm taking His words out of context. What do you think?

-I. R. in Georgetown, SC

ANSWER: I'd rather be a dog than a lost person anytime. Ephesians 2:12 describes our terrible condition on the other side of salvation, *"That at that time ye were without Christ, being aliens from the commonwealth of Israel, and strangers from the covenants of promise, having no hope, and without God in the world."* I can't think of anything worse than having no hope.

In the case of the woman of Canaan, notice that she addressed Him as *"Son of David."* That was the specific promise for the Jews not the Gentiles. However, when she cried out, *"Lord, help me,"* she took the first step toward receiving grace from the Savior, the Lord Jesus Christ. Of course, the moment we become born again we are children of God and are no longer considered "dogs."

ETERNAL PARADISE?

Dear Brother Froese:

I, too, am blessed for several years as a subscriber to *Midnight Call.*

I ponder this question, [which may not be] pertinent to salvation, but I wonder as to your opinion. Really, [I have] two questions.

1)Was man designed to live forever in the Garden of Eden had he not sinned? Genesis 2:17. *"But of the tree of the knowledge of good and evil, thou shalt not eat of it: for in the day that thou eatest thereof thou shalt surely die"* (Genesis 2:17).

Genesis 3:22, *"And the LORD God said, Behold, the man is become as one of us, to know good and evil: and now, lest he put forth his hand, and take also of the tree of life, and eat, and live for ever."* This seems to imply that man was designated to live forever had he not sinned.

2)As Jesus said in John 14:2, *"In my Father's house are many mansions: if it were not so, I would have told you. I go to prepare a place for you."*

In your opinion, isn't our assured home in the heavenly new Jerusalem, or whatever you call our eternal abode, far superior to the Garden of Eden, grand as it may have been?

I suppose God in His foreknowledge, before the foundations of the earth were laid, had this in mind for all those who would accept the provision made by His Son, namely sacrificing His life and blood for us.

-I. E. in Sun City, AZ

ANSWER: Initially, Adam and Eve were created as eternal beings and were instructed not to eat of the tree of the knowledge of good and evil. The "tree of life" is also mentioned twice in the last book of the Bible (Revelation 2:7 and 22:2). Those who are saved will eat of the tree of life not to obtain eternal life, but because they have received eternal life through the blood of the Lamb and, as a result, they can enjoy its fruit.

When Jesus says, *"In my Father's house are many mansions"* or dwelling places, it means that we are eternally apart of God's family. It makes no difference where we abide at any certain time, whether it's a heavenly dwelling place such as the new Jerusalem, or the Garden of Eden. What counts is that we will be in the Lord's presence forever. How to distinguish the various aspects of our existence cannot be fully grasped with our limited intellect, so you and I will have to be patient a little while longer.

DOES BAPTISM SAVE?

Dear Mr. Froese,

In Mark 16:16 Jesus says, *"He that believeth and is baptized shall be saved; but he that believeth not shall be damned."* In 1st Peter 3:21, Peter said, *"...even baptism doth also now save us..."*

In James 2:24, he says, *"...ye see then how that by works a man is justified, and not by faith only."* [This is] the only place in the Bible [where] the words, *"faith only,"* are preceded by the words *"not by."* Won't you please at least teach people about baptism and give them a chance to make up their own minds?

-F. U. in Covington, KY

ANSWER: The Bible clearly teaches that salvation is by faith alone in the person of Jesus Christ. James 2 specifically amplifies that true faith produces works, not vice versa. The faith that does not save is revealed in verse 19, *"...the devils also believe, (have faith) and tremble."*

Mark 16:16 does say, *"He that believeth and is baptized shall be saved..."* but then it adds, *"...he that believeth not shall be damned."* Obviously, the key word is "believe." Through baptism, we confirm what has previously taken place, namely, salvation by faith (See Ephesians 1:13).

KINGDOM GOSPEL

Dear Sir:

I would like to know the complete definition of the kingdom gospel that Jesus taught in Luke 8:1, the Gospel that the 12 apostles taught in Luke 9:12 and the kingdom message the 70 taught in Luke 10:1-9.

Please understand that the kingdom gospel cannot be the death, burial and resurrection of Jesus because it was hidden from the 12 apostles, according to Luke 18:34 and Luke 9:45.

Do you have the same message that Jesus and the 12 and the 70 preached within your organization today?

-R. E. in Neodesha, KS

ANSWER: The message of the kingdom was addressed to the people of the King: the Jews. Jesus continued John's message, *"Repent for the kingdom of heaven is at hand."* He specifically instructed the disciples not to go to the Gentiles. The moment a Christian testifies that Jesus is his Savior, the King of the kingdom is presented in the form of a suffering servant to the sinner. When that person responds, he is added to the heavenly kingdom of God.

ANGELS' WINGS

Dear Brother Froese:

I certainly enjoy reading the *Midnight Call* magazine. There is such a variety of interesting news items in it.

I have heard many references to statements that there are no female angels in the Bible; I have also heard that there are no biblical references to angels with wings.

I am aware that there are several different interpretations for the Scripture that I am enclosing; nevertheless, can we consider that the interpretation is a literal one?

Then we would have female angels with wings.

Zechariah 5:9, *"Then lifted I up mine eyes, and looked, and behold, there came out two women, and the wind was in their wings; for they had wings like the wings of a stork; and they lifted up the ephah between earth and heaven..."*

Comment please.

-T. L. in Pekin, IL

ANSWER: A number of readers have quoted Zechariah 5:9 and I admit this sounds as close as you can get to female angels with wings.

However, these two women are obviously of demonic origin because the event Zechariah observes in his vision is described with the word "wickedness."

It is also interesting that the women have *"wings like the wings of stork."* The stork is an unclean animal. Sorry, they don't qualify as angels.

PETS IN HEAVEN?

Sir,

The enclosed is from a ministry which is on TBN Wednesday evenings at 9:30-10 p.m.

The Bible does not specifically state anything concerning animals being taken to heaven upon death or at the resurrection. However, since God promises that He will not withhold any good thing from those who love Him, I believe that a simple request to the Savior will make loving petitions for our pets a fulfilled request instantaneously. There are multitudes whose beloved pets [have gone] the way of all flesh and died. God is able to bring them back from dust and ashes as simply as He does humans when the dead in Christ rise (1st Thessalonians 4:16-18). However, their restoration will occur only after believers arrive and request their pets. To sum up everything I have said, I believe that we will have the animals we loved with us in heaven, not because of salvation (a spiritual experience), but because our requests produce God's re-creation or restoration of our faithful, loving and loyal furry friends.

We notice in the Bible that Jesus will come on a white horse, so if horses are in heaven, why not our beloved pets? I have pets myself who trust me far more than some family. Please reply.

-Mrs. C.E., East Ryegate, VT

ANSWER: The answer by Rev. E.I. is well worded and seems logical. However, there is no evidence in Scripture that pets will be restored in order to please their former owners. I believe the confusion is because we analyze heavenly things from earthly perspectives. Nevertheless, Romans 8:21 makes a rather profound statement, *"...Because the creature itself also shall be delivered from the bondage of corruption into the glorious liberty of the children of God."* Can we explain this further? I do not think so, but the Bible does say, *"...Eye hath not seen, nor ear heard, neither have entered into the heart of man, the things which God hath prepared for them that love him"* (1st Corinthians 2:9).

MORE PETS IN HEAVEN?

Dear Mr. Froese,

I enjoy the *Midnight Call* magazine so very much and look forward to receiving it each month. I always learn more about God's Word.

In the April issue, page 37, "Regarding Pets...Romans 8:18-23," please explain a little more in detail; I have read several different Bible translations and would like to understand these verses better. Both my husband and I are animal lovers.

May God continue to bless you and the wonderful group you work with.

-D. E. in Austin, TX

ANSWER: When Romans 8 concludes in verse 23 with the *"...redemption of our body,"* it is clear that the animals will participate as well. Verse 21 reads, *"...the creature itself also shall be delivered from the bondage of corruption into the glorious liberty of the children of God."* During the Millennium, the lion will eat straw and the serpent can no longer do harm. Undoubtedly the restoration will include God's entire creation because His unqualified statement regarding His creation was, *"...very good."* However, the question as to whether animals will be resurrected, or if people will recognize their pets, is not revealed in the Bible, therefore it is open for speculation.

CHAPTER 10

ENDTIME PROPHECY

AMERICA IN PROPHECY

Dear Sirs,

Of all the topics in the Bible other than eternal salvation, nothing brings me more joy than the prophetic Word. I wish I had known this stuff as a teenager! If I had, junior high might have been more tolerable! I remember my skeptical brother-in-law asked a rhetorical question: "What if Iraq had won the Gulf War, gained control of the world's oil, and had become a superpower?" I said, "There's no point in arguing the impossible! No matter what happens, Europe will rise to number one!" To which he responded, "How do you know that? You've never been sure of anything in your entire life! Where are you getting this confidence? How are you so sure of yourself?"

Also, isn't there even the slightest possibility that America might be mentioned in prophecy? A teacher once told me that "Tarshish" is England (which seems to fit Isaiah 23:1-2). Secondly, Great Britain's Coat of Arms depicts a lion; could it be that the *"...young lions thereof..."* (Ezekiel 38:13) are former British colonies? And what about Obadiah 1:4? Is there even the slightest chance that this could be referring to Apollo 11, and the fact that since that time, America has lost her place in the world? (I think she has; we're just riding on momentum, smoke and mirrors now.) One person I asked concerning this said, "No, it can't be America, since this verse refers to Edom." True, but the prophetic Word can often be historical as well as prophetic (Hosea 11:1, c.f. Matthew 2:15 and Exodus 4:22-23). One verse can also refer to two totally different events (Isaiah 61:2), or even two different people (Daniel 11:31, for example, which referred to both Antiochus Epiphanes and the Antichrist), and still be properly interpreted. Besides, I believe every nation, with diligent search, can find a prophetic warning for itself in the Bible.

-I.H., Woonsocket, RI

ANSWER: Neither the "young lion" nor the "eagle" have any relation to Britain or the U.S.A. Many other nations have animals such as these included in their state emblems. Prophetic geography begins with Israel as the center. Europe (Rome) ruled Israel when Jesus came the first time and Europe will be in power when Jesus returns. The evidence of this process is quite clear; Europe is economically the most significant and most powerful continent. It has led the world through its Roman laws and systems of civilization.

THE MARK OF THE BEAST

Dear Mr. Arno Froese,

A couple of months ago I ordered the book, *Biblical Counseling* by Wim Malgo. I always looked forward to his column in *Midnight Call*. I regret that he has died and I cannot address my response to one of the remarks he made in his book.

So I come to you. On page 213 he stated that nowhere is it written that they will be lost eternally if they accept the mark of the beast. Had he not read Revelation 14:9-11 which says that if any man worships the beast and his image and receives his mark in either his forehead or his hand, the same shall drink of the wine of the wrath of God? Verse 11 says that the smoke of their torment ascends forever and they have no rest day or night, who worship the beast and his image and whosoever receives the mark of his name.

-I.E., Belle Vernon, PA

ANSWER: Revelation 13:17 lists three categories in the King James translation: 1) "he that had the mark;" 2) "the name of the beast;" 3) "the number of his name." Martin Luther translates this as, *"...the mark, which is the name of the beast, or the number of his name."* Revelation certainly makes it clear that anyone who worships the beast and receives his mark is lost for all eternity but it does not say what happens to those who receive *"...the number of his name."* Based on my understanding of the Scripture, the latter category will enter the thousand-year kingdom of peace, but are not saved.

NEW WORLD ORDER

Dear Arno,

Thank you for the January magazine. I feel compelled to write and share with you something that has been a powerful tool in convincing both Christian and non-Christian alike who is in charge of the worldly kingdom we are surrounded by.

Christians have shown me that the American $1 bill has had the words, "Novus Ordo Seclorum," or "New World Order," printed on it since 1933. The words are in Latin and the seal has Roman numerals on the pyramid. I also found out that the traditional Roman Catholic mass was replaced by the Novus Ordo Seclorum by order of Pope Paul VI, on March 26, 1970 (see, *Keys of this Blood* by Malachi Martin - pages 667-670). Page 667 says that the Novus Ordo has spread by decree throughout the Roman Catholic institution.

On the occult "religious" level, Novus Ordo Seclorum means New World Mass!! Novus Ordo = "New Mass."

When the New World Order is powerful enough to put its insignia on American money for over 60 years, then it is clearly in charge of all the money markets of the world. When the Novus Ordo or "New Mass" is declared by the pope, then the one in charge of all the money is the pope: Antichrist, devil, Satan. We know what Jesus said in Luke 4:5-8, *"And the devil, taking him up into an high mountain, shewed unto him all the kingdoms of the world in a moment of time. And the devil said unto him, All this power will I give thee, and the glory of them: for that is delivered unto me; and to whomsoever I will I give it. If thou therefore wilt worship me, all shall be thine. And Jesus answered and said unto him, Get thee behind me, Satan: for it is written, Thou shalt worship the Lord thy God, and him only shalt thou serve."* Nobody argues with or questions my comments when I explain these facts to them. It helps me to warn people. May God keep you in His care.

-R.T., CANADA

ANSWER: The New World Order is as old as the Roman Empire. The attempt to resurrect it in a new form has also been tried many times throughout the last two millennia. The United States is a product of the New World Order, and a very successful one at that! Our nation is composed of virtually all European nations, with an infusion of Africans and Asians. Our immigrant forefathers surrendered that which is most precious to any person on earth: homeland, heritage, tradition, and culture. Approximately 80% even surrendered their own languages.

The New World Order is actually not "they," but in reality it is "we." The world is already one economically, and each nation has become dependent upon others.

According to my understanding of the prophetic Scripture, this unity will progress and ultimately result in the formation of ten economic power structures. Europe will undoubtedly be the leader.

The New World Order will be the most successful Gentile power structure this planet has ever known. Peace, prosperity and security will be so overwhelmingly real that not only will the people of the world gladly subject themselves to the political and military leadership of the Antichrist, but they will also accept a new, unified religion. The world will worship the image of the beast in unison. There is no doubt that Roman democracy will play a significant role in this endtime scenario.

THE TEN WORLD REGIONS

Dear Arno,

I am midway through, *How Democracy Will Elect the Antichrist,* and am enjoying it thoroughly.

Re: The Ten Kings: I recently read a book about crime on the high seas, written by two former UN staffers. According to them, the world is already divided into ten zones based on maritime use and activities. I find this very interesting, not least because so many references are prophetically made regarding the sea in the endtimes. The one-world/new world is already here!

Here are excerpts from the book, *Outlaws of the Ocean* by G.O.W. Mueller and Freda Adler, 1985:

...UNEP's regional seas program, agreed upon by the member states in 1974 under participation of 120 states, 14 bodies of the United Nations system, and 12 other international organizations. Accordingly, the world has been divided into ten regional seas programs:
- The Mediterranean region (1975)
- The Red Sea region (1976)
- The Kuwait region (1978)
- The wider Caribbean region (1981)
- The West and Central African region (1981)
- The East Asian seas region (1981)
- The Southeast Pacific region (1981)
- The Southwest Pacific region (1982)
- The East African region (1984)
- The Southwest Atlantic region (in the process of formation, 1985)

-E.E., Farmington, MO

ANSWER: Thank you for the interesting outline on the ten sea regions. Whether these correspond to the ten kings mentioned in the Bible is not clear to me. However, I do believe that economy and finance will dictate the final development of the ten kings.

We are certain that they do not represent ten European states. The world will become one, identified by ten specific power structures. Dr. Wim Malgo wrote the following in 1967:

> Let us not look for ten countries being members of the European Common Market constituting the fulfillment of Revelation 17:12. Rather we must look for ten power structures that will develop through the European initiative, but will be world-wide (*How Democracy Will Elect the Antichrist, p.168*).

MYSTERY BABYLON

Dear Mr. Froese,

I have just read your article on Mystery Babylon in the May issue and I feel that your fourfold criteria of the identity of Babylon are both inconclusive and incomplete.

By your own admission, criteria #1 could be Jerusalem or Rome, and criteria #2 could be any city built on a series of hills, including Jerusalem, which is built on the hills of Moriah (one peak of which is Golgotha).

In criteria #3, you quote Revelation 18:3 about rich merchants and delicacies. I ask that you read that passage in conjunction with 1st Kings 10:14-23. Not only does this speak of riches and delicacies, but it is the only passage of Scripture outside Revelation that mentions the number 666. It speaks of Solomon and Jerusalem.

Criteria #4 is ambiguous enough to be any center of commerce.

Finally, you have omitted a most specific passage of Revelation. In chapter 11, verse 8, it says *"...their dead bodies shall lie in the street of the great city, which spiritually is called Sodom and Egypt, where also our Lord was crucified."*

Since we've only one Lord, and since He was crucified in Jerusalem, the identity of the "great city" becomes plain and "Mystery Babylon" is no mystery at all. It can only be Jerusalem, not Rome.

-O.N., Cobden, IL

ANSWER: I agree that Jerusalem could qualify for the first criteria, but we'd have to stretch the truth a little in order to count seven hills as criteria two. In regards to criteria three, you may be overlooking the fact that politics and religion were under one umbrella in Solomon's time by God's decree and did not constitute "fornication."

However, Rome has ruled the world for almost 2,000 years with its ancient laws. Today, Rome is a political entity as much as she is a religious entity. First Kings 10 reports history; Revelation 18 speaks of the future. Revelation 11:18 does in fact identify Jerusalem, but not Mystery Babylon.

COMPUTER

Dear Mr. Froese,

[The number] 555 is the access code for information. Could it be that 666 will be the access code for this world computer?

Think of all the things that can be done with the computer: banking, salary, and retirement funds would be done by computer instead of [by using] paper checks.

We can save for retirement, and also pass funds from one account to another.

Soon we'll be able to purchase food, medicine, and just about anything without a dollar bill passing through our hands and without even leaving home.

I watched a TV program on which someone described the Internet as a kingdom waiting for a king. Since you have a computer and I don't, you know better than I do as to what is here and what is on the way.

But with these few thoughts, I can well understand how no one could buy or sell outside of the computer, or without this mark.

Without Christ, these are scary thoughts. With Christ, I feel comfortable, content and sheltered.

I've also thought about how new laws may need to be passed after the Rapture. Millions and millions of dollars will be floating around from the bank accounts of Christians and Christian organizations.

We're truly blessed and enjoy reading *Midnight Call*.

-T.E., Savannah, GA

ANSWER: Based on Revelation 13, the second beast will give orders to the people to build an image to the beast. This plainly shows that the image will be a man-made object and that this image has received the power to speak and to *"...cause that as many as would not worship the image of the beast should be killed."*

217

The computer is undoubtedly a strong link in the establishment of the Antichrist's New World Order, but this is equally true of all other modern conveniences we enjoy today such as cars, planes, refrigerators, air conditioners and electricity.

As far as the number 666 is concerned, please note that this is the number of the Antichrist, not of a computer system.

DOES PROPHECY MENTION AMERICA?

To those who write *Midnight Call,*

For many years, I've wanted someone to answer a question concerning the part America plays, if any, in the endtimes. I've had someone tell me [America] is not mentioned in Revelation and so it must in some way cease to exist or become of little, if no, importance in the world. Since this is our home, I would like to know more, if possible.

I've often wondered about the passage, "*...the prostitute over many waters,*" and how the angel said it was "*...peoples, multitudes, nations and languages.*" Couldn't this represent America, with its melting pot of many different people and nationalities?

Is it possible that Revelation 18 is in some way referring to America? (What other country is as rich as America?) Since I was a young girl, I've had visions of America's destruction by nuclear war and when I read the passage, "*In one hour your doom has come,*" I get goose bumps. I hope you can tell me that I'm way off base in thinking that this could mean our country.

I've asked pastors what they thought, and many wave me off with the remark that Revelation is too difficult to try to make any sense of. The Bible says, *"...let the reader understand,"* so I'm hoping maybe you'll help me...I've prayed to God about it, and I know He will see that, even if it is not you personally, the right person will answer this question for me. I'm claiming Matthew 7:7.

I wonder at the passage, *"Come out of her, my people..."* because America has become so wicked. Is God trying to tell us (Christians) to leave America in that verse, or just not to partake of the abominations which are so much a part of this country? Or is it speaking to the Jews who still live in America? It may have nothing to do with America at all...help me with this please!

I've also wondered about the possibility of Isaac's descendants (the Jews) and Ishmael's descendants (the Arabs) joining together to destroy America. I'm sure Russia wouldn't mind helping. The false peace could begin with the Arabs and Jews, considering that they're both descendants of Abraham, and [they could]decide to eliminate the Gentiles of America. There's so much anger against America in the Middle East, even from the Jewish people, according to some of the letters that Zola prints in his paper, *Levitt's Letter.*

And last, but not least, can you tell me where the Holocaust is mentioned in Revelation? I can't imagine that it's not found somewhere in prophecy when it had such a big effect upon God's chosen people. Please help us if you can, to understand what we should about these things.

-A.A. Morgan, Topeka, KS

ANSWER: The majority of our ancestors come from Europe. We speak a European language and our laws are based upon Roman law. Our entire civilization is patterned after Europe. Our political system is based on the Greek/Roman system of democracy, which virtually rules the world today.

As a believer, you must make the distinction between three groups of people: Gentiles, Jews and Christians. The country that matters to us is Israel because it is the only one that has received a direct promise from God.

The second group is the Gentiles. Regardless of their governmental system or country name, the Gentiles are all ruled by the prince of darkness: the god of this world.

Nationalism, which is evident throughout your letter, is on its way out, making room for globalism. I see no proof that certain nations will attack the United States or that the U.S. will attack other nations. Why? Because before that great and horrible day, people will say, "peace and safety."

How the world is uniting under the not yet fully revealed "Mystery Babylon" is a subject I discuss at length in my book, *Saddam's Mystery Babylon*.

AMERICA BURNED?

Dear Mr. Froese,

A few years ago, I read a book by a Romanian pastor named Dumitru Duduman. It is entitled, *Through the Fire Without Burning*.

I've re-read it about five times, because never before

had I read any book, with the exception of the Bible, that was so full of the Spirit of God. This man, Dumitru, led the life of a modern-day Paul.

He was sent to America to tell American churches to repent. He completed his assignment and then the Lord took him 'home' about a year ago.

I'm asking you to please get this book. Please ask God's Spirit to grow you some more with the witness of what God has for you in the testimony that is within this book.

I'm enclosing a tract that tells you about this humble man and what he had to endure.

Here are some of the amazing prophecies:

Sept. 1984: From the middle of the country, some of the people will start fighting against the government. The government will be busy with internal problems.

1991: The angel said: Tell the people of America that one day with the Lord is as a thousand years. If they will turn away from sin and turn back to God they will make it through the second day to the third day. If they don't, they won't make it.

Nov. 1993: I opened a great book with the words "BOOK OF THE GENTILES" scrawled on it. I saw all kinds of names written page after page. When I reached the end of the book, I found that there were one and three quarter pages left blank, unwritten.

Jan. 1996: The angel said to me, "Do you remember how many pages were left to fill when I showed you last time? Now there is but one page left. When this is completed, what I have told you will happen to America." He then told me that the time needed to complete this last page will be shorter.

April 1996: In a vision, the Russian and Chinese presidents made a contract to fight against America. A voice said to me, "Watch where the Russians penetrate America." I saw the words written: Alaska, Minnesota, Florida.

Then the man spoke again: "When America goes to war with China, the Russians will strike without warning." The president of two other countries said, "We, too, will fight for you." Each had a place already planned as a point of attack. "Without a doubt, together, we can destroy America...Everything I have shown you is how it will REALLY happen...Then, when it comes to pass, the people will remember the words the Lord has spoken."

-H.E., Mooresville, IN

ANSWER: What all false teachers have in common is extra-biblical revelation. In this case that extra-biblical revelation is Duduman's, *Through the Fire Without Burning.*

America, like any other nation, is a political entity, not a spiritual one. Therefore, the assertion that God has a special message for America is clearly false teaching.

CASHLESS

Dear Arno,

It is now several years ago since I met you at the

prophecy conference at Niagara Falls, Ontario. Many things have happened in the meantime and presently we are confronted with the introduction of the global MARC from Mondex (a microchip card with special features). There are several cities where the card is undergoing trial and introduction; one nearby is Guelph, Ontario. It has been fairly well-received by the public and by some Christians. Some students are protesting and the banks have punished the university.

We know that this card uses a satanic and Freemasonic logo, and by accepting it, we give away alternative forms of payment. It also replaces all of our identification and somehow associates us as members of the Freemasons.

The question I have is whether Christians should accept this device or any other Mondex product, or should we refuse it altogether. When I spoke with the manager at my bank, he stated that the chip implant would come within two years. I know from a reliable source that this date will be brought forward because the banks are going to withdraw cash and checking from the system.

Arno, what should we do? Is there a general consensus among the Christian community as to what we should do? I would like to ask people like David Breese, Grant Jeffrey, Dave Hunt and Peter Lalonde about it, too. Have you already discussed this with them?

This mode of payment and the consequences for Christians will undoubtedly have a great impact on a Christian organization like Midnight Call. That is why I come to you with this request. I expect that this issue has been discussed among speakers of the prophecy conferences.

I would very much appreciate your answer and thank you for it in advance.

-W. E., London, Ontario

ANSWER: Jesus said, *"Render unto Caesar the things that are Caesars."* Don't misunderstand the word "cash." The "cash" we are speaking about is printed paper. Freemason symbols are used on the U.S. dollar, reflecting the spirit of our founding fathers. Whether we use this "cash," debit card, credit card, microchip card, checks or electronic transfer, it is all done outside of our bodies. However, if it is true that "the chip implant will come" then I would refuse.

In order for me to take such a statement seriously, I must know the [bank] manager's name, the name of the bank, their address, telephone and fax number, and any other identification to confirm the reliability of this information. Every reported "reliable" source I have investigated thus for has been exposed as a fraud.

I take this opportunity to ask all of our readers to document statements when sending us information, and not to rely on hearsay.

JERUSALEM OR ROME?

Beloved:

I recently read your book, *How Democracy Will Elect the Antichrist.* May I say how greatly blessed I was by the information contained therein? I have never heard of nor seen this concept addressed elsewhere.

I am enclosing a photocopy of page 98 from the book. Correct me if I'm wrong, but I believe the word "Jerusalem" is an error. I am sure it was either a proof-reader's or printer's gaffe.

Perhaps the next release will reflect as much.

Thank you for your ministry and teaching. May God continue to bless.

Mrs. U.U., Arlington, MA

ANSWER: Jerusalem is correct. The blood of the martyrs of Jesus was first shed in Jerusalem and then in Rome. I agree that the wording is somewhat awkward and will be changed in the next printing. Thanks for your alertness.

CHAPTER 11

FUTURE PROPHECIES

GREETINGS!

Your endeavors have been received with great interest. Allow me to come to my point.

We edit a Christian magazine and are opening ourselves to questions and answers. Recently we received the following question:

Dear Editor,

According to Ezekiel 29-32, Nebuchadnezzar king of Babylon was supposed to scatter the Egyptians, making their land so desolate that no man or animal would pass through Egypt or live there for 40 years, after which they would return and be a weak nation. (See especially 28:8-16; 30:10-12, 20-26; 32:11-15). Was this prophecy fulfilled?

- Spring City Tennessee

Would you mind taking the time to answer this question? We would be most happy to give you proper credit.

Thank you all very much!

-I.E., Wobdury, TN

ANSWER: Although Egypt has experienced several foreign rulerships, including Babylon, the forty-year desolation has not yet taken place. As of 1948, Israel is again a recognized nation, and today they try to "lean on" Egyptians for their peace treaties and political support. Egypt is basically anti-Israel in spite of their lip service. Egypt was never desolate for forty years nor gathered back into the land (this is future).

LOCATION OF THE ARK?

Dear Mr. Froese,

I cherish *Midnight Call* and read it from cover to cover before passing it on to my adult children.

I just finished reading your article, "The Almond Tree," in the November publication. It gave me understanding regarding some of the prophecies you quoted that I never comprehended before. Thank you.

However, regarding the ark of the covenant, on page 14 you stated: "No more mention is made of the ark of the covenant in the Bible. We do not read anything about it after the first temple was destroyed and the second temple was dedicated, neither do we know what happened to the ark of the covenant."

For almost all of the last year, the Lord has led me to remain in the book of Revelation for my evening Bible reading. Without a doubt, many believers in Yeshua have read these passages for many years as I did without noticing a sentence in Revelation regarding the ark of the covenant. I have read many articles over the years speculating what happened to the ark of the covenant, and in the past few months I noticed what God says about the ark in Revelation 11:19, *"And the temple of God was opened in heaven, and there was seen his temple the ark of his testament."*

That is the only ark of the covenant mentioned in the Bible. This must be the same one.

-L. O., B.C. Canada

ANSWER: The ark of the covenant mentioned in Revelation is the one which Moses saw in heaven. In Exodus 25:9, God instructed Moses to do, *"According to all that I shew thee, after the pattern of the tabernacle, and the pattern of all the instruments thereof, even so shall ye make it."* The one in heaven is eternal, the one on earth is no more; therefore, no trace of it has ever been found and probably never will.

EZEKIEL 38 AND 39

Dear Mr. Froese:

I am very interested in endtime prophecy, and I find your magazine goes along with the way I believe Scripture reveals it.

What I can't understand is where Ezekiel 38 and 39 fit into this picture. I believe that this war is different from Armageddon in Revelation 19, since it's an "invasion" from the north. Armageddon is a war against those who have already taken over for at least 3 1/2 years, if not 7 years.

I feel that the Antichrist will be the commander-in-chief over the ten-nation confederacy, but will be a descendant from these people from northern countries (simply put, Muslim descent). Why would his people invade (Ezekiel 38) a nation he already controls?

Please shed some light for me as I have been struggling to understand this for a very long time and no other sources I've checked seem to want to touch it.

E. R., Verdel, NE

ANSWER: The distinct purpose of the Ezekiel invasion is revealed by a set of three protesting questions from the Arabs: *"Sheba and Dedan, and the merchants of Tarshish, with all the young lions... 1)...Art thou come to take a spoil? 2) hast thou gathered thy company to take a prey? To carry away silver and gold, 3) to take away cattle and goods, to take a great spoil?"* (Ezekiel 38:13). This is strictly a materialistic matter.

On the other hand, Revelation 19 has religious character as we see when we read about the four-fold "Alleluia" over the destruction of "Mystery Babylon."

The Ezekiel battle is limited only to the nations mentioned; Armageddon is global.

The Antichrist is clearly a winner. People will ask, *"Who is like unto the beast?"* And indeed, a commander-in-chief as you write, *"Who is able to make war with him?"* However, the "ten nation confederacy" is not limited to ten nations, because it specifically uses the word *"kings."*

That means ten individual power structures, which will undoubtedly be headquartered in Europe, but which will be world-wide.

HOUSE OF WICKEDNESS

Dear Mr. Froese:

What is your interpretation of Zechariah 5:5-11? It would seem to be talking of the endtimes when a house for *"wickedness"* in Shinar is built. When it is ready, the ephah containing the woman-wickedness-will be set upon its base. It would seem to me that era where wickedness began would be established again in the endtimes and then destroyed just as Jerusalem will be saved as God's city.

Your article in the May 1998 issue of *Midnight Call* concerning Mystery Babylon speaks to me as truth about Rome; but then, what is Zechariah 5:5-11 saying about setting wickedness upon its base in Shinar as soon as a house is built for it? I would appreciate your thoughts on this seeming conflict between Rome and Shinar to Babylon in Iraq as the base for endtime wickedness to be destroyed, or will they both be destroyed when Babylon is destroyed in Revelation chapter 18?

The *Midnight Call* questions and answers are a great way to receive in-depth teaching. Sometimes your answers are a bit too brief to be satisfying, but they do cause one to search the Bible to see *"if these things be true."* I couldn't understand what you had against Promise Keepers until you explained more thoroughly in this last issue of *Midnight Call.* Your insight is much needed.

-N. E., Sonoma, CA

ANSWER: In Ezra 6, King Darius decreed that some of the temple treasures be returned to Jerusalem from Babylon. However, the temple treasures were finally carried away by the last Babylon, "Mystery Babylon" (Rome) in A.D. 70. There is no reason to believe that the temple treasures still exist. They were given to the Gentiles, so in all likelihood they were melted down and made into idols, adding more strength to the word "wickedness."

Notice the words, *"This is their likeness through all the earth,"* which show a worldwide Babylon not limited to literal Babylon. Revelation 18 also confirms the global power of "Mystery Babylon."

TWO BLOOD COVENANTS

Dear Mr. Froese:

I have just read (several times) your Editorial in the March issue of *Midnight Call* and I just wanted to tell you I think it is one of the most anointed teachings I have heard in a long time.

I also have a question in regard to "may be able to comprehend with all the saints what's the breadth and length and depth and height." Wouldn't this also be the bringing together of the "two" blood covenants God made with Abraham and Jesus since we are the seed of Abraham?

-O. E. in Tulsa, OK

ANSWER: Ephesians 3:18 expresses the fullness of the Gospel in Christ, which includes only one blood covenant, not two. The first one was done away with by the fulfillment of the last.

There is only one blood covenant that counts. Hebrews 9:12 states, *"...by his own blood he entered in once into the holy place, having obtained eternal redemption for us."*

ABRAHAM A JEW?

Mr. Froese,

In your article on the Antichrist and Israel in the September issue of *Midnight Call*, on page ten, you wrote about Genesis 18:17-18, "He entrusted to Abraham, the first Jew, prophecy, His Word."

Was Abraham a Jew? I thought he was a Hebrew. If Abraham was a Jew and sons are the same heritage as their fathers, would not Ishmael's descendants be Jews also? I doubt if they would want to claim that heritage. I have heard them say that they are descendants of father Abraham.

I thought the word "Jew" was a name used by the tribe of Judah and was first used in 2nd Kings 16:6, where the people of Judah were called Jews.

It is a very good article but I must disagree with the thought of Abraham being a Jew.

-N. E. in Sun City West, AZ

ANSWER: Jesus said, *"...salvation is of the Jews"* (John 4:22) and Abraham is *"...the father of all them that believe..."* (Romans 4:11). Jesus was, is, and always will be a Jew. Indeed, Ishmael is Abraham's son but God said,

233

"...my covenant will I establish with Isaac..." (Genesis 17:21). Ishmael does not count when it comes to God's plan of salvation. God told Abraham, *"...Take now thy son, thine only son Isaac whom thou lovest..."* (Genesis 22:2). Did you notice the words *"thine only son?"* No one counts in God's eternal plan of salvation other than those whom He has chosen: Abraham, Isaac, Jacob, and Judah.

PEACE COVENANT

Letter to the Editor:

My question regards the "peace covenant" of Daniel 9:27. In May 1992, the Israeli government sent a final draft of the "Jerusalem Covenant" to Jewish settlements throughout the world–to be noted, approved and returned to Israel by May 1993.

This having been accomplished, the Israelis inaugurated a huge celebration on May 13, 1993 to announce the importance and intent of the covenant to the world.

Before and since this event–in every piece of prophecy commentary I've read concerning Daniel 9:27–the writers consistently speak of the Antichrist "making a peace treaty" with Israel. The Scripture says absolutely nothing about making a peace treaty! It says, very plainly, that the Antichrist "shall confirm a/the covenant with many..." The use of the word "confirm" seems to imply action on something that already exists.

The 1993 Jerusalem Covenant was no trivial event; it was signed by 17 of the most influential and official men in Israel to proclaim Israel's eternal ownership of

Jerusalem. Jerusalem will remain the basic stumbling block to the "peace process" with the Palestinians. And it will be the Lord's "burdensome cup of trembling" to the nations until the Lord's return.

What more could the Antichrist need but his "confirmation" of the existing covenant to secure Israel's peace before the world–at least until mid-tribulation?

-O.E.O. in Riverside, CA

ANSWER: The Jerusalem Covenant has no political validity and is basically a reconfirmation among some Jews to keep Jerusalem Jewish.

The covenant that is to be confirmed or strengthened by the Antichrist will have great significance through which the Jews will actually accept the Antichrist as their Messiah. Remember that Jesus said, *"...if another shall come in his own name, him ye will receive"* (John 5:43). My understanding of the prophetic Word leads me to believe that this coming covenant will instantaneously solve Israel's internal and external problems and as a result they will exclaim, "peace, peace." This could happen when the European Union accepts Israel as a full member. All other treaties and peace agreements will lead toward the final "covenant."

WHO ARE THE REAL GOG AND MAGOG?

Dear Mr. Froese:

I have studied the Bible for a long time in order to find what is said about the battle of Gog and Magog.

235

I reference Ezekiel 38:9, *"...You will ascend, coming like a storm, covering land like a cloud..."* and Revelation 20:7-9, *"The number is as the sand of the sea."* And *"covering the land like a cloud"* refers to the vastness of the armies. Ezekiel 38:8-12 tells us that the land will have unwalled cities, and the people will dwell in safety without bars or gates. The land will have been waste places that are again inhabited.

This brings up the question of when all of these qualifications could be fulfilled. Israel hasn't dwelled safely since 1948 and it doesn't look as though she will in the near future. Could this waste land that Ezekiel tells about as having been regained have been wasted during the tribulation? I think that it will be a time of safety during the 1000-year rule of Christ. The land could be healed, and the people [could] live in peace without fear. Ezekiel 39 tells about a horde of troops coming down from the north and God's wrath falling on them, and their being devoured by beasts and birds of prey. But I think Revelation 20:7-9 gives us the answer: *"And when the thousand years are expired, Satan shall be loosed out of his prison, And shall go out to deceive the nations which are in the four quarters of the earth, Gog and Magog, to gather them together to battle: the number of whom is as the sand of the sea...."* Please comment on my thinking.

-Y. B. in Wichita Falls, TX

ANSWER: Gog and Magog, found in Ezekiel 38 and 39, are geographically identified as being located in the north of Israel. On the other hand, the Gog and Magog of

Revelation 20:8 encompasses the entire world, *"...the four quarters of the earth..."*. Based on my understanding of this Scripture, it is not dealing with physical nations of people, but rather the nations of demons. Isaiah 14:9-15 records a prophecy in reverse, describing the fall of Satan. Notice that the *"nations"* are mentioned in verse 9 and 12. These are the inhabitants of hell who are oppressed by the apparent power of the *"shining one son of dawn"* who is identified as Lucifer in the King James translation. He is the one who is accused of *"weakening the nations."* However, the devil strengthens the nations in opposition to God's nation and His city, Jerusalem. Also notice that this is an anti-God–not anti-Christ–rebellion, as is the case with the Battle of Armageddon.

THE FOUR BEASTS

Dear Sirs,

I have often wondered about Daniel 7. I have read many books on prophecy and everyone seems to agree that the first three beasts described represent the same kingdoms shown by the first three parts of Nebuchadnezzar's great image.

I have trouble with this interpretation. I believe that his vision is a picture of latter-day countries or kingdoms. Like most fundamentalists, I believe in a literal interpretation unless symbolism is obvious.

The first is a perfect description of America and the second, Russia or the USSR. The third may be a bit harder, however, it is interesting to note that the HQ of the

PLO is in Cairo and the royalty of Egypt was adorned with leopard skins. Also, the Palestinian movement was helped by four main countries (four heads).

The description of the beast that many believe to represent the final kingdom of the Antichrist from Revelation 13 has the mouth of a lion (speaks English?), the feet of a bear (totalitarian law of Russia?), and resembles or maybe has the body of a leopard (the power of the oil reserves in the Middle East?).

-R. S. in Sylvania, GA

ANSWER: Nebuchadnezzar's image of Daniel and the four beasts of chapter 7 show the entire history of the Gentile world. Although America and Russia are great and mighty nations, they do not play any special role in endtime events, but are included in these four power structures: Babylon, Medo-Persia, Greece, and Rome. How do we know there are no more to come? The extended Roman Empire, which is the final Gentile kingdom, will incorporate the substance of "clay," that being the Jewish people. Today, Israel and Jews all over the world are eagerly working toward a full integration in the Gentile world. Therefore, we know that the final "iron-clay" Gentile empire is being established today. The next thing to come is described in Daniel 2:34, *"Thou sawest till that a stone was cut out without hands, which smote the image upon his feet that were of iron and clay, and brake them to pieces."* The present PLO-Israel peace process will only become significant when Rome (Europe) gives its stamp of approval.

238

CHAPTER 12

PAST AND FUTURE PROPHECIES

WHO ARE THE ELECT?

Dear Mr. Froese:

I read your article, "The Disappearing of the Church," in the May issue with interest.

However, I noticed that there were some references you didn't cover. I am no Greek scholar, so I hope you can explain a bit.

First we have Matthew 24:3-42. The main section that seems to go against what you wrote is the following: *"When ye therefore shall see the abomination of desolation...For then shall be great tribulation, such as was not since the beginning of the world...And except those days should be shortened, there should no flesh be saved: but for the elect's sake those days should be shortened...Immediately after the tribulation of those days...and the powers of the heavens shall be shaken: And then shall appear the sign of the*

Son of man in heaven...then shall all the tribes of the earth mourn, and they shall see the Son of man coming in the clouds...power...and great glory. And he shall send his angels...and they shall gather together his elect..." (verses 15-31).

This is a long passage, but it seems to suggest that there is no Rapture before the Tribulation. If there were, how could there be any elect for the angels to gather? That was not talking about the Jews, for they are talked about in a different manner.

You also stated, "The church is the light of the world; thus, sin cannot fully develop" (page 7). If this statement is true, how could God have judged anyone, and how could the world have sunk as low as it has? This isn't making sense to me. The world cannot be judged until there is a standard [to which it can be] compared. *"For until the law sin was in the world: but sin is not imputed when there is no law:"* (Romans 5:13).

If the body of believers left, the Holy Spirit would no longer be here to convict anyone.

Yes, it is possible there would be Bibles, but have you read everything that would benefit you?

If all it took was a Bible to bring conviction to man, this would already be a perfect world.

Sir, any help is already greatly appreciated.

Thank you.

-T.O. in Ada, OK

ANSWER: Regarding Israel, the Bible says, *"he shall send his angels with a great sound of a trumpet..."* But for the

Church, *"The Lord Himself shall descend..."* For Israel, *"a trumpet"* is used but for the Church it is the [last] *"...trump of God."*

Don't mix the Church with Israel even though they are organically connected. The Church will be raptured into the clouds, directly into His presence. The Jews must go back to the land of Israel where they will be gathered by His angels.

Who are the "elect?" Isaiah answers, *"...Israel, mine elect, I have even called thee by name: I have surnamed thee, though thou hast not known me"* (45:4).

If you think sin has fully developed, please re-read Revelation 6:15-16; 9:20-21; and 16:9-11, where you will find the progression of sin.

The Holy Spirit was promised by Jesus to act as the "Comforter" (John 14:16) who would remain with the believer forever.

Don't forget: God, in the person of the Holy Spirit, is omnipresent. He will depart as the Comforter with the Church, but will continue to convict the world of sin.

MILLENNIUM

Dear Brother Froese,

I love *Midnight Call* magazine and look forward to receiving it each month.

My question is: When Jesus comes to set up His throne in Jerusalem, will He bring Gentile Christians for His 1,000-year reign on earth, or will the saints He brings with Him be Jews only? Or both?

Also, in St. John 14:2, Jesus said, *"In my Father's house are many mansions...*" When and where will these mansions be?

-No Name Given

ANSWER: First Corinthians 12:13 answers, *"...by one Spirit are we all baptized into one body, whether we be Jews or Gentiles...".* The Church is His Body and we shall reign with Him.

Martin Luther translates John 14:2 as, *"In my Father's house are many dwelling places...".* This clearly testifies of the fulfillment of Old Testament prophecies which state that God will dwell with man. To your questions regarding when, how, where and why, 1st Corinthians 2:9 answers, *"But as it is written, Eye hath not seen, nor ear heard, neither have entered into the heart of man, the things which God hath prepared for them that love him."*

THE FIVE STONES

Dear Midnight Call,

On the cover of *News From Israel* were the words "David's Five Stones." We have read and re-read from the booklet and the Scriptures but are still unable to come up with an understanding. Could you please help us? Put it in layman's terms. What is the significance?

Thank you with our love and prayers.

-T. N. in Sprague, WA

ANSWER: Norbert Lieth interpreted the five stones of David to represent the world's five continents. Apparently, this was confusing because in America we count seven continents. However, internationally there are only five, as illustrated by the five rings of the Olympic logo: Europe, Asia, Africa, America and Australia.

THIRTEENTH APOSTLE

Dear Arno:

This is prompted by O.E.'s letter, which appeared in the recent (March) issue of *Midnight Call* where the question of the apostleship of Matthias is taken up. I missed the January article that prompted his letter, but I've gleaned enough from it to make the following observations in support of Tom's letter.

Here is the problem: We have 12 apostles, and lose one, then he is replaced. Then comes Paul, who is also an apostle, which makes 13. Thus, we have a problem. Therefore, let's check the Old Testament for a type that might fit this situation.

You will recall that only 12 tribes had an inheritance in the land of Israel, but the full count, including the Levites, totaled 13. The reason for the extra tribe was that the Levites had *"no inheritance in the land,"* but their inheritance was to be *"the Lord."*

In this, the tribe of Levi formed a prophetic type of the church, a tribe (if you will) of priests who have no inheritance in the land (ours being heaven, and with it, the Lord).

So it is entirely possible that Peter, prior to his indwelling by the Holy Spirit, acted according to God's precept, and that Matthias was chosen by God to fulfill the

Scriptures.

Paul came later as *"the apostle to the Gentiles,"* who was promised no throne from which to judge the 12 tribes–as the others were promised–and thus has no inheritance in the land, but rather in heaven, thus fulfilling the type set forth by the 13th tribe, the Levites.

This view clears up a lot of questions that have no answer otherwise, and gives place to another prophetic type and fulfillment that is lost if we assume another view.

-N. A. in Gig Harbor

ANSWER: The "13 tribes...13 apostles" theory sounds fascinating, but Revelation 21:14 reads, *"And the wall of the city had twelve foundations, and in them the names of the twelve apostles of the Lamb."*

MATTHIAS OR PAUL

This question might be important only to me, but I would like your opinion on my thoughts.

Who are the real 12 apostles? Each apostle, including Judas, was called by Jesus; so was Paul. I believe this because Jesus said to the apostles in Matthew 19:28, *"...ye also shall sit upon twelve thrones, judging the twelve tribes of Israel."*

Impetuous Peter (*Webster's Dictionary*–acting with sudden energy and little thought) realized there were only 11 after Judas' death and got ahead of God as usual and "called" an apostle to fill Judas' seat (Acts 1:26).

A year or two later, Jesus called an apostle on the road

to Damascus (Acts 9:5), to be numbered with the 11. I just can't see Matthias' name on the 12 foundations of the new Jerusalem when we never hear about him again. Paul called himself an apostle numerous times (1st Corinthians 15:9). The last one to be called, as one born out of due time.

Love your question and answers and the feature by Arno Froese.

-Y. O. in Oregon, IL

ANSWER: You answered your own question. The apostle Paul was personally chosen by the Lord and is the twelfth apostle. Matthias was democratically elected through the initiative of an unconverted Peter.

Acts 1:26 clearly states, "...*they gave forth their lots...*". Although selection by lot was also used in the Old Testament, it was, "*The LORD'S lot...*" (Leviticus 16:9).

In Matthias' case, it's not the Lord's lot but "they" and "their."

MORE ON MATTHIAS AND PAUL

Dear Midnight Call Ministries:

I've just received my very first issue of your magazine (the January issue) and read your article about Paul. Another writer wrote in about Matthias or Paul in the "Letters to the Editor" section. I know this is not a matter of salvation or anything like that, but you quote in the article (section about the 12th apostle) that Matthias wasn't chosen by the Lord and no other Scripture points to the authority of this decision. What about Proverbs 16:33 or Acts 2:14, in which Peter stands up with the eleven, meaning there is now 12–and Scripture itself calls them twelve in Acts 6:2?

This is after Judas is dead and before Paul was even converted. Matthias was to be a witness like the other 11 original apostles, as stated in Acts 1:21-23 because he saw all these things Jesus did; that's why he was proposed. Paul did not witness all these things and Paul was an apostle to the Gentiles (Romans 11:13), as well as Barnabas, who was also called an apostle in Acts 14:14.

Lastly, along with Proverbs 16:33, they prayed and asked the Lord for His decision and there were 120 believers counting the eleven apostles. Surely the Lord answered their prayer by showing that He decided the lot to fall to Matthias.

I say all this in respect and love.

-O. L. in Minneapolis, MN

ANSWER: The distinction between Matthias and the apostle Paul lies in the fact that one was chosen *"by lot"* and the other by the Lord, *"...he chose twelve, whom also He named apostles"* (Luke 6:13). He chose Paul, not Matthias. The final answer will come when we read the names on the foundation of the new Jerusalem, because that is where *"...the names of the twelve apostles of the Lamb"* will be found (Revelation 21:14).

ELIJAH

Dear Brother Froese:

I am so happy that I started receiving your magazine *Midnight Call*. It has helped me so much.

In the October issue, a Mr. N. asked you about Enoch and Elijah.

I found an article in my mother's Bible some time ago on this matter. So I am asking your response to it.

In 2nd Kings 2:11, Elijah was taken up by a whirlwind into heaven. But to which heaven: 1st, 2nd, or 3rd? This took place in 896 B.C.

Now it says in 2nd Chronicles 21:12 that King Jehoram received a letter from Elijah telling him, in past tense and future tense [he had killed his brothers and made Judah to go a-whoring] that he would die from a disease of the bowels.

King Jehoram started to reign when he was 32 years old. That's from 853 to 845 B.C. He reigned for eight years, so that makes him born in 885 B.C.

If Elijah left in 896 B.C., then he was gone before King Jehoram was born, or was Elijah translated to a place where the sons of the prophets couldn't find him? That way, Elijah would know what had happened to the king in order to write the letter.

I noticed you said Enoch and Elijah didn't experience any physical death.

Now God's Word says in Hebrews 9:27, *"And as it is appointed unto men once to die, but after this the judgment."*

How about our Lord's own words in John 3:13, *"And no man hath ascended up to heaven, but he that came down from*

247

heaven..."

I believe Enoch and Elijah will receive the promise along with all the old patriarchs and us in Jesus Christ at the Rapture.

In Hebrews 11:5, when it speaks of Enoch's translation, that he should not see death, (it) is speaking of availing the second death.

Thank you for your time reviewing this letter.

-R. O. in Indianapolis, IN

ANSWER: The Rapture of Elijah took place in approximately 896 B.C., King Jehoram was born in 885. That means that his letter to the king was of prophetic content. For example, Isaiah wrote about King Cyrus in 712 B.C., but the king's reign began in 536 B.C., which was 150 years before that time.

Which heaven Elijah and Enoch were raptured into is not revealed in Scripture. However, the statement in John 3:13 is explained in Ephesians 4:10, *"He...ascended up far above all heavens...."* Jesus was, is, and forever will be above all things.

I believe that Elijah and Enoch were bodily raptured into heaven, meaning that they experienced the translation *"in the twinkling of an eye."*

While very little information is given about Enoch, we read much about Moses and Elijah, who appeared with the Lord Jesus on the Mount of Transfiguration discussing the Lord's death.

JOEL 2 TO COME

Dear Mr. Froese,

My question is that in the Christian world, it has been said that a great outpouring of the Holy Spirit will come before the Rapture. [Proponents of this view] use Joel 2:28-30 [as their proof]. I feel that [in that passage,] God is talking to Israel just before His return to redeem His people. In my opinion, [the outpouring of the Holy Spirit] will occur in the last 3 1/2 years of the Tribulation when the Jews find out the Antichrist isn't the true messiah. I don't see another Pentecost for the Church. Do you?

-A. E. in Oakville, IA

ANSWER: Joel 2:28-29 was fulfilled at Pentecost. This is a prophecy for the Jews, not the Gentiles. But the events prophesied in verses 30-31 are yet to come. Again, the prophecy applies to the Jews. Incidentally, the Holy Spirit cannot be "poured out" twice–that outpouring is a historical event, just as the crucifixion, death, burial, resurrection and ascension of Jesus. It will not be repeated. Any teaching that places an event before the Rapture is contrary to the Bible.

2ND CHRONICLES 7:14

Dear Mr. Froese:

The churches in our area have been holding citywide prayer meetings, crying out to God for the healing of our nation. They constantly use 2nd Chronicles 7:14, which says, *"If my people, which are called by my name, shall humble themselves, and pray, and seek my face, and turn from their wicked ways; then will I hear from heaven, and will forgive their sin, and will heal their land."*

I am having a difficult time with this, for I do not believe that we can claim this particular Scripture for America. Should we not be crying out to God for His chosen people, the Jews, and for His chosen land, Israel?

While they have good intentions by crying out to God to save and heal our land, I can find no promise in the Scriptures that God ever intended to heal or restore our nation or any other nation besides His beloved Israel.

Please respond, either by printing this letter in your *Midnight Call*, or by sending me your reply. I always look forward to receiving your monthly magazine, as well as *News From Israel.*

-A. E. in Wheeling WV

ANSWER: Daniel prayed, *"O Lord, hear; O Lord, forgive; O Lord, hearken and do; defer not, for thine own sake, O my God: for thy city and thy people are called by thy name."* (Daniel 9:19). No other nation is *"called by thy name."* However, this can be spiritually applied to the Church. May the Lord in His grace open our eyes so that we will see the urgency in fulfilling His command to, *"Go ye into all the world and preach the gospel to every creature."* We do not need to meddle in the national or political affairs of our individual countries, which are under the jurisdiction of *"the god of this world,"* the devil (2nd Corinthians 4:4).

CHAPTER 13

GLOBALISM OR PATRIOTISM?

MILES OR KILOMETERS?

Dear Mr. Froese,

I just received my first issue of *News From Israel*. I like very much your neat little magazine. I am sure you are against (rightly so) the coming one-world government which is rapidly approaching.

I read one time in another prophecy magazine that the coming metric system in the U.S. would bring the world one step closer to the coming one-world government as all other major nations are already using the metric system.

On page 25 of the April issue is a news item entitled "Israel-300 kilometer highway to be built soon?" I was wondering why you would print something that is helping to hasten that which you oppose? That is, using kilometers instead of miles. Thanks for taking time to reply.

-I.N. in Defiance, OH

ANSWER: The metric system is used worldwide. The outdated European system of miles and feet is on its way out. When you buy groceries at the supermarket, purchase a car, use the telephone, or even buy the paper and pen you used to write your letter, you are supporting global corporations. If the United States isolated herself from globalism, she would, almost immediately, experience a total collapse of her economic and financial system, which would result in an unemployment level that would make the Great Depression look like a picnic.

Globalism is a reality today because the world must become one, and that, for me, is extremely good news because Jesus must come even sooner!

METRIC AND Y2K

Dear Mr. Froese,

In the June issue, you state that in the entire world – except the U.S. and Liberia – is "stuck with the old, complicated European system of miles, inches, pounds, etc." You are very much mistaken. The metric system is the one that is complicated. I know for a fact that the British people fought it and it was rammed down their throats anyway. The one-world government advocates are the ones who pushed it in the first place. Why should the U.S., the most successful country in the world, submit to metric? The world should copy the most successful country in the world instead of vice versa.

In your letters section, you answered a question about Y2K indicating that you are not too alarmed about the problem.

I have subscribed to Gary North's *Remnant Review* for 12 years. He is a Christian who is a well-known economist. Ed Lee, President of Lee Ltd. in Merrimack, NH, has called Gary North a present-day Paul Revere for alerting people to the problems of Y2K. I can assure you that Dr. North is not a fanatic, nor is Ed Lee, and many others I can name, including myself. In a report that I read, it is my understanding that the Red Cross has said that the problem could last two years for [that organization].

I believe that you are lulling your subscribers into a false sense of security with your statements and advice on the Y2K problem. [I have received advice and information] from many quarters, including Nick Guorino, who writes *The Wall Street Journal Underground*. His information has been challenged many times and the people who have challenged it have had to publicly admit that his information is accurate, as much as they would like to have proved him wrong.

Most informed people are advising to prepare for the worst in the hope that those measures are not needed. The government lies to the public all the time, and particularly about Y2K, because it doesn't want panic. The banks are also lying to the public for the same reason.

-Mrs. E. P. in St. Johnsbury, VT

ANSWER: You are correct; the metric system is furthering the global world. However, so is the English language that we use to communicate. It has become the most effective way to spread globalism. Does that mean we should stop speaking English?

As far as Y2K is concerned, detailed facts are listed in my new book, *When Y2K Dies*. I am still convinced that the Y2K issue has been flamed by fanaticism accompanied by no reasonable evidence. Of course, we will know the answer come January 1, 2000. [Letter on file, written September 1999].

IS GLOBALISM POSITIVE?

Dear Arno,

I'm reading your article on Mystery Babylon and in it you seem to be commending the Ecumenical Movement for "creating a new atmosphere of trust and fellowship" and you say "we cannot deny the success, neither the good intention of those who propose, support and endorse globalism because of the personal freedom and prosperity this has brought."

But, then you rightly say that this has no relationship to the Church of Jesus Christ and that it's the greatest deception of all time.

Yes, truly, it's the greatest deception and it's a work of the great deceiver, as we know, and we can't commend it in any way no matter if it seems to bring good. That very "good" may prevent people from realizing their need of Christ.

-No Name

ANSWER: Does that mean that the U.S. is the work of the great deceiver, and the founding of this nation was diabolically inspired? I don't think so.

America has made a very positive impact on the entire world. This "united system" is now going back to its European roots, shown by the creation of the European Union.

Is it diabolically inspired? No more and no less than the founding of the U.S.A., the United Nations or the Ecumenical Movement.

However, the moment we involve ourselves nationalistically as Christians, we become ensnared in the affairs of this world and lose clear vision of our purpose and goal. We may fight for socialism or democracy, capitalism or communism, monarchy or dictatorship, but all is in vain.

Christians do not have a "national" calling; our task remains unchanged, we are to proclaim the beloved Gospel of our Lord Jesus Christ to all people and invite everyone to join us in our pilgrimage to our eternal home.

GLOBALISM AND RACE

Dear Brother Froese:

I realize that the content of the enclosed brief article, "What is Godly About Globalism?" is controversial and would require real courage from any publisher to show tangible interest. I sense that you may be that man; therefore, I enclose a copy for your evaluation.

Within the immediate context of Genesis 11 where God established the geographic and grammatical differences between men, Genesis 9 provides the very best understanding for the differences of skin color, etc. Having looked on the nakedness of his father, Noah, Ham was cursed of God; however, the skin difference was not manifested until the birth of Canaan. This asserts the genetic changes in mankind through procreation by Ham.

In Hebrew the name Ham means "black," and Psalm 105 repeatedly confirms that Ham's descendants settled in Africa. Ham's son, Canaan, was to become the servant of Shem (Jews) and Japheth (Gentiles) because of God's curse on Ham's sin. However, the curse of God is on the one who sinned, and not necessarily on his descendants, who merely feel the effect of the curse on Ham...like the drunken father caused the death of his sons through non-provision. The drunken father was the sinner, not his dead sons. All shades of skin are drawn to the U.S.A. for reasons known to the manipulators of this transition. All who live in America are not American in heart, thus ideas contrary to the Constitution are an increasing menace to Americanism. When the liberal principle of "integration" abolishes man's individuality through "intermarriage," the liberal foolishly think that then, and only then, will prejudices disappear; however, this mentality is man "lifting himself up by his own bootstraps." Herein the liberal fails to recall that when America was essentially white, there was not a more prejudicial people anywhere in the world. Until the "Prince of Peace" returns to earth to establish His reign of "peace on earth," as Scripture reveals, there will be only "wars and rumors of wars." The skeptics need only check history and compare this to the happenings of present-day society to confirm these truths.

I am thoroughly aware of the weakening of some fundamentalists toward condition to liberal philosophies that really contradict fundamentalism and biblical truth. Too seldom are these biblical positions graphically and understandingly produced for people's concentration.

It may not be something you want to use, and I understand, but should you see the need and the value, I have discerned that the Lord would have me make the offer to you.

-O. O. in Greer, SC

ANSWER: Globalism is meant to unite people of diversity to form a global union. Undoubtedly, the United States is the most successful globalist nation, for it is comprised of many nationalities, cultures, traditions, and languages all molded into one.

Psalm 105 identifies Egypt as the land of Ham. The *CIA 1998 Fact Book* describes the Egyptian under the heading ethnic groups: "Eastern Hamidic stock (Egyptians, Beduoins and Berbers)." From Egyptian history, we have ample evidence that the sons of Ham, the Egyptians, made use of black and white servants and slaves.

As far as intermarriage is concerned, there is no law against it. The Church of Jesus Christ consists of all born-again people from all nations, races, tongues, and cultures. Your confusion is primarily due to your mixing of nationalism and racism with Christianity. The only segregation the Bible endorses is the Church's segregation from the things of the world!

SAVE OUR NATION

Letter To the Editor,

I direct this correspondence to your publication concerning your articles on *Pre-Trib Perspectives*, authored by Mr. Thomas Ice. Kindly confer.

The struggle to get our nation back under the rulership of our Lord and Savior, Christ Jesus, is the actual tribulation period. It has already been ushered in, and this duration may go on for decades. The real "battle of Megiddo" is getting underway...the action is just starting to heat up.

You must come to realize that the cardinal reason that Satan's forces are running amuck in our nation and around the world is because the so-called "Church" is coaching from the sidelines instead of participating on the gridiron. Your lack of involvement in the action is to your disadvantage – giving your logical deductions of interpretation of the events that are expected to transpire, instead of wading into the troubled waters and joining the soldiers of Christ who have already launched the frontal assault on the actual enemy.

You have allowed the enemy to infiltrate into the ranks of the Church by this nonsensical wishful thinking as you continue to bury your head in the sand, oblivious to what is really going on around you. The sins of this nation lay heavy on us and we are wasting away because of them. You "experts on theology" just watch from the outer court in the sphere of little or no participation or activity, being concerned only with the premise that you will be spared from God's wrath unleashed amid the ungodly as it is brought upon our civilization. God's wrath is being poured out in measure as we speak. It is high time for you to get involved in the pursuit to restore righteousness and truth back to our nation of people instead of dwelling on insignificant rhetoric that has no bearing on our future as a nation or as a people with Jesus as our conscious expression!

-A. E. in N. Jackson, OH

ANSWER: The Bible does not bestow any type of political or geographical promise upon believers. The attempt to "get our nation back under the rulership of our Lord and Savior Jesus Christ" is folly for two reasons. First, it never was under His rulership. Second, the Word of God makes no provision for an earthly nation or political identity to become subject to our Lord during the time of the Church. It is quite clear from Scripture that all nations are ruled by the god of this world regardless of what form of government rules.

You are right, "Satan's forces are running amuck" in the political world, but for those who have been redeemed by the precious blood of the Lamb, he is a defeated foe. Today, more than ever, we must follow His exalted order to, *"Go ye into all the world and preach the gospel to every creature."* All other things can indeed be classified as "insignificant rhetoric."

PATRIOTISM AND THE BIBLE

Dear Editor:

I give you credit for the understanding you have in

regards to the biblically foretold one-world order, final beast government system that will rule over mankind. Truly it is the most obvious sign of the endtimes.

However, as a devoted Christian American citizen, I see you have a serious misunderstanding in regards to American patriotism! God's Word states that as men and women of faith in Jesus Christ the Lord, we must obey the government of man in the land we live in.

In America, our "Constitution," as our founding fathers gave us, is the "LAW OF OUR LAND!" This is our government—"our constitutional republic!" It is the duty and right of all sovereign national American citizens to obey and defend the Constitution since this Constitution was based upon the laws of God!

As God's Word says: When man's laws become contrary to the laws of God, we must then obey God's laws instead of man's laws. "Resistance to tyranny is obedience to God!" Indeed the one-world order government is a tyrant and contrary to our Constitution and the laws of God!

-P.I. in Kingson, NY

ANSWER: You are mixing politics with religion. Basically, all governments are patterned after the laws of God. You will not find a civilized form of government that sanctions adultery, theft, and murder, or encourages children to be disobedient to their parents.

While the Constitution is a fine document, it has no religious foundation in Bible-based Christianity, nor does it mention the name of Jesus. Political governments will continue until Jesus comes and makes an end of all governments, including ours.

As believers, we have only one example, the Lord Jesus Christ who was born in a country that was ruled by a foreign dictatorial power. He never suggested that the people oppose the prevailing government; just the opposite is true. He told the people to pay their taxes according to the law of Caesar, thereby endorsing that government.

It is only what we do for Jesus that will count for eternity. Nationalism and patriotism have absolutely no relation to Christianity! A patriot may be a Christian, but there is no such thing as a Christian patriot.

TURN U.S.A. AROUND?

Dear Mr. Froese,

I am outraged at your statement, "...Vain attempt...to install a righteous government."

Daniel was taken as a servant from a defeated nation, and the time of the Rapture may still be another thousand years away.

God has given us choices. Our people chose to turn away from God, His moral base, our Constitution, into political corruption. Christians don't just give up as your article suggests; we work to turn it around.

There are many righteous men who can lead our nation well. With God, all things are possible.

-N. E. in Trona, CA

ANSWER: It is a noble cause for you to "work to turn it

(America) around;" however, the Bible offers no indication of a national or geographic promise for the Church, leading us to believe that our task is to establish a righteous form of government. You write, "God has given us...." Who is "us"?

Mixing tradition with truth will always lead to error. The only nation with a political and precise geographic promise is Israel.

The Church is scattered among the nations, just as the Jews were for approximately 2,000 years. Today, the Jews are returning to the land of their fathers and the Church will be returned to the Father. Based on the prophetic Word, it will not take a thousand years as you indicated in your letter.

CHAPTER 14

BIBLE CODES, Y2K, AND PROMISE KEEPERS

"2000"

Dear Mr. Froese,

I read the question and reply about the year 2000 computer catastrophe we are facing. Your comment about the year 2100 being a likewise potential recurrence is not valid, because the solution to the problem is having computers that require 4 digits for the year instead of 2.

When the system is fixed, it will not need to be fixed again because "00" will no longer be entered for the year, but 2000, 2100, 2200 etc.

The problem exists and I hope you have time to read the enclosed material.

I wrote the one entitled, "The Wise Shall Understand" to Christians and disciples. In it I attempt to correlate the computer crisis with the final event that will put the Antichrist in control.

If we look at events in the Mideast, Russia and China,

we can see that the foretold events regarding the ushering in of the tribulation period are all coming to an intersection like the spoke of a wheel.

But the computer crisis is the one event that can make all the nations hand over their sovereignty to one person! I have been astonished that no prophetic scholars have related this to prophecy.

[In]each issue of the publications I receive, I search for any indication that the light has come on somewhere – but so far there hasn't been a word.

Excuse my handwritten note, but I thought it was important to get this information to you for your evaluation. I can see that you do not truly know what this problem means for the entire world. I believe Christians need to be aware.

Mrs. R. E. in Sarasota, FL

ANSWER: You are correct regarding the two- and four-digit computer program. However, my answer "assumes" that if the two-digit program remains (which will be the case for some), then the same problem will occur in the year 2100.

Regardless of this fact, most organizations have already fixed the year 2000 problem and the rest still have 549 days to do so. Undoubtedly there will be problems for those who fail to prepare. I will keep your material in my file and if the Lord has not returned, we can compare notes on January 1, 2000. [Letter was written September 1999].

YEAR 2000

Dear Mr. Froese,

I have been hearing on TV that at the stroke of midnight at the year 2000, the computers will roll back. Could that be fulfillment of the Scripture in Revelation where it speaks of a day's wages for a loaf of bread? Prison doors will open; could that be the evil turned loose on earth?

If it is not too much trouble, I would like a letter from you on your opinions on the situation or an article in *Midnight Call* about it.

Thanks for the birthday card and thanks for the magazine.

-D. C. in Bledsoe, KY

ANSWER: I see no evidence in Scripture referring to the year 2000; therefore, I conclude that it will be just another year.

In regards to the computer problem, there is no direct relationship to the year 2000 because the potential problem would also apply to the year 2100. At this moment, businesses, organizations and governments all over the world are reprogramming their computers. I am convinced that the majority will be ready when 2000 comes.

Of course, there will be those who have failed to prepare, which is always the case every time the April 15th tax return deadline rolls around.

There may be some problems where large corporations have overlooked some aspects of this rather complicated software problem, but that won't cause a lack of bread or prison doors to be opened as your letter suggests. [Letter on file, written August 1999].

NUMBERS

Dear Brother Arno:

Just a quick note to your readers to give them some food for thought.

If you take the year we are living in, 1998, and divide it by the holy Trinity, which is 3, you will come up with the number 666, or the number of man. Could this be the year our Lord is coming to get us off this planet?

Numbers can reveal much. I believe that this is why there is a book in the Bible called Numbers.

I would also like to tell you I get a lot out of your magazine. Keep up the good work for our Lord!

-L. E. in Shade, OH

ANSWER: Because the Bible does not advise us to use mathematical formulas in relation to the Lord's coming, I am forced to consider this "666-1998" theory insignificant. I don't see where Scripture encourages me to "count;" however, it does say, *"Blessed is he that readeth, and they that hear the words of this prophecy..."* (Revelation 1:3).

YEAR 2000

Dear Brother Froese:

Many favorable words have been written about the benefits of computers, with almost none in opposition.

In just 11 months, the computer world will enter the year 2000 with few computers equipped for the digital change. Most people, including myself, have said, "What's

the big deal?" I have since learned the possible consequences of being indifferent to this seemingly simple
problem and have become convinced that this minor
"glitch" could be the instrument that could give the 666
man of Revelation control of the world with the blessings
of a grateful populace. It could even force a peace treaty
between Israel and the Arabs.

For example: This one-world commercial system that
man has created is controlled by computer chips high
above the earth and the ocean floor. Since computers must
work in unison with each other, mal-equipped ones will
either not function at all or else give false information.
Imagine the chaos of a world that has no computer to
operate its power plants.

No electricity means no water or heat for homes, no
pumps to pump gasoline and oil for transportation, no
telephones, no mail service, no stock market; banks and
hospitals will be paralyzed. Panic could reign supreme.
The one who controls electricity in today's society controls
the world. This would be the most opportune time in history for the Antichrist to emerge with a solution and
become man's master. An eager and willing world would
gladly accept him as God and his 666 mark in order to
survive.

Please give some remarks on this possible scenario.

-R. E. in Oakland, MD

ANSWER: The scenario you have given regarding the
entrance of the Antichrist is unrealistic. The Bible says that he
will *"come in peaceably"* and *"by flatteries"* because he *"shall*

work deceitfully"(Daniel 11:21,23). These verses clearly reveal the democratic principles by which he will enter.

Also, keep in mind that the computer is not the final authority; men control computers. From the information I have gathered, there are definitely potential problems in some areas. But this has no direct relation to electricity, gasoline, telephones, the stock market, and hospitals. None of these (and many others not mentioned) rely exclusively on one certain chip which could cause havoc.

For example, our ministry operates many computers. Although some may be over a decade old, they do, in fact, recognize the year 2000. In your case, your subscription is active until December 2001.

Credit cards issued with expiration dates past the year 2000 are all functioning. The fact that there will be some problems cannot be denied; after all, there will always be some people who neglect to fix the problem and will suffer the consequences. [Letter on file, written February 1999].

Y2K

Dear Mr. Froese:

Thank you for allowing *Midnight Call* to be made available on tape through Clearer Vision Ministries in Orlando, FL. That is how I "read" your magazine. I appreciate the quality and excellence of your clear Bible teaching. However, your casual, irresponsible position on the Y2K problem must not go unchallenged. You and many other Bible teachers should not be afraid to lose credibility by considering scenarios that go against conventional teaching.

A more definitive statement on Y2K would be quite instructive should you choose to make it for the record.

I won't detail the potential magnitude of Y2K, as hundreds of pages on the Internet already outline that. The mainstream media is beginning to pick up on the problem to a small degree, indicating that Y2K is at least of some importance.

I happen to believe it will change our world and the way we live like nothing else has in hundreds of years. However, let me be moderate for a bit.

My in-laws were without electricity and water for nearly a week in late June due to severe storms. They were unprepared and didn't even have batteries for a transistor radio. Suppose Y2K is no more of an inconvenience than that storm. Wouldn't some moderate preparation be in order? What would you do if you knew such a disruption was coming? What about Paul's admonition to Timothy in 2nd Timothy 5:8? I've heard it argued that preparing for Y2K is laying up treasures on earth. I hardly think taking personal responsibility for the safety of your loved ones can be so described. Furthermore, it in no way has to detract from spreading the Gospel in these increasingly more uncertain and urgent times.

The reason Scripture does not speak of the year 2000 is that is does not predict much, if anything, about the Church Age [in which we] live, as you should well know. Did Scripture predict the Dark Ages? The Black plague? Adolf Hitler and the killing of 6 million Jews? Did Scripture predict the automobile? Airplane? Nuclear bombs? Computers? Your theology hinges so much on computers, smart cards and a possible virtual reality beast of Revelation, but please be open-minded about this. Where were the computers when the Romans taxed and registered people at the time of Jesus' birth? Are they absolutely necessary for the mark of the beast? To answer "yes" may be 1) spiritualizing Scripture, 2) overestimating man's greatness, and/or 3) underestimating the supernatural works of Satan and God.

I believe Y2K's catastrophe will happen in part due to man's greed and shortsightedness. Major corporations have known of potential problems for quite some time, but they have been reluctant to do anything to hurt their bottom line. Furthermore, we've come to take technology and our way of life for granted and denial is a natural response to anything that threatens or upsets our comfort zone.

Suppose the inevitability of the Y2K disaster fits into the intents, if not plans, of the power elite. As you know, many environmental extremists would love to see our planet de-industrialized and de-populated. You can be certain there are those in high places who will not be so adversely affected because of the preparations they've made.

Can you envision a scenario where things are so bad the Church must be rescued by Rapture before or after such a tremendous calamity? What if total chaos results from the Y2K problem? Doesn't it seem likely that the world at large will call for a miracle worker to rescue them? For example, the stage may be set for the appearance of the Antichrist in a more meaningful way than you may believe it is now.

Think about these things, but don't wait until January 1, 2000, and please don't encourage others to do so. Their very lives might be at risk. Would you want that on your conscience?

-H.T. in Hallsville, MO

ANSWER: We do not deny the fact that Y2K may cause a problem; however, problems were meant to be solved. On May 4, 1998 an article appeared in *The Wall Street Journal* which stated "...the Y2K problem has already been recognized and though the remedies are not easy, people know what to do, and for the most part, are doing it before the year 2000 arrives."

I am not too alarmed by the Y2K problem primarily because it is being amplified by fanaticism. Rather than being based on facts and debated rationally, it seems to be the product of over-exaggerated scenarios fueled by doomsday prophets. My concern is for the Gospel that the Lord has entrusted me to proclaim. Time is too precious to be invested in other things that are not essential to the faith. [Letter on file, written April 1999].

BIBLE CODES

Dear Arno:

It will interest you to know that information has been found in the Bible codes that indicates the signing of the false seven-year "peace covenant" with Israel – by the Antichrist–will occur on September 15, 1999! The Bible code names Bill Clinton and Ehud Barak as signers of that covenant. Since Clinton sent Carville and his "thugs" to Israel to buy votes for Barak in this last election, it isn't surprising he could get Barak to sign a false peace covenant, which Clinton will break 3 1/2 years later.

In addition, the Bible codes give overwhelming indication of Tishri 1 (Rosh Hashanah, between sundown 9/10/99-9/12/99) as the date for the Rapture of the Church. Now, I know some people hesitate over finding a date for the Rapture because they claim "no man knows the day or the hour." However, this reference from Matthew 24 has to do with the:

1) "Second Coming of Christ" (at the end of the seven years to set up His kingdom on the earth for 1,000 years) and the

2) "end of the world."

Neither of these two events have anything to do with the "Rapture" (Marriage Supper of the Lamb). Therefore, any date God gives in His "codes" for the Rapture is not a violation of His Word. Plus, since one can count seven years from the signing of the peace covenant by the Antichrist with Israel to the exact day of Christ's Second Coming, the reference in Matthew 24 is, therefore, really only applicable to not knowing the date/hour for the "end of the world."

To biblical prophecy buffs, it appears that Bill Clinton is being named by God as the infamous "Antichrist!" As though to provide further confirmation, the information about Clinton appears right next to the word "666" in the Bible codes.

This is extremely significant in light of a comment by Larry Nichols, one of Clinton's former associates (now in hiding for his life) warned in his 6/16/99 report that "Clinton is going to try and take over the world. He is not going to stop with our nation. He has his eye on the world!"

If the researchers are correctly interpreting the information recently discovered in the Bible codes, then Clinton does end up ruling the world! God help us all!

For your benefit, I have enclosed a copy of the applicable information on Bible codes about these recent findings so you can check it out for yourself.

You have cause to rejoice, Arno! Your struggles will soon be over. Whether or not you believe it, be ready just in case! In the meantime, keep looking up, "your redemption draws nigh."

-C. H. in Castro Valley, CA

ANSWER: The fact that you have been misled into believing that September 15, 1999 is the date of the Rapture and that Bill Clinton is the Antichrist should be sufficient proof. The Bible clearly states that the Antichrist cannot be revealed until the Church is taken out of the way first. The Great Tribulation and the kingdom of the Antichrist are only made possible by the removal of the light of the world which is the Church.

The Bible codes have absolutely no relation whatsoever to the Bible because this computer game can be played by using a tabloid paper—with amazing results. It's ironic that an atheist (Michael Drosin) is the author of the best-sell-

273

ing book, *The Bible Code.* Our Lord Jesus never said anything about hidden codes, but he surprisingly asked, *"Have ye not read the Scripture...?"* In Revelation 1:3, we have this wonderful promise: *"Blessed is he that readeth, and they that hear the words of this prophecy..."* Also, in regards to Clinton breaking the covenant with Barak after 3 1/2 years, do you not know that Clinton will not even be in office in three and a half years?

MORE ON BIBLE CODES

Dear MCM,

I'm writing this letter to let you know I really enjoy your magazine, *Midnight Call.*

I wish I could afford to order all the prophetic issues that you carry, but I can't. I'm praying that in the near future, I'll be able to order your *News From Israel.*

I also wanted to see if you would find out about a certain situation which I had recently heard on TBN's "Praise the Lord" program.

Rabbi Yacov Rambsel has done some intense study concerning the Bible codes and he has discovered some information about Y2K.

Along with this [information] he had also come across the word "Rapture."

As you probably well know, everything that falls in a chapter scenario will come to pass, that is, if you believe these codes, and I do.

So far, these codes haven't lied and the chances of having codes surfacing, like these codes have, is almost zero.

Not one book has been found yet that can tell names, places, and events, like the Bible codes.

The thing that I am wondering is whether or not he is saying, by his findings, that the Rapture could be happening in the year 2000.

Of course, he didn't say a certain day or hour but he did find the year. The Lord also said no one knows the day or hour but we would know about His return, even at the door. I believe we can know the year or the season but not the day or hour.

-D. E. in Jacksonville, FL

ANSWER: I disagree wholeheartedly with the Bible code concept because it has absolutely nothing to do with the Bible.

The reason why names appear, which may seem to indicate prophetic value, is due to the fact that these people are searching for them. Did you know that those same words can be found in other books as well?

It stands to reason that more people are searching the Bible because it is still the best-seller and over 25% of its content relates to prophecy.

I suggest you get a copy of the book *Decoding the Bible Code* by John Weldon, published by Harvest House.

To assume there are "hidden codes" in the Bible is to say that the full message of the Scripture hasn't been available to us for almost 2000 years, and that we needed a computer to give us additional confirmation. I reject such a theory.

We don't need any code to understand the simplicity of

the Word of God such as John 3:16, *"For God so loved the world, that he gave his only begotten Son, that whosoever believeth in him should not perish, but have everlasting life."*

PROMISE KEEPERS

Dear Brother Arno Froese:

I believe what your writers have to say about endtime events. I am in agreement with your stance on what is to come. But please...stick to the theological interpretation of the Bible.

I was taken aback by your comments concerning the Promise Keepers in your "Letters to the Editor" column dated February 1998.

What right do you have to say such things about the great work that takes place by this organization?

The biggest division taking place in the Church today is the controversy that exists over the very subject your magazine is written about!

Our communities are so full of Pre-Trib, Mid-Trib, Post-Trib, No-Trib debates.

Stories of the Antichrist [appear with] the tail of every comet...

Doomsday reports of black helicopters parked in the garages of our neighborhoods...

Help...who do I believe?

All I am simply trying to say is this: "Hats off to Coach McCartney and his leadership team for striving for unity in a Church that is being torn apart by every wind of doctrine."

I thank you for your magazine.

-Rev. D.E., Duluth, MN

ANSWER: Your praise that Mr. McCartney is "...striving for unity in a Church that is being torn apart by every wind of doctrine" reveals to me that you believe that we have the capacity to establish a visible manifestation of the Church of Jesus Christ on earth.

I strongly disagree that the Church is being torn apart by every wind of doctrine as your letter suggests. On the contrary, the Church is perfectly united in Him.

The assumption that we are capable of bringing about the perfect unity our Lord prayed for is presumptuous.

You are overlooking the fact that the Church exclusively consists of born again believers who may be found in virtually all churches–whatever their denomination or affiliation may be.

The gross error of believing that we can establish a unified "churchianity" will only lead to the fulfillment of Revelation 13, "*...all that dwell upon the earth shall worship him,*" that is, the Antichrist!

If we try to establish "the power of biblical unity" through visibly manifested organizational means, then we are producing something outside of the works of our Lord. Jesus testified, "*I in them, and thou in me, that they may be made perfect in one.*" You are trying to break through an open door when you attempt to build a unity that our Lord has already perfected!

PROMISE KEEPER

Dear Sir,

My understanding of the unity which Promise Keepers strives for and your understanding of it vastly differ.

I've never understood [the organization]to call for a unity of compromise but rather a unity of repentance, that we should come together by coming in line with the Word of God. Turning away from sexual sin, arrogance, hatred, bitterness...all things that Satan would devise to drive a wedge between Christians. And yes, the group emphasizes first and foremost, being born again.

Is this call for unity within the true Church of born-again believers scriptural? Paul calls for Christians to repent of their arrogance when they say, *"I'm of Paul"* or *"I'm of Apollos."* These statements are divisive to the true Church. We are often admonished in the Word of God to be of one mind, to endeavor to keep the unity of the Spirit in the bond of peace, and so on. This would seem to indicate that the total unity that Jesus desires for us is not automatically complete now and forever when we are born again. This kind of unity must be sought after through repentance. See also Ephesians 4:13.

Thank you for providing Christians with a source for keeping on top of endtime events. I would admonish you to never be a source of divisiveness among true believers within this very important ministry that God has given you. But, by all means, never compromise the Word of God and never compromise the convictions that the Holy Spirit has taught you from the Word.

-E.L., Cuyahoga Falls, OH

ANSWER: The words "unity of repentance" which you have written in your letter are foreign to the Scripture. No mechanism for mass repentance is provided in the Bible. Repentance is a personal act. Another item you wrote, "Come together by coming in line with the Word of God," sounds somewhat peculiar because we are already admonished in Scripture to not forsake the assembling of ourselves together. This includes the whole family: parents, grandparents, and children. I fail to see where Scripture admonishes us to come together as men only, to physically embrace each other, hold hands, openly display emotionalism, and then claim that this behavior produces unity within the Church.

I do agree that unity must be sought after and James tells us how: *"Humble yourself in the sight of the Lord...."* But the only way to seek unity is by coming closer to Jesus.

The fact that people are coming to Jesus through the work of PK is wonderful and I greatly rejoice.

BIBLE CODE AND PROMISE KEEPERS

Dear Brother Froese:

First, I wish to thank you for sending me the information on Bible software.

Next: I have just finished reading a book by Michael Drosnin called *The Bible Code*, published by Simon & Schuster. A Christian friend from California called me several nights ago, very excited about this book. It is found in secular bookstores and according to the clerk at my local bookstore, it is one of the hottest selling books on their shelves. The author is a non-believer and writes from a secular point of view.

Several years ago, a Christian Jew who is also a famous mathematician, with the use of a computer, discovered a hidden code in the Old Testament original Hebrew. This hidden code unlocks the past, present and future, and predicts a nuclear holocaust in Jerusalem during the year 2000.

If you haven't heard of this book, you must obtain a copy of it ASAP and read it.

I am very eager to know your opinion of the book. I highly respect your spiritual insight in such matters.

The third thing I would like to mention is that I attended the Promise Keepers rally or "Sacred Assembly" in Washington, D.C. this past weekend. I have read what you have had to say about Promise Keepers in the *Midnight Call*.

I had heard and read a lot about Promise Keepers in the past and decided to attend the "Sacred Assembly" in person to find out firsthand if it is of God or the devil.

By 6 p.m. Saturday evening, I was churching with mixed emotion. There were close to 2,000,000 men present. There was a group of men approximately 1/4 mile wide by 3 1/2 miles long.

To open the meeting, we sang, "A Mighty Fortress is Our God." For several minutes, almost two million men were praising God at the top of their voices with one accord.

The thought crossed my mind [that] this is just a small

foretaste of what it will be like on the day of the soon-to-come Rapture of the Bride, when we will all praise the Lord in unison with one heart and mind. I cannot describe the feeling.

Many souls accepted Christ that day. One young man accepted Christ on our bus on the way home and gave one of the most heart-stirring testimonies I have ever heard, before a group of 55 men. We were all humbled by this young man's honesty before the living God.

Back to the "Assembly." As the meeting progressed, the theme turned more and more to UNITY. Our mission to preach the Gospel started to become secondary as UNITY became the primary theme.

When Bill McCartney [founder of Promise Keepers, and former football coach at the University of Colorado] spoke, the hair on the back of my neck started to stand up. He asked us to openly accept the Roman Catholics as full brothers in Christ...unity, unity, unity!

Compromise for the sake of unity, straight down the road to the one-world religion of the unholy trinity.

Brother Froese, I have believed for a long time that we are living in the last of the last days before the Rapture of the Bride of Christ.

As I walked down the fast-emptying streets of our nation's capital, I was almost shivering as I realized how close we are to a one-world religion. I was also frightened to realize that most of the people with whom I had attended the rally were buying into McCartney's program, pastors and lay people alike.

Satan is inspiring man with a grand and noble plan to

bring a pseudo-healing and unification of the nations, a task that only Christ can do when He returns with the saints to set up his kingdom on earth.

On the other hand, it is very exciting to realize that the soon return of Christ for the Church is imminent!

-R.E., Burlington, IA

ANSWER: Regarding the Bible code: Jesus asked, *"Have ye not read the Scripture...?"* Also, Revelation 1:3 says, *"Blessed is he that readeth, and they that hear the words of this prophecy...."* Nowhere do I read that we must wait for a hidden Bible code in order to understand God's message.

Critics have clearly revealed that, depending on the system you use, you can get any message from virtually any type of literature.

In regards to Promise Keepers: When controversy regarding the preaching of the Gospel existed, Paul said, *"What then? notwithstanding, every way, whether in pretence, or in truth, Christ is preached; and I therein do rejoice, yea, and will rejoice"* (Philippians 1:18). Therefore, I am happy and thankful that souls are being saved.

However, it is unfortunate that compromise often brings success, and with success comes compromise. As a result, confusion is born.

For example, Promise #6 of, "The Seven Promises of a Promise Keeper," says, "The Promise Keeper is committed to reach beyond any racial and denominational barrier to demonstrate the power of biblical unity." This "promise" ignores the fact that churches, denominations and ministries are not the Church, although they may contain the

Church if two or three born again believers are gathered in His name. Promise Keepers assumes that the breaking of "denominational barriers" will produce a "demonstration of biblical unity." That presumption is not even alluded to in the Bible.

Unity must always be in Him and His doctrine, not based on an organizational level. The visible religious union that Promise Keepers seeks to promote will ultimately lead to the open arms of Rome.

GOD BLESS PROMISE KEEPERS

Dear Mr. Froese,

In the December 1999 edition of *Midnight Call* is a letter from a lady asking about the Masons and Promise Keepers (in the same breath). I have tried to ignore your answer to her for the past several months, but I have decided that I cannot. Yes, Freemasonry is definitely of the occult, and was the basis of the "Blood Oaths" in the Mormon Church, which is also of the occult! It is your answer about Promise Keepers that has compelled me to write.

The Roman Catholic system probably is the "Whore of Babylon." However, Scripture does implore, *"...Come out of her my people..."* (Revelation 18:4). But how can they come out unless they hear the truth that can set them free! They most likely won't hear it from the Roman Catholic system, since they preach "another gospel" based on "works." How can they preach, except they be sent? As it is written, *"How beautiful are the feet of them that preach the* gospel," (Romans 10:15) *"once delivered unto the saints"* (Jude 3b). [The Promise Keepers] have speakers such as Charles Swindoll, James Robinson, Tony Evans, E.V. Hill, and Jack Hayford, just to mention a few. Nothing in their services even remotely resembles a Roman Catholic "mass." They also have altar calls, and invite men to rededicate their lives to Christ, or, for those who have never done so, to accept Christ as their Lord and Savior, and acknowledge Him "before men." (Some Protestant churches don't do that!)

The Catholic Church has taught parishioners that to attend any other church is a "sin." If a Catholic man can attend a PK meeting without feeling threatened, he just might get saved! And, of course, God is *"...not willing that any should perish, but that all should come to repentance* (2nd Peter 3:9b). Once saved, the indwelling of the Holy Spirit will then lead him into all truth!

If reaching beyond racial and denominational barriers is anti-Christian, it appears the apostles Paul and Peter must have been anti-Christian. They had to contend with Judaizers who were trying to say that Gentiles had to be Jews first, then they could become Christians. In other words, they were trying to start different denominations in the early church. In my opinion, denominations are anti-Christian. Why not just believe in the ENTIRE Bible!

The ecumenical movement is the "world" and false religion coming together in a one-world political, religious system, of which, no true Christian would participate!

You seem to have the idea that since Christ said, *"I will build my Church,"* we should do nothing! I don't think so!

The great Commission was given to everybody! Your magazine and seminars help build the Church, as well as preachers, missionaries and Christian workers around the world. And so does Promise Keepers. These ministries are not ours, but God's ministries working through us in the power of the Holy Spirit. If Bill McCartney was called and sent to do this by God, we should not touch the anointed of the Lord. Let us not forget who the enemy is. God bless Bill and Promise Keepers.

-Rev. E.L., Las Vegas, NV

ANSWER: "Reaching beyond racial and denominational barriers" is not anti-Christian; however, the assumption that by doing so "demonstrates the power of biblical unity" is. Promise #6 follows the line of Vatican philosophy that assumes that an organizational structure can represent His Church on earth. Promise #5 requires "...honoring and praying for his pastor by actively giving his time and resources." Thus, the Promise Keeper is bound to support his Catholic priest, his Mormon cult leader, and in some cases his homosexual pastor. Are you aware that it is not permitted to discuss doctrine among PK? Without doctrine we have no faith and from such developments the Bible admonishes us, "...*come out of her, my people....*" Did you know that Promise Keepers has recently renounced the doctrine of justification by faith alone? This gross abandonment of a pillar doctrine aligns the movement with the teachings of the Catholic Church.

The fact that the Promise Keepers organization is to be commended for seeking a closer relationship to the Lord and that many souls have been added to the Church is not the issue. The point in question is the issue of unity without doctrine. The Catholic Church welcomes such unity; therefore it is not surprising that Catholic clergy encourage parishioners to attend Promise Keepers. (Enclosed is a letter from Cardinal Mahoney Archbishop of Los Angeles highly recommending Catholics to attend Promise Keeper meetings).

INTERDENOMINATIONAL CRUSADE

Dear Brother in the Lord,

Recently our church began pushing a citywide interdenominational crusade. The pastor asked if we had any questions. I asked, "How can we join hands with some of the churches who deny the Gospel and could lead to a one-world church?" Well, I was rebuked. "We Christians need to join hands and set doctrine aside," they said. Maybe this is the Holy Spirit's moving and now I feel discouraged in my faith.

I do want unity but many of these churches don't preach the Gospel. I have prayed on this subject and so far have one brother in the Lord to agree with my stand.

To me, it's an offshoot of Promise Keepers, which I quit over a year ago.

How can we really be sure when God is in it? I am dealing with a Mormon man now and have been for the past ten years.

He did go to our church today and many of his people are turning against him.

I need some "good ole wisdom" and help from someone who has more insight on these movements. Since we are so close to the endtimes, I want no part of the Antichrist movement for the sake of love and unity in Christ Jesus, for many will say "Lord, Lord," but He will deny them.

-R. E. in Oakville, IA

ANSWER: Second John 9 warns, *"Whosoever transgresseth, and abideth not in the doctrine of Christ, hath not God. He that abideth in the doctrine of Christ, he hath both the Father and the Son."* We must never compromise doctrine. Doctrine is the fundamental of faith and enables us to identify false teachings.

Regarding the interdenominational crusade, I would give my support if the evangelist preaches the doctrines of Christ. Many souls have found the Lord during such crusades. I have met people all over the world who have testified that they were led to the Lord through a Billy Graham crusade. Many other denominational and interdenominational evangelists are doing a tremendous job.

If you mean literal "hand holding," I must agree that I am not in favor either. Our unity must not be directed horizontally, but vertically. The closer I come to Jesus, the nearer I am to my brother.

CHAPTER 15

CHURCH ISSUES

GIFTS FOR TODAY?

Dear Mr. Froese,

I have three questions:

First: Do you believe that tongues, healing and prophecy are for today or that they were to confirm the Gospel in the days of early Christianity and therefore have passed away?

Second: Please explain what you deem false teaching of the Pre-Wrath Rapture and Post-Trib Rapture. What do these terms mean to you?

Third: If the foundation of the Catholic faith is "good," according to your response in the December 1994 *Midnight Call* newsletter, why do you align yourself with Dave Hunt, who reports in his book, *A Woman Rides the Beast,* that this Catholic Church is the apostate church of Scripture? He quoted in one of his newsletters that the Protestant church used to adamantly teach against the Catholic faith. They seem to use the terms of Christianity, but wherein are they told they must be born again? I want to know how you view the Catholic Church and are you still speaking with, or would you align yourself with, Dave Hunt? How can two walk together unless they agree?

Please respond.

-K.N., Jacksonville, FL

ANSWER: The signs (Mark 16:16-17)(all five) that should follow those who believe were indeed fulfilled by the apostles in the early church (Mark 16:16-17). The Bible says that the Jews require a sign. Later, Paul explained, *"Faith cometh by hearing the word,"* not by signs. Can God demonstrate these signs today in His Church? Absolutely! But why should He?

The Pre-Wrath Rapture means that Rapture will occur in the midst of the seven-year tribulation. The Post-Trib Rapture means that it will take place after the tribulation. Both are false because the Rapture can take place at any time. We are to wait for Him now, not after a certain event has taken place.

Indeed, the Catholic Church has a good foundation; unfortunately, she has built cultic practices upon it, such as the infallibility of the pope, adoration of Mary, prayers to dead saints, holy water and the sacrifice of the mass, just to name a few.

I do not see where we disagree with Dave Hunt except in terminology, which is of lesser significance. Our unity with all born again Bible-believers is grounded in a person, the Lord Jesus Christ. We will always have disagreements amongst ourselves, just as the apostles did (compare Acts 15:2,7 and 39).

TONGUES

Dear Brother Froese,

I am so thrilled to be getting the *Midnight Call* magazine.

I can hardly wait for it to come in the mail each month. It has enlightened me in God's Word so much. May God bless you all. I have a question.

I was raised in the Church of God most of my life. I don't know if you're very familiar with this denomination or not. But the Lord has been dealing with me about some of the things that go on in this movement.

First, they teach we must be born again, which I truly believe. They say we have to get down at an altar and cry and plead for God to forgive us and save us. They also teach that we have to seek the Holy Ghost the same way, and we don't get the Holy Ghost if we don't speak in tongues. If we don't, then the next service we should repeat the actions until we do. People all around us are yelling and screaming in our ears so we can't think straight. They also shout, run around and jump up and down, speaking in tongues all at the same time. They fall out, in the spirit, so they say. I'm very confused. God is not the author of confusion. I'm not saying they're wrong, but for the life of me, I can't, and I've searched my Bible through, find where Jesus or any of His disciples ever acted this way. Yet, we're supposed to go by the teachings of the apostles. They never taught this. To me, this is a gospel other than the Gospel of Jesus Christ. Please comment on this.

-I.N., Englewood, FL

ANSWER: The apostle Paul asked seven questions which are all categorically answered with the word "No." Consequently, the teaching that speaking in tongues is a sign of rebirth is false.

The confusion between the baptism of the Holy Spirit and the filling of the Spirit has caused much harm in the Church. The baptism of the Holy Spirit is our rebirth. *"In whom ye also trusted, after that ye heard the word of truth, the gospel of your salvation: in whom also after that ye believed, ye were also sealed with that holy Spirit of promise"* (Ephesians 1:13). We don't have to go to any altar to be saved. As a matter of fact, there is no such thing as an altar other than the one in heaven where we have direct access through His precious blood. The filling of the Spirit is a repeated process. The believers described in Acts 4 were forbidden to preach in the name of Jesus. As a result, they held a prayer meeting and became empty of themselves, meaning they had only one prayer objective: to fulfill the task the Lord had given them by preaching the Gospel. They didn't ask for political changes, new morals in their nation, or prayer in public places, but simply, *"...Lord, behold their threatenings: and grant unto thy servants, that with all boldness they may speak thy word"* (Acts 4:29). As a result, we read in verse 31,*"...they were all filled with the Holy Ghost..."* Believers, filled with the Spirit, are the last ones to say so. The attempt to force the Lord's hand to be *"filled with the Spirit"* contains the danger of being deceived by a false spirit.

SPEAKING IN TONGUES

Dear Mr. Froese:

I am a regular reader of *Midnight Call* and *News From Israel.* I enjoy both tremendously and do so appreciate having the truth put forth—truth that we will never learn from the secular sources.

There is a subject heavy on my heart, and I would appreciate your comment on it.

I am a senior citizen with grandchildren. I was taught, as a child, to pray and study God's Word daily. I have always felt that I "knew" the Lord, and certainly have a strong desire to know Him even better. I have had miracles occur in my life which have proven to me, beyond any doubt, that God is real. Jesus is alive and He intervenes in our lives, frequently in answer to prayer.

There is a very famous minister who often appears on TV. I enjoy hearing his Bible studies, but one day he made a statement that I am truly concerned about. He said, "If you don't speak in tongues, or you haven't been 'slain' in the Holy Spirit, then God does not hear your prayer—you are wasting your time praying."

God has blessed me mightily; but I don't speak in tongues, and I've never been "slain" in the Holy Spirit! I would never denigrate either happening, for both are biblical. I wonder if perhaps God has always known that He didn't have to "slay" me to get my attention; I do not know.

293

I am concerned because this man is a Christian brother and his voice reaches millions. His comment has not diminished or destroyed my faith, but I am concerned that others might be discouraged or even stop praying entirely. I pray for this man, as I do believe him to be wrong.

I admire your intelligence and your willingness to be faithful to His holy Word. Thank you in advance for your integrity and your comments.

-O.R., Springfield, MO

ANSWER: First Corinthians 12 makes a clear distinction between the Body of Christ and the different gifts. Paul asks, *"Are all apostles? are all prophets? are all teachers? are all workers of miracles? Have all the gifts of healing? do all speak in tongues? do all interpret?"* (Verses 29-30). Obviously, all questions were answered categorically with the word "NO." Anyone who teaches that everyone must speak in tongues is teaching that which is contrary to the Scriptures.

In regards to being "slain in the spirit," this is a relatively new concept not found in Scripture.

One of the obvious errors I have detected during many years in the ministry is a lack of discernment when distinguishing between the baptism of the Holy Spirit (the rebirth-see Ephesians 1:13) and the filling of the Holy Spirit. Careful reading of Acts 4 makes this matter plain. These Christians were born again but now they were *"filled with the Holy Ghost."* Why? Because they acted in accordance with the instruction of the Lord to preach the Gospel of Jesus Christ, but they were forbidden to do so.

There is only one Holy Spirit baptism, *"For by one Spirit we are all baptized into one body, whether we be Jews or Gentiles, whether we be bond or free; and have been all made to drink into one Spirit"* (1st Corinthians 12:13). But there are many fillings. This has no relation to speaking in tongues or being slain in the Spirit.

HOLY SPIRIT BAPTISM

Dear Arno Froese:

Since you seem to be so learned in the Scriptures, I was surprised that you made an error in your cover story on page 13 of the December issue, regarding Acts 2:2-4. After which you stated, "This is a one-time event, the birth of the Church, never to be repeated."

I would like you to respond to Acts 10:44 and 45. Also, Acts 11:15 (Peter speaking), *"And as I began to speak, the Holy Ghost fell on them, as on us at the beginning."* Also read the following in verse 16. *"Then remembered I the word of the Lord, how that he said, John indeed baptized with water; but ye shall be baptized with the Holy Ghost"* (My Bible has a reference to Matthew 3:11).

Also, I refer you to Acts 19:6, *"And when Paul had laid his hands upon them, the Holy Ghost came on them; and they spake with tongues, and prophesied."*

I believe this baptism of the Holy Ghost is not a requirement for salvation, but is a help in witness. So whether or not one has received this baptism of the Holy Ghost in no way reflects on one's salvation. Faith in Jesus is the only requirement although works should follow faith.

This last Scripture I believe will clear up your comments on "The Danger of Deception," page 7 in *Midnight Call.*

-C.F., Ontario, CANADA

ANSWER: There is a distinct difference between Acts 2 and Acts 11. You will notice that verses 1-33 of Acts 2 are missing in Acts 11. The Gentiles heard the Gospel of salvation, and as a result, *"The Holy Ghost fell upon them as on us at the beginning."* So there was no second Pentecost.

You are confusing the filling of the Holy Spirit with the baptism of the Holy Spirit, which is the rebirth. Ephesians 1:13 confirms this, *"In whom ye also trusted, after that ye heard the world of truth, the gospel of your salvation: in whom also after that ye believed, ye were sealed with that holy Spirit of promise."*

BIRTH OF THE CHURCH

Arno Froese:

While reading your cover story, I came upon some areas that need clarification. In "The Danger of Deception," you quote from Matthew 7:22. I suggest that you also read Matthew 7:15 where Jesus is speaking of false prophets who come in the guise of sheep while at heart they are voracious wolves, and then goes to the verse you quote. Do you recall when Jesus cast out demons and the Pharisees said, *"Through the ruler of the demons He casts of demons,"* and Jesus answered in Matthew 12:22-26 that a house divided against itself cannot stand?

Then, in "The Birth of the Church," you say that the

pouring out of the Holy Spirit at Pentecost was a one-time event. What about Acts 10 where the Holy Spirit is poured out on some Gentiles? Also, in Acts 19:6, some Ephesians were baptized by the Holy Spirit. They were believers, but they had not been baptized by the Holy Spirit.

How can you do away with prophecy? (Please read 1st Corinthians 14:3. Prophecy is for edification, exhortation, and comfort). We still need it today.

The baptism by the Holy Spirit is the same now as it was during the age of the apostles. If your writers and contributors are saying differently, then you are speaking against the Holy Spirit.

-R.T., Sandpoint, ID

ANSWER: The birth of the Church is reported in Acts 2 and was signified by the appearance of *"cloven tongues like as of fire."* These Jewish believers were prepared and waiting for this event.

In Acts 10 we read, *"While Peter yet spake these words, the Holy Ghost fell on all them which heard the word"* (verse 44). Notice that this time there were no *"cloven tongues like as of fire,"* nor did Peter testify as he did in the case of Acts 2, *"...this is that which was spoken by the prophet Joel"* (Acts 2:16).

The baptism of the Holy Spirit, which results in the rebirth, is not a repetition of Pentecost, but a result.

We no longer need to wait for Pentecost; it's past history. People are saved when they hear and believe the Gospel, *"In whom ye also trusted, after that ye heard the*

297

word of truth, the gospel of your salvation: in whom also after that ye believed, ye were sealed with that holy Spirit of promise" (Ephesians 1:13).

Matthew 7 reveals that deception does not necessarily come from the outside, but rather from within.

Hindus, Muslims, Buddhists and other false religions neither practice nor claim to "prophesy," "cast out devils," or perform "wonderful works" in the name of Jesus. Thus, we need to beware of the "workers of iniquity" within the Church, particularly those who demonstrate supernatural signs and miracles.

HEALING THE BODY

Dear Mr. Froese:

I was surprised when I read the comments to "See A Doctor" in the May issue of *Midnight Call*. It appears that one of the greatest prophecies in the Old Testament was not considered. I refer to Isaiah 53:5 which was fulfilled by Jesus Christ at Calvary. (Read also Matthew 8:16-17.)

By the reasoning that was stated that sometimes God heals through faith and other times through doctors, then God saves people sometimes through Jesus Christ and other times through pastors, priests or the pope! Of course this is foolishness. The Bible tells us that all deliverance from sin, sickness and disease was taken care of at the cross by Jesus Christ.

Doctors do not need to become shoemakers, for the world and Christians who have not been taught the truths of the Bible need doctors and medical science. I understand that the medical profession makes over 100,000 mistakes each year in their treating of patients. I am sure God did not raise up this kind of profession for those who will trust Him by His Word. I knew a doctor who would ask his patients if they wanted prayer according to Matthew 18:19, Mark 11:24; 16:18 or James 5:14. Otherwise, he would treat them by the medical skills he learned. The first option was free; the second option he would have to charge them. The local churches ostracized him for his convictions and faith in God's Word. Like Jesus told Peter when he sank, *"...O thou of little faith, wherefore didst thou doubt?"* (Matthew 14:31).

I know several so-called "men of faith" who turned to the medical profession when they were tested with an illness. However, that does not make God's Word null and void. God's Word is truth. It is truth whether you or I believe it or not. It is not true because we believe it but because it is the inspired Word from God Himself (2nd Timothy 3:16).

I send them and you this letter in Christian love and pray that you will receive them in like manner. I do enjoy reading *Midnight Call* as part of my studies of endtime events. Not many periodicals carry current events around the world like you do.

May your faith continue to grow as the Lord blesses you through His Word.

-R.S., Colorado Springs, CO

ANSWER: All healing is divine. A physician does not have the power to heal, he only prescribes the necessary medication or treatment to prepare the hurt for healing. Nevertheless, the body will get sick and ultimately die. Jesus said, *"It is the spirit that quickeneth; the flesh profiteth nothing..."* (John 6:63).

The Lord *"...healed all that were sick..."* for a specific reason, *"That it might be fulfilled which was spoken by Esaias the prophet..."* (Matthew 8:16-17). The body has no special promise. Flesh and blood shall not inherit the kingdom of God. Our old nature is under the law of sin and will only go in one direction, to the grave. Apparently, the great apostle Paul carried a sickness all of his life. He was also powerless regarding the sickness of Epaphroditus (Philippians 2:25-27) and *"...Trophimus have I left at Miletum sick" (2nd Timothy 4:20).*

The healing of the physical body has been overemphasized to the point that a great number of ministries have fallen prey to the spirit of lies replacing the preaching of the Gospel with so-called healing services. However, there is a provision in Scripture regarding those who are sick. *"Is any sick among you? let him call for the elders of the church..."* (James 5:14).

MUSIC LEADS TO CHAOS?

Dear Arno,

All musical roads are leading to chaotic noise. Some roads are longer than others and take longer to arrive, but the destination is the same. Rebellious noise has an appeal to rebellious hearts.

The morality of a country can be no greater than the

quality of its music. We are ...rotting at the core. Your book, *How Democracy Will Elect the Antichrist* makes a lot of sense to me. Thanks!

-E. A., Valencia, PA

ANSWER: Music is one of the most powerful avenues through which the world is being united and will ultimately worship the image of the beast. However, not all music leads to chaos. Revelation 15:2-3 reads, *"...having the harps of God. And they sing the song of Moses, the servant of God, and the song of the Lamb...."* Now that's good music!

I LIKE ROCK MUSIC

Dear Brother in Christ,

In the January and March issue, I read two articles in the "Letters to the Editor" section which shocked me. They were written by two people who made reference to the fact that "rock" music was sinful and demoralizing our country. I was shocked to see that a Bible-believing magazine would agree with such statements.

Don't misunderstand me; I do not condone all "rock" music. I'm 16 years old and am unwillingly exposed to some of the current rock and heavy metal bands such as Marilyn Manson and Korn. It truly saddens me that my peers are listening to this satanic garbage and actually believe that it does not affect them. Unfortunately, there are many popular bands who openly degrade the name of Christ and all Christian morals; however, today, there are dozens of Christian rock bands all over the country spreading the Gospel of Jesus Christ.

I have experienced both sides of the coin. I have attended traditional church services with organs, pianos, and choirs for years. I have also attended many Christian "rock-pop" concerts as well. I condemn neither as long as they are reaching people for Christ. Personally, I have seen more people truly repentant and on their knees crying out for God at Christian rock concerts than I ever have in all of my "hymn-church" attending. If you have never attended a Christian rock concert, let me relate a typical one to you. At almost every Christian rock concert, regardless of where and when, a presentation of the Gospel is made. These musicians know that a significant percent of their crowds consist of unsaved teenagers just looking for a fun time. They turn the music up loud and have a great time singing about God, but they know most of the unsaved people are not really listening to what they are saying. To reach them, they always have a time at the end where they calm the crowd and relate the Gospel so that it appeals to young people (most of the time, they are young people themselves). The response is almost always enormous. Teenagers who may never have even thought about God are humbly crying out to Him to save them. Many times, I have seen up to 20 percent of the crowd respond to an invitation. Perhaps they were not all sincere, but that problem has never stopped Billy Graham.

Also, many people assume that just because the "noise" of rock music doesn't remind them of their familiar hymns, the lyrics are not equally worthy of praise. I think that some of the most beautiful and inspiring songs ever composed were written by rock bands. Some of these songs were written by bands such as DC Talk, Three Crosses, Jars of Clay, Third Day, Smalltown Poets, and Caedmon's Call. Many people are guilty of stereotyping bands when they have not even listened to the lyrics. Just because these lyrics do not contain as many complicated words such as "diadem" and "disconsolate," does not mean they are of lesser value. Truthfully, I would rather sing a song that is relevant to me and that I can understand than a beautifully crafted song that I cannot. Many of the hymns and church songs mean nothing to teenagers because they do not understand them and they seem irrelevant to their lives. Christian rock tries to fill that gap. They know that if they do not hook teenagers onto Christian rock, the teenagers will resort to bands such as Marilyn Manson for their music.

Please, do not mistake my point. I am not degrading hymns. Many times when I have actually thought about the words to those "same ol' hymns," I have realized the timeless truths and contextual beauty contained in them. However, the only problem with hymns is that they do not reach young people for Christ, and without Christian youth, the Church in America will die.

I believe these two letters were also incorrectly referring to contemporary Christian music that is performed during worship services in many churches today. I currently attend one of these churches myself. Sometimes we play more upbeat music (far from rock), sometimes we sing slow music, and sometimes we even sing hymns. It does not matter to us what we sing as long as it leads the people into a sincere worship of God. Many times people prematurely assume that because these songs do not sound like hymns, then they must not be godly. The questions come up, "What makes hymns godly? What are the right songs to sing on Sunday morning?" The usual response is, "We have always done it that way." Hymns are steeped in tradition. They lead you into a spiritual state of worshiping God; however, I believe many people do not sing them for this reason. It is my belief that many people sing hymns just because they do not want to change.

I don't understand your stand and what you believe. However, I have spent the time typing this letter just for you (I'm a slow typer), and so I expect, out of mutual respect for each other, that you will read it carefully, pray for God's wisdom on the subject, and give it some major thought. I, for the next week after this letter is mailed, will do the same. If after all this, you genuinely feel that you and God feel the same about the subject, then I respect your beliefs. After the "roll is called up yonder," maybe we will meet and have some good "slap-on-the-back" laughter about which of us was wrong. I will close with a statement that I once heard singer Rich Mullin say. He said that we should stand firm on what we believe is the truth of God, but yet we should also be slightly skeptical of it. As long as we are never absolutely sure it is the truth, we must constantly compare it up to God to make sure it is true.

This letter was not written specifically for publication. If it is published, I can imagine it will probably be edited for length. As a brother in Christ, I am pledging my full faith that you will edit it justly.

-E.L., Orangeburg, SC

ANSWER: You present your case well. There is much to be said about outdated hymns. The unbearable hardship, incurable illness, lack of nutritious food, and constant fear of war that our forefathers experienced and are expressed in many hymns is relatively unrealistic for young people today.

However, there is a conflict. In general, the older generation dislikes "Christian rock," while the younger generation seems to welcome it. You correctly state that without modern rock music, we "...do not reach young people for Christ, and without Christian youth, the Church in America will die." But there is a question we must answer: "Is music only a matter of fashion or would the great deceiver, the father of lies, use music, as he did in Nebuchadnezzar's case, to deceive the masses of people into a false worship?" If the devil deceives the old generation, he is betting on a losing game because older people are dying one by one. But if he can reach the younger generation, then potentially, he can get the Church into his camp.

Surely, we agree that music contributes to the setting of the mental state for "worship." Let's look at two examples: 1) Would people feel comfortable with the hymn, "My Faith Looks Up To Thee, Thou Lamb of Calvary" during a rock and roll concert? I think not. Humble music does not prepare the audience for mental and emotional participation in a rock concert. 2) A successful rock performer leads the audience into such a mental and emotional state so that it begins to actively participate with bodily motions. Elvis Presley, credited as one of the great promoters of rock and roll, "[brought] sex into the open through music." Whether or not we like rock and roll is not the question. What needs to be addressed is this, "Is this a tool we should use to preach the Gospel?"

During the Spanish Christian Booksellers Convention in Miami, I tried to be objective when I attended a Christian rock concert at that event. Believe me, I remained objective for as long as I could, but after a while, it was impossible to be an honest observer in the audience without being totally shocked, disgusted, and even frightened. Quite frankly, it felt as if demons themselves were dancing on the stage. Only when I walked out, went back to my hotel room, and prayed did peace return to my soul.

I am warning against Christian rock because of its potential of deception. I fear that many young people are being led to a conversion to "another Jesus" and "another Gospel." Please be aware of the possibility of such a development.

FORBID ROCK MUSIC

Dear Mr. Froese,

If I may, I'd like to comment on Mr. W.J.E's letter in the January issue about church music. Please assure him that he's not the only one and it certainly isn't his age.

I'm 47 and grew up with rock and roll, but some of the things I hear in church these days makes me want to clench my jaws and wince.

If it was up to me, I'd get rid of the noise-makers, keep the piano and organ, and forbid the performance of any work composed after about 1900. You can't beat the grand old hymns!

-R.W., Atlanta, GA

ANSWER: Your prohibition of composing music would silence dedicated servants of the Lord who have the gift of expressing God's love, glory and power through music. Otherwise, I say "Amen!"

CHRISTIAN ROCK MUSIC

Dear Brother Froese,

I really enjoy *Midnight Call* magazine, especially the "Letters to the Editor" column. This time I would like your opinion, and I'm sure I am not the only one.

The reason was your article about "His glory."

Something that has bothered me for a long time has to do with the so-called "new" songs that have been popping up for the last 10 years. They have originated in the circles of "Christian rock" and have been sung along with traditional hymns in many evangelical churches (less and less of those, I might add).

The only "rock" I recognize is Jesus my Savior, and that's not just because I am 72.

The reasoning goes that this is the only way to retain

or attract the youth. I am all for attracting youth, but I feel strongly that some of these songs are lacking in many ways.

The most important way is *scripturally*. For example, we often sing a song which says something like: "Father [we] love you, [we worship] and adore you. Glorify your name in all the earth." I wholeheartedly agree with that.

The next verse says the same about Jesus, and I wonder about that and the last one, of course, says the same about the Holy Spirit and here I know for sure that this isn't biblical.

There are many other examples. The problem, no doubt, is a version of Paul's warning to Timothy: "...*not to appoint those too new in the faith.*"

However, we let them crank out songs which are frequently added willy-nilly to the worship list.

We have accepted the synthesizer and the drums and have put up with some new songs that are difficult to sing. Whenever I bring this up, I am told that it's just my age. What's your opinion?

-W. J.E., CANADA

ANSWER: I fully agree with your statement regarding contemporary music being sung in the churches. I don't understand it, and I don't like it. To me, it is just unintelligible noise.

You write, "We, however, let them crank out songs," and with that point I separate myself from "we" because I don't have the authority to "let" or "forbid" anyone anything except for my family.

When I hear this new type of music: I am reminded of Daniel 3 in which the whole world had to fall down and worship the image of the beast at the moment they heard the unifying music Nebuchadnezzar had installed.

Today, rock-and-roll music has such a unifying consequence like no other music has ever had.

In fact, the mindless noise of this modern music has such a unifying effect that millions of young people all over the world are buying it without even knowing its content.

What are we to do? Serve the Lord with fear and trembling for He is coming again soon!

CHAPTER 16

TESTIMONIALS

CHRISTIAN PERSECUTION

Dear Mr. Froese,

I am originally from Burma (renamed Myanmar) in S.E. Asia, where my people, the Karen Christian ethnic minority group, had been persecuted by successive Burmanese governing powers for our faith in our Lord and Savior Jesus Christ and our obedience to His command to spread the Gospel.

The persecution intensified after 1948 when the British granted independence to Burma. Since then, persecution has taken on a new subtle form.

Although all denominational churches were suppressed, the Catholic Church alone was given a little favor: the Baptist churches, being the largest and most evangelizing, were the hardest hit.

We were made to understand and accept the idea that the Catholic Church, being founded by Jesus' disciple Peter, was the true church; whereas the Baptist church was the breakaway church.

I am so glad to know that St. Peter's church was born in Jerusalem and not in Rome.

So, I am satisfied and at peace to be a humble Baptist, filled with the Holy Spirit, and waiting for the fulfillment of Bible prophecy that my Savior Jesus Christ will return to Jerusalem.

I am also satisfied that God has chosen Israel to preserve the Bible.

If He had chosen the Karen's, the Bible would have been adulterated and lost a long time ago.

Yes, salvation is of the Jews, a very brave and hard people.

And by divine authority, God has given Jerusalem to the Jews.

I was reading an article in *The Washington Report* and was confused by arguments as to why Jerusalem should be an international city, divided between Jews and Gentiles.

I opened the Bible to Joshua 18:21-28. *"Now the cities of the tribe of the children of Benjamin, according to their families were...And Zelah, Eleph and Jebusi, which is Jerusalem..."* What God had given by Joshua, who would dare take away? May the God of Abraham, Isaac and Jacob be praised!

-O.W., Port Lavaca, TX

ANSWER: I appreciate your report, and praise God for the wonderful protection and grace He's given to you, your family and the church in Myanmar. It's amazing how the Lord builds His Church despite persecution or dictatorial oppression. Thank you for your note on Jerusalem; truly, it's the great controversy and as a result, the nations of the world will be judged because of their stubborn refusal to heed the Word of God. Zechariah 12:2-3 is yet to be fulfilled.

KUWAIT FREE?

Dear Brother Froese,

I've been in Kuwait for the past five years. Some other brethren and I began a small church. We endeavor to teach and preach the full counsel of the Word of God, and reach the field with the truth. The use of videos is very effective here. I have contacted several ministries for permission to copy their audio and video products locally here in Kuwait for free for replacement tapes. We ask this only because of our special situation here in Kuwait. All have been very gracious.

Everything we have, from Bibles, tracts and videos to song books, has to be hauled in by personal luggage and effects. God has seen to our safety thus far. Even though your production has no copyright warning on the tape, I still would feel better asking for permission to copy and distribute your video here. Please allow us to do so. We use computer-generated labels to identify each tape. Not with our name, of course, but with the ministry's name and address so that wherever the tape ends up, the originator can be contacted.

The Lord allowed me the pleasure of leading four black "chain gang" workers to His saving grace while on vacation in Bennettsville, S.C. They desperately need to see this tape. Actually, so does everyone in S.C., especially the black community. If they could only see the true Islam here in Kuwait, they would change their minds very quickly. The tape is very true indeed. The Kuwaitis are very rude and cruel in their dealings with other people here.

Kuwait is a country of only 700,000 natural citizens. Nearly two million more are expatriate workers from many different countries: India, Pakistan, Bangladesh, China, Sri Lanka, UK, France, Italy, Russia, Romania, African nations and Americans. We have found, "The Jesus Film," and "The Gospel According to Luke," to be very effective tools for witnessing to these other people. Yes, it's a charismatic production, but it is available in more than 300 languages, 26 of which we are authorized to distribute here. We have been able to track nearly 300 decisions for Jesus Christ in the past year, with nearly 1000 films distributed. We have received good reports from other countries where our work has leaked into, others turning to Jesus Christ's saving grace. Many religious backgrounds are represented here, and are hearing of the Lord Jesus Christ in many ways. Our work is underground of course.

I hope you will write in agreement to support our work in this small way. If the answer is negative, believe me, we will understand and not copy your product.

-Name Withheld

ANSWER: With this letter, we gladly grant you the permission to duplicate and distribute any of our products in accordance with your outline. We praise the Lord for your dedication and faithfulness, and pray for His protection over you and all who are on the front lines testifying that Jesus is the Savior.

PERSECUTED SAINTS

Dear Mr. Froese,

A few days ago, I posted a letter to you requesting renewal for subscriptions to *Midnight Call* for myself and three other Christians. I gave a change of address for Mr. Peter Ikwulono. This Peter Ikwulono is indeed a man of God. He has and is pointing many Catholics and Muslims to Christ. About 18 months ago, a lady wrote telling me of how, through Peter's earnest prayers and his powerful preaching of the Word of God, many people in her village had turned from their idol worship and evil ways to worship and serve the living God. She, her husband and children were so happy after confessing their sins and accepting Jesus Christ as Lord and Savior, they felt a peace they were unable to explain.

Last August, I received terrible news that this dear soul was beaten to death while helping 3 men (new Christians) spread the Gospel. The men were badly beaten (one was not expected to live) and were hospitalized.

They were unable to pay the bill, and Peter, feeling responsible because he was the one who led them to Christ, sold the very few possessions he had in order to help pay the bill. Now Peter has lost his job, and his wife and two children are crying because there is no money to pay the rent.

Peter has been hospitalized twice after being attacked and beaten; his Bibles, hymn book, tape recorder and hired bicycle were stolen. In spite of all this suffering and worry, he has not turned away from God, but is still out trying to point people to God.

One lady who was until recently, a Muslim, wrote to tell me about Linda (the lady who was beaten to death) and that she would be willing to take Linda's place and die for Christ's sake. All this shows me what a weak, weak Christian I am!

Unfortunately, some letters (some containing bank drafts) that I had sent to Peter have been opened and contents stolen, or letters have not arrived. Contents are also being removed from parcels. Satan and his force are working overtime. I hope that prayer relief will come soon for God's suffering servants.

Peter informs me that he needs the *Midnight Call* magazines – the information is so rich.

May God arrange for all *Midnight Call* subscribers to receive their copies each month.

My thanks to you for Midnight Call publications, books, tapes and your help.

God bless all the Midnight Call staff.

How comforting to know that at the end of the straight and narrow path, there lies heaven and Christ for the Christian.

-N.A., New Zealand

ANSWER: Thank you for your letter. It was a strong

reminder that in our present day, physical persecution is a reality in some countries. We are admonished in Hebrews 13:3, *"Remember them that are in bonds, as bound with them; and them which suffer adversity, as being your-selves also in the body."* May the Lord bless you for the kindness you are showing to the persecuted brethren. We publish your letter with the hopes of bringing additional prayer warriors into the field.

SAVED THROUGH SUFFERING

To Whom It May Concern,

Words can never thank you enough for your magazine. What power it has and what teaching in each and every article there is, in understanding endtime prophecy.

I do suffer so much with an illness for which there is no human cure. I am partially paralyzed and must use a wheelchair, leg braces and crutches. I live in tremendous pelvic pain and have been placed on morphine injections every two hours.

So I live in tremendous suffering, yet because of my suffering I have accepted Jesus Christ as my Lord and Savior and I've gained tremendous understanding of the Bible and endtime prophecy.

My late husband died...He was very much involved in in-depth study of [the] endtimes. He taught me a tremen-dous amount about endtimes and he only wanted to live until the Rapture. He did not make it. But he gave me so much to go onward. Together we have grown in Christ, and were able to witness to the children and two of the three have accepted Christ as their Savior. My family, being Jewish, has totally walked away from me and it is a shame. I pray for them constantly that they will accept Christ as their Lord and Savior.

You are in our prayers, we love and cherish you and we do pray that the Lord may come soon, so that all Christian suffering is over and we are out of pain and with Jesus Christ eternally.

With all our love in Christ,

Name withheld, Meza, AZ

ANSWER: What a tremendous testimony! I was deeply touched when I read the sentence, "...because of my suffering, I accepted Jesus Christ as my Lord and Savior." The Lord knows your fears; He also knows what is best for you, although at this very moment, neither you nor I are capable of fully grasping it.

You are experiencing the very painful words," ...*we must through much tribulation enter into the kingdom of God"* (Acts 14:22). I have prayed to the Lord for you to give you the necessary grace to hold on to Him because your reward is great.

I noticed when you wrote about your late husband and his waiting for the Rapture that you said, "He did not make it." That, dear sister, is not really the case, because he is in the presence of the Lord. Remember, when the Rapture takes place, the dead in Christ shall rise first. Time ceases to exist in the presence of the Lord because we have entered eternity.

Only at the moment of the Rapture will we receive our

glorified bodies. Those who have gone home to be with the Lord before us are first in line.

YOUR WORK IS APPRECIATED

My Dear Brother Froese,

We are grateful to you for continuing to send us *Midnight Call* for the last seven years. The *Midnight Call* magazine, which is sent from the Evangel Publishing House, is arriving in good condition. I want you to put us in your next year's budget and inform our brothers to continue sending us the magazine from Kenya.

The *Midnight Call* is playing a great role in our spiritual well being and closer contact to what is happening to the saints in other parts of the world. It is very encouraging to me as an evangelist, seeing that the very spiritual encounters I'm going through are the same things that other saints are passing through.

If you would keep in touch through the *Midnight Call,* it would take away my fear and I would continue even more courageously to spread the Word of truth to these people whom Satan has blinded through the spirit of Islam, that they receive their sight and the eyes of their hearts may be enlightened.

Even though I'm passing through many difficulties, I'm not going to abandon my attempt to continue translating the *Midnight Call* into Cibemba. Because it is not by might nor by power, but by the Spirit of God, the work of God will be completed and there will be a big celebration. The typewriter you blessed me with sometime back in 1992 is not working well;

319

please pray for me that God may bless me with a computer.

I appreciate you. We are reaching an unreached group of people with the help of Midnight Call Ministry.

Evangelist E.M. Mulenga, Zambia

ANSWER: Your letter is published here to alert our readers of your need. Contributions may be sent in care of our office or can be sent directly to P.O. Box 220863, Lubengele, Chililabombwe, Zambia.

WORDS OF ENCOURAGEMENT

Dear Fellow Servant of Christ,

It is my sincere prayer and heartfelt desire that this finds you all in the very precious care of our Lord and Savior Jesus Christ.

I cannot tell you just how much I appreciate your magazine ministry known as *Midnight Call.*

There are numerous articles on a variety of topics but there is always the ever-underlying truth of every page and paragraph from start to end. Amen.

The more I read, the more I see that the staff must depend on checking the Scriptures as well as the news articles of any given daily press sheet, always remembering to keep the truth and authority of God's holy Word as supreme and priority.

Keep up the good work.

I just felt I had to write this; you see, not enough people in today's society are willing to speak out for good and right.

So, as long as you will keep your work within God's will, I shall continue to lift you up in word and prayer. Likewise, should you falter, I know prayer will be made for that too.

I know within my heart you won't falter as long as you keep Christ and the ministry He gave you in perspective. Amen again.

-Rev. K.R., Sr., Windsor, VA

ANSWER: Thank you for your kind words. Your letter was an ointment to my soul.

CHAPTER 17

SIGNS, WONDERS AND THE ANTICHRIST

IS MAFIA THE BEAST?

Dear Editor Arno Froese:

I'd please like to know if it's possible that the future Antichrist will rise from the Sicilian mafia as an heir or descendent of the Julio-Claudian blood-line with a mind like Caesar Nero instead of Benito Mussolini's fascism with a Neronian agenda based on Nero's evil ideals of anti-Christian hatred, anti-Semitism and loyal obedience to Caesar as "god."

But a Sicilian mafia ruler who enters politics can fit the description of being the man of sin since the mafia is an organization of underworld sin like Nero's underworld of iniquity (2nd Thessalonians 2:3; Daniel 8:23).

I think that the Julio-Claudian bloodline is not dead, as most people think. [It is] very much alive like the fossil fish that was considered extinct until a living species was caught in 1938 by [an] African fisherman (Revelation 13:3-14).

Let it be noted that there is a Sicilian boss of bosses [who is] imprisoned in Italy, known as a mafia boss, his own followers had called [him] the beast!

They will show their true ancient Roman colors soon, when the underworld comes to the surface to rule the revived Roman Empire much like Caesar Nero [did] by starting out as a good political leader until he turn[ed] into a vicious tyrant.

The Sicilian mafia is a big vicious underworld that's a powerful political tyranny [which] owns just about everything, more than the Jews; while it's richer than the U.S. government or big oil companies, including all of the nations of the world.

Sicilians are the most feared people in the world, which means that the Neronian system is very much alive within the mafia because they're keeping the Neronian ideal alive underground until it's time for Rome to rule again with a strong brutal leader with striking features like Nero's.

Antichrist will be the seed of Satan (Genesis 3:15) being of the Julio-Claudian bloodline. So that's all I have to ask and say. Please be sure to write back soon.

-K.N., Smith River, CA

ANSWER: The Antichrist will not be revealed until the Church is taken out of the way. Because the Antichrist is the greatest deceiver of all times, we are looking down the wrong road when we seek an evil, mafia-type criminal character.

The Bible says, *"...the world wondered after the beast."* *"...They worshipped the beast, saying, who is like unto the beast, who is able to make war with him?"* It is evident that he will be the most celebrated, benevolent leader the world has ever seen.

ANTICHRIST JEWS

Dear Brother Arno,

In the May issue of *Midnight Call*, Brother Thomas Ice stated on page 39, in the first column under "First" that Scripture teaches that the Antichrist will be of Gentile descent.

Fruchtenbaum also agrees. I have to disagree, according to Daniel 11:37, [which] states, *"Neither shall he regard the God of his fathers, nor the desire of women."* You and I both know that wherever the phrase *"God of fathers"* [occurs] it is either referring to Abraham, Isaac, Jacob or the Jews' ancestors. [It is] never referring to the Gentiles. That verse clearly teaches that the Antichrist will be a Jew and that President Clinton can't be, as he has a great desire for women!

If you can, please respond to this in the *Midnight Call*.

-H.T., Asheville, NC

ANSWER: I agree with you that the Antichrist must be a Jew; otherwise, the Jews would not accept Him. After Jesus admonished the Jews to *"search the Scriptures."* He made this prophecy in John 5:43, *"...if another shall come in his own name, him ye will receive."* Undoubtedly one described as "another" who comes in his own name must have scriptural qualifications, such as coming from the tribe of Judah. I don't believe that the Jews would accept him if they could not identify with them.

PREPARING FOR ANTICHRIST

Dear Mr. Froese:

I truly believe that the present preoccupation this age has with "alien invasions" is a tool used by Satan to prepare people for the future.

The movie "Independence Day" gives a graphic picture envisioning a global invasion that is to overtake the world. The movie stimulates thoughts and ideas of the possibility of a single force with global dominance. The movie sows seeds in the minds of its viewers of having to accept the control and rule of an unwanted global force.

Another new movie instills even more of the same thoughts in the minds of those people viewing it. In the Star Trek movie "First Contact," the message of the "borg" is remarkable. The "borg's" motto is "resistance to assimilation is futile." The message is one that shows a battle for life as the borg seeks to take over and assimilate all.

It seems uncanny how this portrays the future and end-times. Just as the borg proclaims "resistance is futile," the Antichrist will have the same philosophy with his mark.

The message of these movies clearly portrays the idea of global and worldwide control/rule. It is a message that subconsciously stimulates the acceptance on a one-world order.

Is Hollywood being used as a tool to blind, numb, and

prepare this age for the drastic times ahead?

Are "subliminal" messages being generated now to ease the acceptance of a one-world order and the mark of the beast?

Christians can read their Bibles to learn about the future. Are the lost going to the movies to learn and become prepared for what is to come?

It is plausible that people who accept the idea of not being able to resist assimilation/dominance in thought will come to easily accept the mark of the beast when it comes. Resistance is futile; there will be martyrs.

Please let me know if I'm out in left field.

-M.R., El Cajon, CA

ANSWER: I only recall going to the movies twice since I became a Christian, seeing "The Hiding Place" and "Schindler's List." However, your analysis is right on target. The promotion in our daily newspapers and magazines clearly convey the message of the great preparation that is going on right now.

Therefore, we do well to avoid the visible and turn to the invisible, our coming Lord, *"Whom having not seen, ye love; in whom, though now ye see him not, yet believing, ye rejoice with joy unspeakable and full of glory"* (1st Peter 1:8).

ANTICHRIST

Dear Brother Froese,

I agree with you that Tommy Ice's article was well written and an excellent article, even though I fail to agree with either him or you in certain details. I seriously doubt if any two students of the Bible will agree with each other on every teaching of God's Word. I do appreciate you as a student, writer, and publisher. Your magazine, *Midnight Call,* is an excellent publication and I receive a lot out of it. I have also recommended it to several others. I learned a long time ago that I am not infallible, nor is any person infallible. Now we see through a glass darkly but someday we will fully understand the entire teaching of the Word of God. You and I disagree upon this interpretation but someday we will fully understand.

I am answering because I felt your letter was evasive while teaching on the subject. You built a "straw man, or nationalism" and then tore down the straw man. Nationalism does not enter into the study of the Word of God, except that all nations have failed. The straw man of nationalism was irrelevant, immaterial, and not pertinent to the subject. First Peter 2:9 belongs not to any earthly nation but to the born again believers of all nations.

CONTEXT: Daniel 2 is in the first half of the book where the first six chapters deal with the historical aspect of the book. It was a dream or vision given to Nebuchadnezzar and deals with the four great world empires throughout the entire history of nations. God revealed this dream to Daniel and he interpreted it to the King. The Roman Empire is the fourth of these beasts.
Daniel 7 is in the prophetic section of Daniel (chapters 7-12) and it was a vision given to Daniel of the rise of the man of sin from among the nations and that he is of the fourth empire mentioned in Nebuchadnezzar's dream, or

the revised Roman Empire.

CROSS-REFERENCE: I noticed you conveniently disregarded the cross-reference in Revelation 13:2, where the Antichrist (out of the Roman Empire) brings into submission the same three beasts mentioned in Daniel 7. At the end of Daniel 7, Christ arrives on the scene to defeat the man of sin and to reign over the earth.

TOPOLOGY: It appears that you disregarded any topology concerning the beast of Daniel 7, except as we both agree, the fourth is the Roman Empire under the domination of the Antichrist.

Brother Froese, I realize that there will be times we disagree and I do not plan to change you, nor will you change my understanding of the Word of God. The only One who should change either of us is the conviction of the Holy Spirit. There may be times in the future when I feel strong convictions to write. My respect for you or the *Midnight Call* is not lessened because of not agreeing upon this portion of the Scripture, but someday we will each fully understand all the truths of the Bible.

May He continue to use you for His honor, praise, and glory.

-R.O., Evansville, WY

ANSWER: In relation to nationalism, the apostle Paul had every reason to emphasize his nation. He was of the stock of Israel, the chosen nation of God, of the tribe of Benjamin, which was the first tribe to be integrated into the royal tribe of Judah. He was a Hebrew of Hebrews, the nation through whom God gave the Law to Israel and the world. He was "free born," a Roman citizen, but when comparing these advantages with Christ, he said, I "...*do count them as dung....*" Why? Because Paul recognized the eternal value.

I see no relationship between Daniel 7 and Revelation 13. Daniel 7 identifies the four Gentile super-powers: three which are identified by animals, but the fourth is so diverse that no animal could appropriately represent it. The Antichrist is revealed in Revelation 13. He doesn't bring the three beasts into submission, but the characteristics of the three beasts: leopard, bear and lion are part of the beast. Notice that the listing is in reverse: beast, leopard, bear, and lion. Daniel 7 begins with the lion, followed by the bear, the leopard, and then the beast. The power and authority of the four-fold Gentile super-power structure comes directly from Satan, "...*the dragon gave him his power, and his seat, and great authority*" (Revelation 13:2).

Your statement, "Christ arrives on the scene to defeat the man of sin" presupposes that a battle will take place in which Christ will have to fight in order to win. This is not the case because Jesus is the eternal Victor. He does not need to prove Himself. Remember, darkness is always exposed at the appearance of light, "*And then shall that Wicked be revealed, whom the Lord shall consume with the spirit of his mouth, and shall destroy with the brightness of his coming*" (2nd Thessalonians 2:8). You are most certainly correct when you conclude, "Some day we will each fully understand all the truths of the Bible." That day may not be too far off.

VISIONS FOR TODAY

Dear Editor,

I notice that you don't believe persons today can have visions. Joel 2:28 reads, *"...I will pour out my spirit upon all flesh; and your sons and your daughters shall prophesy, your old men shall dream dreams, your young men shall see visions."* Please explain what this is referring to. Thank you.

-T.E., Grasston, MN

ANSWER: Of course people have visions today. Muslims, Buddhists, Hindus, and Christians have visions, but they are meaningless.

The apostle Peter testified that the events taking place in Jerusalem after Pentecost were the fulfillment of Joel 2:28, *"This was that which was spoken by the prophet Joel."* There are no words about additional fulfillment of the same.

SIGNS, WONDERS AND FRUIT

Gentlemen:

Regarding your frequent referral to "fruit" and to the Scripture that some day the Lord will reject those who did great things in His name but who were not His disciples, what is the acceptable fruit the believer is to bear?

Also, I think it is time the charismatic and evangelicals got together and decided on the correct interpretation of the Scriptures. On one hand, we are bombarded with miracles just for the asking and "God's will for our lives." It seems Texas preacher John Hagee gives the impression that even attending a church service and enjoying the singing and preaching is the sin of complacency. He as much as said we should get "off our duffs" and reclaim America for God. I am a disabled 80-year-old and still don't know what God expects of me. I've been through the grinder in life and still can't glory in it except to keep on suffering. Please shed some light on all these dilemmas. Thank you.

-Mrs. S.K., Berwyn, IL

ANSWER: The "fruit" Jesus speaks of is identified in Galatians 5:22-23, *"But the fruit of the Spirit is love, joy, peace, longsuffering, gentleness, goodness, faith, Meekness, temperance: against such there is no law."* Surely, there is no need to interpret these simple words.

The prevailing confusion in Christianity is not about the fruit of the Spirit but the gift of the Spirit demonstrated in signs and wonders: *"He that believeth and is baptized shall be saved; but he that believeth not shall be damned. And these signs shall follow them that believe: In my name shall they cast out devils: they shall speak with new tongues. They shall take up serpents; and if they drink any deadly thing, it shall not hurt them; they shall lay hands on the sick, and they shall recover"* (Mark 16:17-18).

The fulfillment of these signs during the times of the apostles is recorded in the book of Acts. Notice that the Lord says, *"they."* This refers to the Church collectively, not to individual believers. Today's "miracle performers" highlight the fifth sign, restoring health to the sick. This

332

has caused even greater confusion because it is practiced contrary to the Scripture. The instruction is plainly conveyed in James 5:14, *"Is any sick among you? let him call for the elders of the church; and let them pray over him, anointing him with oil in the name of the Lord."* Notice that the individual believer is to call on the elders of the church, not the pastor. Confusions will be eliminated when we follow these basic instructions.

"Reclaiming America for God" is not biblical. Remember that all nations are under the rulership of the devil, who is the god of this world; there is no such thing as "reclaiming," that is known as Dominion or Reconstruction theology.

However, there is a higher way to demonstrate living faith in the living Lord, *"...blessed are they that have not seen, and yet have believed"* (John 20:29). We all desire to be physically fit and often go the utmost to keep our health; yet the Bible says, *"Forasmuch then as Christ hath suffered for us in the flesh, arm yourselves likewise with the same mind: for he that hath suffered in the flesh hath ceased from sin"* (1st Peter 4:1). I have prayed that the Lord will give you the needed grace to follow Him despite your suffering.

NEED A MIRACLE?

Dear Arno Froese,

I am enclosing some mail I received last week. I read it and I read it again. Am I wrong to feel this is endtime deception?

I have never heard of an angel/prophet. Maybe I am the one who is misjudging?

I know Jesus said at the endtimes, there would be false religions and to beware. I am interested in knowing what you think on the enclosed. Thank you.

After looking the enclosed over, you may just toss it in the rubbish. By no means do I intend to follow through, but I would be grateful to know your thoughts on this. No doubt, others out there got this too.

Here are some excerpts of the materials: "You must have the seven miraculous gifts God chose for you!"

ENCLOSED

Need a miracle? The penny you hold in the palm of your hand can be responsible for the realization of the personal miracle of your choice...

See for yourself...you will soon experience miracles of love, money and good luck...!

Seven miraculous gifts of the Spirit have been selected by the hand of God especially for you. These miraculous sacred icons will lead you to the blessed path to miracles.

These are powerful, blessed images and sacred icons that radiate the power of the Father, the Son and the Holy Spirit.

I, Asariel, the angel prophet, solemnly vow that your next 365 days will be filled with miracles of love, money, success, and good luck as a result of the revelation of angels that I will send you....

-C.L., East Ryegate, VT

ANSWER: We are admonished to deny ourselves and follow the Lamb, which doesn't always lead to health and wealth, but which often leads to great disadvantage.

(Many of our brethren who live in countries where persecution is real can testify to that.)

The Bible says the following regarding good luck and money: *"Your riches are corrupted, and your garments are motheaten, Your gold and silver is cankered; and the rust of them shall be a witness against you, and shall eat your flesh as it were fire. Ye have heaped treasure together for the last days"* (James 5:2-3).

First Timothy 6:10 drives this point home, *"For the love of money is the root of all evil: which while some coveted after, they have erred from the faith, and pierced themselves through with many sorrows."*

You have done well to reject such deception, which originates with the father of lies.

PROPHET AND PROPHECY

Dear Arno:

What do you think of this prophet and prophecy as stated in the article I have enclosed with my letter?

I must add, this man has trained hundreds of thousands to "work the works of God." Here is what it says:

"In 1989, while I was traveling from Perth, Australia, God woke me up in the middle of the night, told me to get out of bed, and revealed two specific things to me: 1) God said, `Tell My people that the 90's is My Decade of Destiny; 2) `The 90's is My Decade of the Holy Spirit.' Based upon the incredible revelations God shared with me during that time, I wrote one of the most powerful prophetic books God has ever given me – 5 *Major Cries and 5 Major Waves of the Holy Spirit coming in the 1990's.*

In the middle of 1995, the Lord spoke to me another revelation, which seemed to contradict the first. God said, 'The Decade of the Holy Spirit is about to close.' It seemed strange to me that the Lord would tell me a decade was 'about to close' right in the middle of it.

'Lord, how can a decade close in the middle?' I asked, Then He showed me that the Church today has not yet seen a real manifestation of the Pentecostal power that we read about in Acts 1. 'Now,' God told me, 'My power is about to be released. There will be a tremendous, pure stream of My power, and it will last for three years.'"

Your answer is appreciated. Thank you.

-J. R. O., Milan, NM

ANSWER: The Bible does not state that in the last days, God would elect a prophet who is supposed to convey to the Church that "the 90's is My decade of Destiny." Obviously you are a victim of your own imagination. However, the Bible does tell us that *"God, who at sundry times and in divers manners spake in time past unto the fathers by the prophets, Hath in these last days spoken unto us by his Son..."* (Hebrews 1:1-2).

God's full counsel to us is recorded from Genesis to Revelation. The Church is not in need of any extra-biblical revelations. The above verses expose additional prophecies as false prophecies. No amount of success qualifies anyone to go above and beyond the Scriptures.

HEAVENLY VISIONS?

Dear Mr. Froese:

Your editorial in the October *Midnight Call* had many interesting points. I have not seen the things God has prepared for us yet. But Jesus said He went away to prepare a place for us.

I would like to tell you about some of my brother's many wonderful experiences in the spirit. You know the Word of God is able to divide asunder between soul and spirit. God has separated my brother's human spirit apart from his soul and body and taken his spirit into heaven, to Mount Zion.

Angels came into the church one evening and beckoned him to go with them. When his spirit left his body and went over to them, his spirit, which was about the same size as his natural body, was clothed with some type of white garment similar to theirs. Only his garment had a hood on it. He went with them right out through the side of the brick building. He then was taken into heaven and shown many wonderful things, things difficult to put into human words. He said Mount Zion was made of huge slabs of precious stones. God allowed him to see many other wonderful things.

He saw mansions and monument-type spires. He said the flowers are maybe ten feet in diameter and the colors are not the ones we know here. There is no gravity, so that the water flowing down Mount Zion doesn't rush. It flows the same on the side of the mountain as it does on the level. He said there is nothing refuse there. There are trees and what might pass for what we know as well-manicured grass. He said there was a light shining past Mount Zion. He believes it was coming from New Jerusalem. He says he really doesn't have words to adequately describe the things he saw. Remember Paul said it was not lawful (possible) to utter his experiences in the third heaven.

Later on, my brother saw a vision of New Jerusalem high in the heavens, but he did not go there. He said the streets of the city are clear, and the light was shining down right through the street as he looked up at the city.

My brother's spirit has also been taken into eternity, past the heavens, into pure God. He says his spirit goes many times faster than the speed of light. Once there, he rested in God for ten days with some type of buffer between him and God. God is consuming fire. No man can be in direct contact with Him. I believe that is why he appeared in theophanies when He wanted to talk directly to His children.

Remember God appeared to Moses in a burning bush and later on in a thick darkness up on Sinai. Remember how God also came as one of three men to talk to Abraham in Genesis 18. The Lord manifested Himself to Hagar as the angel of the Lord. So many ways God has chosen to talk with His children.

One time he was before God's throne, and he saw the spirits of just men made perfect. These spirits of just men were leaning in, toward God, listening carefully, so that they would not miss the answer God was giving to my brother's question: "How do I approach your throne?" God's answer was Luke 11:9.

I have seen Jesus twice. My brother has seen Jesus 34

times. And he also has six angels who work with him all the time and whom he has seen. Many of my friends have seen angels; I have had visions of angels as they ministered to others in another place. I have felt their presence near me, even though I could not see them. I believe we have only begun to enjoy the things that God has prepared for us. I am looking forward to many experiences in Him while I am still here on earth before I go to heaven.

Even though we may be "limited in our tabernacle of flesh and blood" we can, through the Spirit, look into many things God has prepared for us. I want to be open to all such experiences God has for me as His child. God gave Paul and John the Revelator many experiences, which they wrote about. As Spirit-filled children of God, we can expect spiritual experiences too. *"The Spirit itself beareth witness with our spirit, that we are the children of God"* (Romans 8:16). We must have God's own Spirit in us as the apostles in Acts had if we are to receive these things out of the Spirit.

You know the Roman church started the belief in God as a trinity of three persons. You will not find the word trinity in the Scriptures. God is really One omnipresent Spirit. As I understand it, the Roman church also started baptism. They instituted sprinkling as a convenience. These were not done in the church of Acts. I have also heard that the Roman church claims all the churches that baptize in the name of the Father and of the Son and of the Holy Ghost as part of their church. We will soon be finding out, won't we? If we will look at the word "name" in Matthew 28:19, we find it is singular.

The great eternal Spirit is "the only true (pure) God" (John 16:3). That is, pure without any mixture. But Jesus is God and man. Not pure God and not pure man. The Eternal Spirit was manifested in flesh, but still He was the One and only eternal God. Remember how God's glory shone through the flesh of Jesus on the Mount of Transfiguration?

May God enlighten the eyes of our understanding and give us the spirit of wisdom and revelation in the knowledge of Him, I pray in Jesus name. There is much to be known of Him.

-A.I,, Granite City, IL

ANSWER: Based on the Scripture quotations in your letter, it is obvious that you read your Bible, which I commend you for. However, you have apparently overlooked 1st Peter 1:8, *"Whom having not seen, ye love; in whom, though now ye see him not, yet believing, ye rejoice with joy unspeakable and full of glory."* If the Bible tells us that we have not seen Jesus and you tell me that you have, then I am forced to come to the conclusion that something is wrong. Have you read 2nd Corinthians 11:14? *"And no marvel; for Satan himself is transformed into an angel of light."* How about Paul's repeated admonition that we walk by faith, not by sight or experiences? Doesn't the Bible also say that faith comes by hearing the Word of God?

Regarding baptism, we are given clear instruction by the Lord Jesus, *"Go ye therefore, and teach all nations, baptizing them in the name of the Father, and of the Son, and of the Holy Ghost"* (Matthew 28:19).

First John 5:7 reveals the Trinity, *"For there are three that bear record in heaven, the Father, the Word, and the Holy Ghost: and these three are one."* Even the first three verses of our Bible clearly demonstrate the Trinity; God the Father, God the Spirit, and in verse three, God the Word. Who is the Word of God? Read John 1:1 and 3.

Incidentally, God only called one Moses, one Paul and one Peter. Imitation is never the real thing.

THE CHURCH SUBTLY DECEIVED?

Dear Mr. Froese:

Christians look forward to the Rapture when Christ will appear in the clouds and call us up – this I believe is imminent. Thank you so much for a wonderful publication, the *Midnight Call.* Of all the Christian publications that I receive, yours is the best. Why? Because you are not afraid to take a stand – always standing fast upon the precious Word of God.

I have real concerns today about those who embrace false Christian organizations; for example, the Roman Catholic Church, Mormonism, you name it. Evangelical born again Christians present a real concern. This drift into apostasy, I believe, is caused largely by the charismatic (or neo-Pentecostal) movement. It appears to me that they place their emotional experiences before the Word of God, like reviving the "sign gifts," that I believe are no longer present in this age. The video, "Protestants and Catholics-Do They Now Agree?" is a real eye-opener.

Not everyone who "believes" in Christ is saved and certainly if they are depending on works (such as the Roman Catholics teach for salvation) they can't be saved (Ephesians 2:8). I realize there are some Roman Catholics and others in cults, who are born again.

Do you have knowledge of any publications or books written by born again Christians that deal with the subject of sign gifts (not for this age) and ecumenism that you could recommend to me? Somebody who takes a solid position as you do? These various movements today are so subtle, it takes a while to see them drift away from the Word of God.

-R.E., Vancouver, WA

ANSWER: The deception of the endtimes is undoubtedly in full swing today. While it is true that even believers are deceived by "emotional experiences" which are promoted primarily through the new charismatic movement, it does not mean that the more conservative denominations are immune to evil influence. The great tragedy is that believers think that they are secure because they have recognized certain identifiable deceptions within the Church, but fail to realize that the great deceiver is always preparing a newer, more refined form of deception. The Bible admonishes us, *"Wherefore let him that thinketh he standeth take heed lest he fall"* (1st Corinthians 10:12). A well-written Bible study on the subject of signs and gifts is, *The Church Subtly Deceived,* written by Alexander Seibel.

CHAPTER 18

CATHOLICISM

CATHOLIC INSULTED

Dear Mr. Froese:

I am a new subscriber to the *Midnight Call* and was enjoying it and even speaking highly about the May issue. Then I read your letter on page 45. I am a member of the Roman Catholic Church and feel most insulted to be declared as ungodly, unbibilical and a non-believer in Jesus Christ. Scripture is read daily in Catholic churches and is considered top priority. A recent proclamation from the pope encourages even more interest and study of the Scriptures as we approach the end of the millennium. I attend Bible study throughout the year; studying all versions to get fullness of meaning is encouraged. Clergy, religious orders, and pious lay people make Scripture part of their daily prayer life in the liturgy of the hours.

Might I suggest you read Paul's letter to the Ephesian church, chapter 6, and note verses 11 and 12. Paul said, *"We are not contending against flesh and blood* (people, each other) *but against principalities, against the powers, against the world ruler of this present darkness, against the spiritual roots of wickedness in the heavenly places"* (Satan and his troop of fallen angels).

I have had membership in both Catholic and Protestant churches over the years. I have found that the Holy Spirit dwells in both places and Jesus Christ, the Word, and the Almighty Father are praised and glorified. However, I have seen the powers of darkness lurking there as well. Satan seems attracted to the holiest of people and places to attempt to further his work.

We Christians cannot afford to give comfort and aid to the enemies of Christ by needless and loveless conflict between ourselves.

-N.E., Janesville, WI

ANSWER: Thank you for your letter expressing your deep concern for Christian unity. However, there is an error. It lies in your mixing the organizational structure of the church, (Catholic, Baptist, Methodist, etc.) with the Church of Jesus Christ. Your statement, "The Holy Spirit dwells in both places" reveals that fact.

As a Catholic, you should know that the Vatican officially curses anyone who believes that salvation is obtainable through faith in Jesus outside of the Catholic Church.

Here is what, [the] *Cateschisme de L'Eglise Catholique* (Libreria Editrice Vaticana, 1993) states: "Man can obtain a knowledge of God's Word only from the Catholic Church and through its daily constituted channels" (*A*

Woman Rides the Beast, page 339). The Catholic Church clearly bashes Christians.

I do not doubt that born again Christians are members of the Catholic Church, but I cannot deny that Catholicism incorporates a cultic tendency in its doctrine.

I would be guilty before God if I simply brushed away, for the sake of love and unity, the institution's doctrinal errors, such as the infallibility of the pope, the sacrifice of the Mass, purgatory, prayers addressed to Mary and a host of other saints, or the unbiblical system of priests and nuns. These and many more blatant violations and contradictions of the Holy Scripture sanctioned by the Roman Catholic Church must be warned against emphatically.

To summarize, don't mix human organization, by whatever name, with born again believers who are called Christians.

IS CATHOLICISM A CULT?

Dear Mr. Froese:

I thank you for your ministry. I have learned so much about God's Word from your videos, prophecy conference and magazine, *Midnight Call.*

In the May issue, "Letters to the Editor," you lumped the Catholics together with false religions such as the Mormons, Hindus, Muslims, and Freemasons. You wrote, "But their God is surely not the God of the Bible."

I was raised Roman Catholic. My family is still practicing Catholicism, but I disagree with the statement you made concerning their god not being the God of the Bible.

I respect your knowledge of the Word and would ask that you explain your reason for such a statement.

-D.R., Orange, CA

ANSWER: Addressing prayers to saints, including Mary, celebrating Mass and referring to it as a perpetual sacrifice, the office of the pope, his claimed infallibility and the system of priests and nuns are all blatant violations against the Holy Scripture and have no relation to biblical Christianity.

CATHOLIC BIBLE?

Dear Mr. Froese:

Peace in the Lord Jesus Christ!

On page 50 of the October edition of *Midnight Call*, you state that the Roman Catholic Church is cultic in practice and violates sacred Scripture.

Did you check this out in *The Catechism of the Catholic Church*? I hope you have a copy of it in your reference library. Just check out each one of your assertions and you will find that each one [of Rome's teaching] is scripturally based, is clearly evidenced in the writings of the early church fathers, the patriotic writers; and is taught today very clearly in the writings of Pope John Paul II, Pope Paul VI and in the documents of the Second Vatican Council.

Also look at the Apostle's Creed from the 1st century of Christianity and in the Nicene-Constantinople Creed from the 4th century.

Also check out how we know what is the canon of

sacred Scripture. It was given to the world by the Roman Catholic Church.

Protestantism's three pillars are: 1) Sola Scriptura [Scripture only]; 2) Private interpretation; and 3) faith alone without works. All three are unscripturally based. You need a divinely founded church that preceded the New Testament to be your authority and that is the Catholic Church.

Without it, you are floating in the wind and opposing Christ who said He would always be with His Church, and it would never fail to always teach His saving truth. [And yet you] blaspheme the Holy Spirit by saying He contradicts (lies) Himself.

We see in the U.S.A. about 25,000 Christian churches teaching contradictory beliefs and all presumably based on the Bible and someone's private interpretation.

We obey Jesus in sacred Scripture and in the church He founded. "He who hears you (the apostles and their successors), hears me." That's authority and it is preserved in His church today.

God bless!

-N.T., Vienna, VA

ANSWER: Frankly, I had to chuckle when I read, "...the canon of the sacred Scripture...was given to the world by the Roman Catholic Church."

The only "sacred Scripture" we have was given to us by the Jews, written for the Jews. *God, who at sundry times and in divers manners spake in time past unto the fathers* [not Roman Catholics] *by the prophets*" (Hebrews 1:1).

347

The Jewish apostle clearly testified, *"...holy men of God spake as they were moved by the Holy Ghost"* (2nd Peter 1:21). Who were these *"holy men"*? Roman Catholics? No! They were Jews!

I appreciate your self-revelation, which clearly shows the error of your beliefs: "You need a divinely founded church that precedes the New Testament to be your authority and that is the Catholic Church." Wow!

Acts 2 documents the birth of the Church, which didn't take place in Rome, but Jerusalem. Peter, the Jew, said, *"Ye men of Judaea and all ye that dwell in Jerusalem."*

In verse 36, *"Therefore let all the house of Israel know assuredly..."*

In chapter 3:12, *"...Ye men of Israel..."*

Chapter 4:10, *"Be it known unto you all, and to all the people of Israel...."* He was not addressing the Romans; he was addressing the Jews.

Later, in Acts 10 we read of *"...Cornelius, a centurion of the band called the Italian..."* He was the first of the Gentiles to be added to the Jewish Church and that caused much controversy.

The existence of His Church (not Catholic or by any other name) is guaranteed by the Lord and has no direct relation to Catholicism or any other denomination.

The Church is found wherever two or more born again believers gather in His name. Those believers may be scattered amongst the 25,000 different churches and denominations as you claim, but that does not change their individual position as belonging to His Church, which is not identified by any name.

You must decide whether to believe in an organizational structure with a primarily man-made doctrine, or trust the Jewish Holy Scriptures. The Author of our Bible is not Rome, but the Lord Jesus who testified, *"Salvation is of the Jews"* (not of Rome). One is true, the other false.

EUCHARIST

Dear Mr. Froese:

I'm writing in reference to an answer to a letter writer in the January issue of *Midnight Call*, on page 45. The answer to "Bashing Catholics" by Y.A..

In the answer, you said, "...the worshipping of Mary, celebration of the Eucharist, and many other unscriptural practices."

My Bible tells me that the Eucharist is not "unscriptural" and should be observed in remembrance of what Christ's crucifixion meant. Your answer reads that it is unscriptural. Would you please explain? Thank you.

I'm a life subscriber and enjoy *Midnight Call* and *News From Israel* very much.

-N.I., Lake Ariel, PA

ANSWER: Page 368 of, *The Catechism of the Roman Catholic Church* says, "The holy Eucharist completes Christian initiation." Under Section 1324, the Eucharist is described as "the source and summit of the Christian life." And "in the blessed Eucharist," the Catechism says, is contained the whole spiritual good of the church." These man-made doctrines are not scriptural.

When you read the Catechism and the Scripture carefully, I think you will agree that the "Eucharist" has nothing to do with Lord's statement, *"This do in remembrance of Me."* A believer is not sanctified, his sins are not forgiven, nor is anything added to his salvation by participating in the Lord's Supper.

BASHING CATHOLICS?

Dear Midnight Call,

Had you not selected to bash the Catholic faith in at least two magazines I received, my husband and I would have definitely renewed our subscription to *Midnight Call.*

I found the magazine very informative. It is a real shame that *Midnight Call* chooses to stoop that low and bash certain denominations.

My husband and I were appalled.

When you decide to repent and put it in print that these are brothers and sisters in Christ your ministry has offended, only then will we renew our subscription.

You are persecuting the Body of Christ whether you want to admit it or not.

Until then, I will inform all of my brothers and sisters from various denominations in Christ not to support your ministry.

-Y.A., Humble, TX

ANSWER: We are clearly instructed in the Scripture to warn of false doctrine regardless of denomination.

For example, no Christian can defend the institution of

the pope, his alleged infallibility, the worship of Mary, celebration of the Eucharist, and many other unscriptural practices.

How you can call these things biblically based is beyond my understanding.

All "brothers and sisters in Christ" are clearly admonished in Scripture to "...*reprove, rebuke, exhort with all long suffering and doctrine*" (2nd Timothy 4:2).

CATHOLICISM AND PROMISE KEEPERS

Gentlemen:

I am writing in reference to your March issue and an article under the "World Focus" section on the United States. The article is entitled "Promise Keepers Unity Promotes Romanism."

As a former Roman Catholic, I am curious about what was written in that brief article, especially in view of the growing popularity of Promise Keepers. I am concerned that we may be supporting the Ecumenical Movement, albeit indirectly, through that ministry.

I would appreciate any further information that you may have that would provide additional insight as to the role of Roman Catholicism in Promise Keepers and its leadership.

-R.M., Oregon

ANSWER: A copy of a letter sent to us by *The Berean Call* not only confirms that "Promise Keepers Unity Promotes Romanism" but it goes one step further, "Romanism promotes Promise Keepers":

Dear Steve:

Thank you so very much for your letter of June 26, concerning the group called "Promise Keepers."

I was very impressed with the group at the meeting in Anaheim, and I am very intrigued by the whole concept. After all, it is the bringing of our discipleship with Jesus Christ into our daily lives that is at the very heart and soul of our spirituality.

It is obvious that the Promise Keepers have advanced this practical discipleship in a very substantial and affirming manner for men, and I commend all of you who are involved in this superb effort.

I would be very interested to know how the Archdiocese of Los Angeles and I could be of assistance in the fuller promotion of Promise Keepers, and how we might be able to work closely together to encourage this deeper level of discipleship for our Catholic men throughout the Archdiocese.

I would be open to any suggestions that you, Father Joe Shea, or Father Christian Van Liefde might have on moving forward with an expansion of the Promise Keeper concept among our Catholic men. It seems to me that there are many options available to us, and I would surely be interested in exploring those with all of you.

Thanking you for the witness of your own life of faith in Christ, and looking forward to pursuing this possibility even more fully.

Fraternally yours in Christ,
Cardinal Roger Mahony
Archbishop of Los Angeles

cc:Father Joseph Shea
Father Christian Van Liefde

P.S. This seems to me to be a wonderful way to prepare for the Third Millennium of Christianity which begins in the year 2000.

VOICES

Brother Froese:

I need some help and so I turn to you.

During the night, fairly recently, I was awakened by a voice saying, "Pray for those in hell!" My inner feeling was that I was being asked to pray for ALL who will go to hell: past, present and future. Although I instantly recoiled from this request, the voice came to me once more, "Pray for those in hell!"

I asked myself, "What could I possibly pray for?" Not for their salvation. They had their opportunities when they were living on earth.

Then, Brother Froese, the following monologue started going through my mind. "God says that all His children should be merciful and compassionate. They should do good to those who hate and abuse them; they should be kind to the unthankful and to the evil" (this seems to be from Luke 6).

If God expects His children to do these things, why shouldn't He do the same? Yet, He is condemning those who reject Him and His Son, not only to hell, but to an eternity of pain, torment and suffering in the lake of fire. That suffering has to be beyond the imagination. PLUS, after death, they will be cast into the lake of fire. How can

He actually sit on His throne and watch their torment and suffering-His angels watching with Him! (I checked this out and it comes from Revelation 14:10, I believe).

Surely, the view of the lake of fire and the horrible suffering of those in torment must desecrate the beauty and the perfection of His throne room and heaven!

This is what I ask you to pray for. It is true, the Scriptures tell us that these condemned are to spend all eternity in this torment and horrible suffering, but the Scriptures also tell that, due to intercessory prayers of God's children, He DOES change His mind! Pray, then, this prayer for those in hell, that God will extend this most merciful act to those in torment.

Brother Froese, I have tried and tried to determine, to my own satisfaction, whether or not this is a spirit I should listen to. I can't fathom an "evil" spirit making such a request, can you? What do you think? What is your conclusion? Shall I continue to offer this prayer to God that He be so merciful to those in hell - and, perhaps, count on you adding your own much more powerful prayers to my own? Or do you think I should stop?

I greatly anticipate your answer. My *Midnight Call* is priceless to me! Thank you so much! May God continue to bless you on the tremendous calling He has given you.

-L.R., Durant, OK

ANSWER: My advice is that you immediately renounce this false spirit in the name of Jesus. Also, ask the Lord to forgive your inability to discern between true and false. You are experiencing evil spirits camouflaged with truth.

For example, a lady possessed by a demon pro-claimed,"...*These men are the servants of the most high God, which shew unto us they way of salvation*" (Acts 16:17). Was there something wrong with proclaiming the Gospel truth? Yes, there was! *"Paul, being grieved, turned and said to the spirit, I command thee in the name of Jesus Christ to come out of her. And he came out the same hour"* (Acts 16:18). Please, prayerfully read 2nd Corinthians 11 and pay particular attention to verses 4, 13, 14 and 15. Indeed, there is a false Jesus, a false spirit, a false gospel, false prophets and false ministers. Why? Because Satan himself is transformed into an angel of light.

CATHOLIC MARY

Dear Mr. Froese,

The idea of Mary having had other children beside Jesus comes, of course, from the passage in the Bible where His listeners tell Him that His brothers and sisters were waiting outside to see Him. Mary and Joseph natu-rally had relatives, so He had aunts and uncles and cousins. In [the usage of] their language, close relatives were frequently called brothers and sisters, not necessar-ily [indicating that they were] born of the same mother.

In all of the early church history, there is nothing to indicate that Jesus is not the only son of Mary. I think it is inconceivable that a person so closely attached to Christ could have any connection to a foreign god. Your dislike of Mary must be very deep to think such an idea.

Mary was always around at important dates. She was

terribly worried when Jesus, who doing His own thing, went to the temple without telling anybody. She walked all the way to Calvary with Him. She was present in the Upper Room with the disciples waiting for the Holy Spirit to come down. It is assumed that she went with the apostle to Asia Minor and presumably died in Ephesus, from where her body was taken up to heaven. There were, at one time, pilgrimages to the assumed gravesite.

If you adhere strictly to the Bible, you should also recognize that Jesus left an assurance that His Church would be protected from false teachers when He told Peter to watch over His brethren. He even brought him to Rome, the center of the Empire, indicating thereby that he was the first among equals, protected from error by the Holy Spirit for all time. There was a chapel built over his grave, later replaced by a larger church. This was finally replaced in the 16th century by the monumental St. Peter's Basilica, which is still over the place of Peter's burial.

You may object to papacy, that some of the chosen were not worthy of the honor, but there are a great number of saintly popes, many wonderful teachers, and even martyrs. If some failed in our estimation, let's not forget that they were all human. Even Peter wasn't perfect, yet he was chosen. All of them, with the grace of God, brought His Church through 20 centuries of turmoil and she is still here, in full recognition of her duty. All the popes of the last 200 years were holy priests and worthy leaders. The fact that after 2 millennia His church is still here and growing should be proof enough that the "gates of Hell" are powerless against the Holy Spirit!

Dear Mr. Froese, I am praying for you.

-E.S., Irvington, NY

ANSWER: When any organization claims to be the exclusive dispenser of salvation to man, it is classified as false teaching. The true Church, consisting exclusively of born-again believers, will be protected and indeed *"the gates of hell"* shall not prevail against her.

You would have to do a great deal of twisting to make Mark 6:3 say something other than what it says, *"Is not this the carpenter, the son of Mary, the brother of James, and Joses, and of Juda, and Simon? and are not his sisters here with us?..."* If *"brother"* doesn't mean *"brother"* and *"sister"* doesn't mean *"sister,"* is *"son of Mary"* also invalid? Let's stick to the Word of God, Mr. S. The Bible is not confusing; man-made doctrines are.

I was shocked to read your statement, "your dislike of Mary must be very deep...." I can assure you that this is definitely not the case because I praise God for the selection of her. Scripture says, *"Blessed are thou among women and blessed is the fruit of thy womb."* There is no conflict. However, in your letter, you are identifying another Mary who, quite obviously, is of demonic origin. When you pray in accordance with the Catechism's instruction, "Holy Mary Mother of God pray for us sinners," you are worshipping a Mary not found in the Bible, but one who originates from hell.

Jesus said, *"I will build my church"* and He is doing so. He is the way, the truth, and life. The Bible says, *"For there is one God, and one mediator between God and men, the man*

357

Christ Jesus" (1st Timothy 2:5).

MORE ON CATHOLIC DOCTRINE

Dear Mr. Froese,

In the October issue of *Midnight Call*, your response to a writer's letter, "Catholicism a cult," was accurate as far as it went, but did not really answer the question.

Being a former Catholic myself, I believe they do claim to believe in the God of the Bible, but they do not understand salvation or a "believer's" relationship with Jesus Christ.

My reference to Catholic doctrine is per the 1994 publication, *Catechism of the Catholic Church-Libreria Editrice Vaticana*. Articles 1427 and 980 state that, "It is by faith in the Gospel and by Baptism that one renounces evil and gains salvation;"

"This sacrament of Penance is necessary for salvation for those who have fallen after Baptism." This says that man's actions of baptism and penance are the way to forgiveness of sins and eternal life, and not the blood of Jesus Christ through God's grace, as described in Ephesians 1:7, *"In whom we have redemption through his blood, the forgiveness of sins, according to the riches of his grace."*

How does an infant who is baptized have faith in the Gospel? The faith of someone else cannot save you!

And as an add-on to your cult (false doctrine) thoughts, how about the following:

Article 968-969: "This motherhood of Mary in the order of grace continues uninterruptedly from the consent which she loyally gave...."

"Taken up to heaven she did not lay aside this saving office but by her manifold intercession continues to bring us the gifts of eternal salvation." This says she is a Co-Redemptrix with Jesus!

Article 82: "The church, to whom the transmission and interpretation of Revelation is entrusted, does not derive her certainty about all revealed truths from the holy Scriptures alone. Both Scripture and Tradition must be accepted and honored with equal sentiments of devotion and reverence." This means the Word of God is not absolute Truth – how about the Book of Mormon or the Qur'an?

Also, only God, through His Spirit can accurately interpret the Word!

Why has the Catholic Church eliminated the second commandment dealing with the prohibition of graven images (Deuteronomy 5:8-10) from its teachings? (See pages 496-497 in the catechism).

-I.A., DeSoto, MO

ANSWER: Thank you for the additional documentation regarding the Vatican's interpretation and tradition. That is clearly a violation against the doctrine taught in the Scripture.

Regarding the second commandment, it is quite obvious that God's Word, *"Thou shalt not make unto thee any graven image..."* is contrary to their practice.

SALVATION BY THE CHURCH

Dear Mr. Froese,

Referring to an article appearing on the editorial pages of the *Midnight Call* in November, I am differing with you strongly in your assessment of Mother Teresa's commitment to Jesus Christ.

It is astounding that such an educated (presumably) man as you, would, in your anti-Catholic prejudice, make a statement such as; "I am sorry to say personal faith in Jesus Christ and trust in His substitutionary work on Calvary's cross is nowhere in evidence" regarding the future saint.

How you fail to see that such giving of one's life to others, the fulfilling of the great commandment, is a mystery to me, and I am sure, to many of your readers who do not share your myopic view of the salvific nature of Jesus' life, death and resurrection.

In your Bible-based ignorance you do not see that being a Catholic, dedicating oneself to the Catholic Church, the pope, and a religious system of benevolence is belonging to Jesus Christ, following Him in the one church that He established while He walked this earth.

Following the law of love to the extent that Mother Teresa did requires an outpouring of the Holy Spirit that comes when one has truly given their life to Jesus Christ.

In a narrow-minded view, one could assume, like you do, that one cannot be saved by professing the Catholic faith.

Judging from your fierce rejection of the church, the mass and the sacraments, I fear for your ignorance of the very institutions that were established by Jesus.

By your apparent obsession with the human errors within the church several hundred years ago and the resulting distortions of "the Reformation," you have lost sight of the truth and have thrown everything aside in your hatred and confusion.

You state, "Then, only those who have put their faith in the Lord Jesus can look unto Him," inserting a comfortable (for you) interpretation and condemning those who do not think your way. You do not see that faith alone, "sola fide," won't guarantee eternal life. It is the grace of God that is required.

I would venture to say that you would do yourself and your followers well by removing the blinders and seeking the truth. It won't be found in "Sola Scriptura," so you will need to look elsewhere beside the Bible to find the true teachings that have survived the ages. Try the one, holy, catholic and apostolic church: The Catholic Church. It alone is the church of Christ, founded 2,000 years ago by Him, and, you may discover, it is the path to eternal life.

I would also venture that Mother Teresa knew this and tried to follow its teachings, the teaching of Jesus, with all her heart and soul.

Both you and I have a long way to go to even approach the level of faith and trust in Jesus the Christ that Mother Teresa demonstrated in her life on earth. We will need for her to intercede for us before God. I pray that He will have mercy on us, Mr. Froese.

-R.N., Hesperia, CA

ANSWER: Your statement in the latter part of your letter is rather revealing: "Try the one, holy, catholic and apostolic church: the Catholic Church. It alone is the one church of Christ, founded 2,000 years ago by Him, and, you may discover, it is the path to eternal life."

This gives me enough reason to believe that you are serving "another Christ," one to whom you do not have direct access. Apparently you need Mother Teresa to "intercede" on your behalf.

This "other Jesus" has given the authority to "it," in your case, the Catholic Church, "...it is the path to eternal life."

The Jesus that Bible believers proclaim is the one who said, *"I am the way, the truth, and the life: no man cometh unto the Father, but by me"* (John 14:6).

We do not need Mother Teresa or any other so-called "saint" to intercede on our behalf because *"...there is one God, and one mediator between God and men, the man Christ Jesus"* (1st Timothy 2:5).

The Jesus Christ we proclaim is the Jew who called His Jewish apostles, and caused both the Old and New Testament of the Jewish Bible to be written.

He founded His Jewish church in Jerusalem (not Rome) and sent His Jewish apostles and saints throughout the world into Samaria, Syria, Turkey, Rome, Spain, Greece and the entire world to preach the Gospel.

That is the Jesus we proclaim. You must admit that the Jesus of the Bible isn't the one you have written to me about.

362

FALSE DOCTRINE?

IGNORE WORD-FAITH?

Dear Midnight Call:

I have enjoyed reading *Midnight Call* while appreciating the work you do. But I have to agree wholeheartedly with the letter to the editor in the September issue from H.D. of Campbell, California.

Like H. D., I am bewildered by your total lack of stories dealing with the Word-Faith teachers. You call yourself "The Prophetic Voice for the Endtime," yet you completely ignore one of the most dangerous, devilish phenomena of these endtimes; that is, the increasing popularity of the Word-Faith blasphemers, and the damage they're doing to the Body of Christ. Why? Why do you ignore them? Or is it just that you're "asleep at the wheel?" I almost get the impression you're on the payroll of Fred Price, Rodney Howard Brown and all the rest of them.

You say if you followed Mr. H.D.'s advice, your magazine would be filled with articles about the errors of others. Then fine! Let's be honest, your magazine is already filled with articles about the errors of others anyway...as it should be (for example, Roman Catholicism and political liberalism). You have a column titled, "Signs of the Times." If ever there was a topic dealing with the signs of the times, it's the Word-Faith movement. Unfortunately, you won't find it in the *Midnight Call!*

People's lives have been ruined by this teaching. To show love does not mean you ignore error. The Word-Faith movement is one of the most diabolical cancers spreading in the Christian church today, while "The Prophetic Voice for the Endtimes" chooses to totally ignore it. What a shame.

-V.K., CANADA

ANSWER: After having carefully checked the 48 pages of the September issue of *Midnight Call,* I could only find one page that would qualify your statement, "...your magazine is already filled with articles about the errors of others..." Also, you are getting the wrong "impression" when you assume I am "on the payroll of Fred Price, Rodney Howard Brown, and all the rest of them." As a matter of fact, I don't know these people, nor have I ever read anything they've written or heard them preach. Who am I, then, to take it upon myself to show that the above-mentioned are responsible for "diabolical cancers spreading in the Christian church"?

You overlook the fact that each servant of the Lord and ministry has a certain task. Not all are supposed to do the same things. For example, Dave Hunt has written extensively on the Word-Faith movement and does an excellent job in documenting their errors.

Jesus gives a very personal warning to His disciples, *"Take heed that no man deceive you."* This applies to an individual: "you," not "others". The devil is no fool; he has prepared a much more refined deception for the good solid Bible-believing church people as well. If the "Word-Faith movement" and 10,000 others instantly disappeared today, do you think Satan would throw his hands in the air and give up? Not at all!

How can we escape deception? By continuously drawing nearer to Jesus. Therefore, our primary goal is to preach the saving Gospel of our Lord to people everywhere. The Bible says, *"Whom the Son makes free, he shall be free indeed."* Remember that there is a group of people who deliberately choose, according to itching ears, to reject the truth, *"And for this cause God shall send them strong delusion, that they should believe a lie"* (2nd Thessalonians 2:11).

Also, I choose to heed the advice of Matthew 13:30, *"Let both grow together until the harvest: and in the time of harvest I will say to the reapers, Gather ye together first the tares, and bind them in bundles to burn them: but gather the wheat into my barn."*

FULL MOON POWER?

Dear Brother Froese,

Thank you for all you do and for the magazine. It's

helped me a lot.

At a ladies' Bible study, I was surprised at the number of women that believed: 1) the occurrence of the full moon somehow figured into when women began their labor for childbirth; and 2) a lot of the ladies – teachers, nurses, office workers and others – agreed that on the full moon more problems on the job and just everywhere could be expected, such as children being more disorderly in the classroom, trouble with co-workers, frustrations and so on. Would you please comment on this?

Name withheld, Georgia

ANSWER: Since the beginning of time, pagans have believed that the sun and moon were divine, presumably because of the illumination that comes from them. All types of beliefs have arisen, attributing events and the behavior of people on earth to the influence of the heavenly bodies. Colossians 2:16 says, *"Let no man therefore judge you in meat, or in drink, or in respect of an holyday, or of the new moon, or of the sabbath days."*

BROWNSVILLE REVIVAL

Dear Sir,

I want to take a moment to ask for some encouragement or advice in some things that seem to be popular movements under the guise of Christianity. These movements being Promise Keepers, the Brownsville Revival, the [Christian] militia, and the laughter thing [known as the "Toronto blessing"] spreading in the charismatic movement. (Any others you might be aware of?)

I have doubts about these things. However, I do believe that in the last days, God will manifest a greater frequency of miracles. Maybe my belief is unscriptural, I don't know; but many churches profess this. I am well-settled that most of these movements are deterrents to truth and encourage wimpy Christianity as it fills a need to follow something we see, not faith in an invisible God that we should know by relationship. Myself, I seek not after signs and wonders but they should follow me, and I don't look back.

The Brownsville Revival is new to me and has outstanding reports of a cleansing. However, I watched a church in central Ohio go from a wholesome family gathering place to cultic behavior in a few short weeks after the pastor returned from Brownsville. He shut down all children's programs, Bible studies, and actually prayed a curse on anyone who would take a drink of alcohol, to mention a few observations.

This became too bizarre and I took my family out. In attending another church, they caught wind of this Brownsville thing and spoke about it as a true move of God. I respect the pastor and the congregation at the latter church, but I have true concerns (about) this Brownsville movement. Any insight you may have on this will be greatly appreciated.

-I.O., Delaware, OH

ANSWER: Your statement, "He shut down all children's programs, Bible studies, and actually prayed a curse on anyone who would take a drink of alcohol..." is most certainly "cultic behavior." We must be extremely cautious whenever and wherever the attempt is made to propagate visible manifestations as proof of the working of God's Spirit. The oft-repeated idea that in the last days, God will manifest a greater frequency of miracles is not to be found in the Scripture. Scripture clearly states that demonic miracles will be manifested in greater frequency in the last days. The success of the Antichrist lies in the avenue of deception through signs and wonders. *"Even him, whose coming is after the working of Satan with all power and signs and lying wonders, And with all deceiveableness of unrighteousness in them that perish..."* (2nd Thessalonians 2:9-10).

Incidentally, miracles do not produce faith, they produce unbelief, which is evident when reading Israel's history, and they are given to us as an example. Where does faith come from? Romans 10:17 says, *"...faith cometh by hearing, and hearing by the Word of God."*

JESUS ONLY

Dear Sir:

My son, having been grounded in the Word all his life, recently renounced his Baptist heritage, called his family liars, and has made life miserable for his wife and toddler son. He has joined a "Jesus Only" (oneness) group called Apostolic Faith Chapel. I do not know much about this "cult," but he gave up everything and is following it faithfully. He uses Acts 2:38 as some kind of "magic" formula and says he can't find "our" baptism or salvation in the

Bible. I have been saved 42 years, but he says I am going to hell because I cut my hair. He is now taking his little son to these meetings "to get the Holy Ghost and speak in tongues." Can you help me to help him somehow? He has had several hours of "brainwashing" and has a ready answer for all of us in his family, as well as the community. Thank you for the article in this issue (May) on the "Baptism of the Spirit." When I was saved and baptized, I remember the pastor using, "In the name of the Father, the Son, and the Holy Ghost," but my son says those are just "titles" for the name of Jesus and Acts 2:38 in the ONLY way! Please explain all of this. Thank you.

-I.O., Winnsboro, LA

ANSWER: I am sorry to hear about your son falling into the clutches of a false teaching. This is a tragedy that affects not only himself, but also his family and friends. The Bible warns that if we are not deeply grounded in the Word of God, we are in danger of falling into a false teaching. What can you do? Quite frankly, nothing! Your arguments and Scripture quotations will not help because he chooses to believe a lie. My advice is not to talk to your son about God, but speak to God about your son. Nothing is impossible with God. Your son may still experience the restoring grace which saves even the worst of sinners and rescues the one fallen into the deepest pit. Also, search your heart before the Lord so He can reveal to you where you have failed; then leave all things in the hands of the Lord who does all things well.

369

JEHOVAH WITNESS

Dear Sir,

Glorying in the so-called damnation of a 72-year-old grandmother in Singapore who had (page 28) Jehovah Witness material is not the thing for a Christian to do. Whoever wrote the article used Romans 13:1-2 as a club to hit her over the head. The apostles disobeyed their government by preaching Christ.

It is written, you shall not kill. Mary and Joseph ran off with the baby Jesus to Egypt to keep Him from being killed. The government wanted to kill him; did they do wrong?

It is also written, "To rescue the perishing." If being a J.W. is too much of a cult, then she should be rescued from it by Christians.

-C.R., Knox City, TX

ANSWER: Having re-read the article in question, I fail to see where we "glory in the ...damnation of a 72 year old grandmother..." This lady, who is following the cult of the Jehovah's Witnesses, has simply brought the punishment of her government for disobedience upon herself, based on Romans 13:1-2. Incidentally, the apostle did not disobey the government, but the religious authority. To serve in the military of a country and kill someone, even in the line of duty, are two different matters. When soldiers came to John the Baptist asking, *"What shall we do?"* He did not tell them to refuse military service, he said, *"Do violence to no man...and be content with your wages."* Indeed, Jehovah's Witnesses need the Lord because they too, as anyone else, can be made free, for the Bible says, *"Whom the Son shall make free, ye shall be free indeed."*

SOUL SLEEP

Dear Mr. Froese:

I love the *Midnight Call* Magazine and need an answer to my question. I have a friend who is very nervous and despondent since her sister died and I keep telling her she is with Jesus and will see her again. She has been a Christian all her life, as have I, but she believes in "soul sleep." I told her Jesus' reply to the thief on the cross, but she said, "that's paradise."

I thought paradise and heaven are the same. I lost my husband 27 years ago and am now 80, but I know he's with Jesus and very much alive and this gives me great peace and joy. What specific verse or verses can I give her to show her our loved ones are alive and well in that glorious heaven. I can hardly wait to go there. God is so good!

(Name withheld) Crete, IL

ANSWER: Second Corinthians 5:1 states, *"...we have a building of God..."* And verse 8 makes it clear, *"...absent from the body...present with the Lord."* Even now, *"...our conversation is in heaven; from whence also we look for the Saviour, the Lord Jesus Christ"* (Philippians 3:20). At our rebirth we become eternal beings. We will receive our glorified body at the Rapture.

SOUL SLEEP CONFIRMED IN THE BIBLE?

Dear Mr. Froese,

When a person dies, it is like a sleep. The dead do not know anything (Ecclesiastes 9:5). At the Second Coming of Jesus, the dead in Christ shall rise first (1st Thessalonians 4:16-17; Revelation 20:4-6). They are brought up in the clouds to be with Jesus, then the righteous that are alive are brought up to Christ to be with him in heaven for 1,000 years (Jesus never touches foot on earth).

The wicked who are alive at Jesus' Second Coming will be slain by the very presence of Christ (2nd Thessalonians 1:7-8, Psalm 68:2). The wicked remain dead in the grave until the thousand years is over (Revelation 20:5). Then they will be raised from the dead and Satan shall deceive them to do battle against the New Jerusalem (Isaiah 65:17; 2nd Peter 3:13; Revelation 21:5; Revelation 21:2-3). But God destroys all wicked people, including Satan (Revelation 20:9-10; 21:8; Malachi 4:3). Then God's people enjoy eternity with Christ on the new earth (Revelation 21:2-7). Amen!

-T.H., Renton WA

ANSWER: When the Bible says, *"...absent from the body, and...present with the Lord"* (2nd Corinthians 5:8), it gives no indication that the soul is unconscious.

In Philippians 1:23, Paul testifies, *"For I am in a strait betwixt two, having a desire to depart, and to be with Christ; which is far better."* The verse in Ecclesiastes is referring only to the physical body of flesh and blood.

The Rapture is the moment that the Church is caught up to be in the presence of the Lord. After seven years, Jesus will come back to earth with His saints and we shall rule with Him for 1,000 years. This constitutes the kingdom of God on earth under the rulership of the Lord. The earth will then be filled with the knowledge of the Lord.

After the thousand years have elapsed, the final execution upon Satan and his angels will take place. Peter explains it this way, "...*the heavens being on fire shall be dissolved, and the elements shall melt with fervent heat*" (2nd Peter 3:12). The final state, "...*Behold, I make all things new...*" (Revelation 21:5) will be implemented. Therefore, the apostle admonishes us, "...*we, according to his promise, look for new heavens and a new earth, wherein dwelleth righteousness*" (2nd Peter 3:13). Believers will be in the presence of the Lord, "...*and so shall we ever be with the Lord*" (1st Thessalonians 4:17).

MASONIC CHRISTIANS?

Dear Friend in Christ,

We received your new book, *How Democracy Will Elect the Antichrist*, and have read every word. It is well written and very much enjoyed by yours truly.

There is one sentence on page 162 that is untrue. You say, "Our first President, George Washington, and many of the Founding Fathers were members of the occult religion of Freemasonry." Freemasonry is not a religion, it never has been a religion, and it will never be a religion. It is a fraternal organization of which I am very proud to have been a member for more than sixty years. Please know that we do not expect to convince you that it is anything different from what you say it is. We also have the anti-Masonic video, "From Darkness to Light." It is filled with statements which are totally false. As Mark Twain said years ago, "Most of what people know just ain't so."

We are also aware that it is not uncommon for a minister to be "down" on Freemasonry. My stock answer is that almost everyone is "down" on everything they're not "up" on. Undoubtedly, you are aware that the Southern Baptists made an attempt to expel all Freemasons from the denomination. They were unsuccessful in the effort so far. In my opinion, they will try again.

Let me say also that I have served as secretary of my Lodge for nine years. It may have been wasted effort, but I sent out a tract with each dues notice. A few samples are enclosed. In every Masonic Lodge there are men who are saved, and there are men who are unsaved. By the same token, in every Christian church, there are those who are saved, and there are those who are unsaved.

In addition to the untrue statement mentioned above, I strongly resent what appears to be a "put down" of George Washington. He was possibly more responsible for the many freedoms which we enjoy today than any other individual on earth. He was a God-fearing man - a man of prayer. He also refused a suggestion that he become King George the First.

-P.A., Weston, WV

ANSWER: In his book, *Morals and Dogma*, Albert Pike, a

33rd-degree Mason, wrote the following on page 213, "Every Masonic temple is a temple of religion." The fact that you equate the Church with the Lodge reinforces the religious nature of the Lodge.

Indeed, George Washington was a great, courageous man of high moral standards, but the fact that he feared God and was a man of prayer does not make him a Christian.

Unfortunately, I must agree with you that many anti-Masonic books and videos are not based entirely on facts and that certainly does not help the cause of Christ.

However, the issue is whether Freemasonry can act as a substitute for religion, in this case, Christianity. Please don't confuse true Christianity with any benevolent organization or movement. Christians work toward our heavenly home while virtually all other religions and movements attempt to establish heaven on earth.

Of course, we cannot deny that George Washington, the bulk of our Founding Fathers, staunch anti-Nazi German Chancellor Konrad Adenauer, British statesman Winston Churchill, or Christian political rights champion Jesse Helms, who are all Freemasons, have in fact accomplished great and heroic acts for the benefit of all people in the free world. But the freedom we proclaim as Christians cannot be obtained in a lodge, or anywhere else for that matter. The Bible states, *"If the Son therefore shall make you free, ye shall be free indeed"* (John 8:36).

GIGGLING FOR GOD? REPRISE

Dear Mr. Froese:

I was considering subscribing to *Midnight Call* until I read the short insert entitled, "Giggling for God?" It is quite evident that you have not been to Toronto to the Airport Vineyard Fellowship or spoken with any of the many pastors in Toronto who are now coming together monthly in a church-wide renewal meeting.

I was very impressed by the order of the meetings and by the careful screening process that those who pray for others must go through.

These are the last days, Mr. Froese, and the Lord will do many things He's never done before. This movement seems to be an outpouring of the Spirit to heal God's people both emotionally and spiritually-and sometimes physically, too (a Church without spot or blemish). The "joy of the Lord is our strength." I would think you would be interested in the results of the small percent who are overcome with holy laughter (there are many varied manifestations).

Just like anything the Lord does in a supernatural way, there will be persons who go home and begin to misuse or distort what they've experienced or heard about at Toronto or other renewal meetings. This is sad, but it's human nature (and a way for Satan to create skepticism).

How do you explain thousands of churches in England and Germany now having nightly meetings as a result of the Toronto blessing?

How can you explain night meetings of 1,500 to 2,000 people with people from 15 to 21 countries being present?

Why are pastors and Christian leaders making such great financial sacrifices to go to Toronto?

You had better be careful what and whom you criticize with the body of Christ – and especially what you print. The Lord will hold you accountable because of your influence.

-S.S., Altoona, PA

ANSWER: The Bible says, *"Prove all things..."* (1st Thessalonians 5:21). John admonished us to, *"...believe not every spirit, but try the spirits whether they are of God..."* (1st John 4:1). And the commendable Bereans, *"...searched the scriptures daily, whether those things were so"* (Acts 17:11).

Yet you threaten me with the words, "You had better be careful what and who you criticize..." and, "The Lord will hold you accountable because of your influence." Is the Scripture, which admonishes us to prove all things, wrong?

Where in the Bible do we find the "outpouring of the spirit to heal God's people both emotionally and spiritually?"

Where does the Scripture describe "a small percent...overcome with holy laughter?"

And where in the Scripture do we find that a "careful screening process" is required for admittance to meetings or allowance to pray?

We have received about a dozen letters defending this "giggling for God" and all were, as yours, based on experience, not Scripture.

SOUL SLEEP

Dear Sir,

I have noticed in one of your articles in the issue of November 1997 an item regarding a dead woman whom you said is now with the Lord. In my study of the Bible, your statement isn't in conformity with the teaching in the Bible. Genesis 2:7 says, *"And the Lord God formed man of the dust of the ground, and breathed into his nostrils the breath of life; and man became a living soul."* This is what happens at birth.

When a person dies, Ecclesiastes 12:7 says: *"Then shall the dust return to the earth as it was: and the spirit shall return unto God who gave it."*

Ecclesiastes 9:5-6, *"For the living know that they shall die: but the dead know not any thing, neither have they any more a reward; for the memory of them is forgotten. Also their love, and their hatred, and their envy, is now perished; neither have they any more a portion for ever in any thing that is done under the sun."*

In the New Testament we are told that *"a dead person sleepeth."* Matthew 9:24 and John 11:11 give us this condition.

However, the Word of God gives us the hope of eternal life if we die in Jesus. So for the present, all dead persons except for Moses and Elijah and a few others who were resurrected when Jesus died on the cross (see Matthew 27:52) are all here on this earth awaiting either of two resurrections.

The first resurrection is for those who will be saved at the Second Coming of our Lord Jesus Christ, which I think will be very soon. This is what St. Paul tells us in 1st Corinthians 15:5-58.

Those who will be saved will be with Jesus in heaven for a thousand years, after which God will establish the new heaven and earth.

The second resurrection will be for those who will be burned by fire for their sins and will have eternal death.

I hope that this will clarify your understanding of the state of the dead.

-S.U., Riverside, CA

ANSWER: As far as our physical bodies are concerned, you are correct, we *"sleep,"* (which is a metaphor for dying). The apostle Peter confirms this when he says, *"Knowing that shortly I must put off this my tabernacle..."* (2nd Peter 1:14).

Paul also speaks of the physical body when he says, *"For we know that if our earthly house of this tabernacle were dissolved, we have a building of God, a house not made with hands, eternal in the heavens."* In verse 8 he explains, *"We are confident, I say, and willing rather to be absent from the body, and to be present with the Lord"* (2nd Corinthians 5).

The real you and I are the spiritual substance which is so genuine that Paul could say, *"And [God] hath raised us up together, and made us sit together in heavenly places in Christ Jesus"* (Ephesians 2:6).

CHAPTER 20

THE RAPTURE

RAPTURE AND CLINTON

Dear Brother Froese,

I have just finished reading my January *Midnight Call*, and as always, enjoyed it very much. It is always edifying and uplifting. But I do have a question about the article, "Salvation in the Tribulation" by Brother Thomas Ice. Perhaps he just didn't put it down at my level. But I am of the opinion that while many will be saved during the tribulation, they won't be added to the Body of Christ. The Church was complete at the Rapture. Those saved during the tribulation will enter the kingdom as those of all the nations that will say, *"...Come, and let us go up to the mountain of the LORD, and to the house of the God of Jacob; and He will teach us of his ways, and we will walk in His paths..."* (Micah 4:2).

Also, while I am writing, I would like to run something by you, as I truly value your opinion. For some time now, I have pondered the possibility that Bill Clinton might be the devil's counterfeit copy of John the Baptist. I felt so strongly that this possibility should be thoroughly examined that I wrote a letter to the editor of my local newspaper. It was printed in today's paper. I further likened all of his supporters to the Herodians (Mark 3:6).

King Herod bootlicks, lawyers (professional liars) and spin doctors...are identified in the Scripture by their like-mindedness. (Jude 8,10-13; 15-19; 2nd Peter 2:10-19; 2nd Thessalonians 2:10 and Psalm 1:4-6).

The ungodly...and their way shall perish. Today's Clintonites, who are consistently polled, the 60-75% would again, this day scream out "Give us Barabbas!"

If this assertion is even near right, it should speak volumes as to what's about to happen.

-U.E., Rome, GA

ANSWER: You are correct. The Church is the Body of Christ and when it is complete, the Rapture will take place and no one will be added.

However, there are other groups of saved people, such as the saints of the Old Testament, of which John was the greatest but the least in the kingdom of heaven when compared with the glory of the Church.

The tribulation saints are described in Revelation 7:9 and 14. Notice in verse 15 that *"they...serve him day and night in his temple."*

However, according to Revelation 21:9-10, the Church in its glory is veiled in the holy Jerusalem.

It is important to add that regardless of the group, all are saved one way, through the blood of the Lamb.

I don't think that President Clinton, or any other U.S. president, plays any significant role in the endtime development of Bible prophecy. The center nation was, is and always will be Israel. The power structure that envelopes Israel is Europe. That is from where world rulership will emerge.

As far as corrupt politicians are concerned, we've always had them, we have them today, and will continue to have them in the future.

As to the significance of the nations of the world, including the United States, the Bible says, *"All nations before him are as nothing; and they are counted to him less than nothing, and vanity"* (Isaiah 40:17).

FIRST RESURRECTION

Dear Mr. Froese:

I enjoy receiving *Midnight Call* and the articles and information.

I have a question after reading your article in the May issue "The Disappearing Church–Rapture."

What about Revelation 20:4-6? It says this is the first resurrection and it includes the people killed because they didn't take the mark of the beast. If they are included in the first resurrection, then is this not the same resurrection spoken of in 1st Thessalonians 4:16-17 and 1st Corinthians 15:51-54? If not, then it would be the second, not the first resurrection.

-L. N. in Wetumpka, AL

ANSWER: Revelation 20:4-6 is the finalizing of the first resurrection. Salvation is only obtainable through Jesus and all who ever have and ever will be saved belong to the first resurrection. This includes all categories of believers: the saints of the Old Testament, the Church and the Great Tribulation saints. However, each group is distinctly different. As the Body of Christ, the Church is also His Bride. According to Revelation 21:9-21 the glory of the Lamb's wife is hidden by the heavenly Jerusalem. The tribulation saints worship God "in his temple" day and night, but the Bride is in the place where there is *"no temple"* (Revelation 21:22).

Jesus is the firstfruit of the first resurrection and the Rapture is the fullness of the firstfruit of the first resurrection.

"I AM READY"

Dear Arno:

I love you and your magazine but you know what? I get newsletters and magazines from all kinds of humble, sincere Bible teachers whom I respect... But all of them argue and debate on when the Rapture will occur: "Pre-Trib Rapture" versus "Mid-Trib Rapture." It's gotten to the point that I don't care when it will happen. It will happen when it happens; it's on the Father's timetable. This topic is causing division in the Body of Christ, and I feel we're wasting God's valuable time instead of just concentrating on hearing the Lord's voice, bringing the lost to Christ, praying without ceasing, and staying on our knees to make sure our own hearts and walks are right in God's eyes.

My brothers and sisters in Christ in other countries are having their families torn apart, are imprisoned, are going through horrific tortures and are being murdered - all because they refuse to deny Christ. The Rapture is the last thing on their minds; they just focus on spreading the Gospel.

And we should also pray for and provide for Israel and the Jews. Instead of worrying about when the Rapture's going to happen, every morning I just look up and say, "Lord, I'm ready. But in the meantime, use me. Show me how to bring someone to Christ today." I'm sending a letter like this to all the Bible teachers whose newsletters and magazines I get. Thanks Arno—I love your magazine!

-V.C., Utica, MN

ANSWER: Your statement, "Every morning I just look up and say I am ready..." demonstrates the biblical truth of the imminence of the Rapture.

However, I doubt very much that "the Rapture was the last thing on the minds" of those who faced death as martyrs for Jesus. I believe just the opposite; the coming of Jesus was their great comfort.

When the Church is taken away, the Holy Spirit, in the office of the Comforter, will also be taken away. That means that during the Great Tribulation, there will be no comfort of an imminent Rapture because it will already have taken place!

2ND THESSALONIANS 2

Dear Mr. Froese:

I need your input. I know a lot of people say we (Christians) will be gone before the seven-year tribulation begins. Then please explain the following verse. Second Thessalonians 2:1-3: *"Concerning the coming of our Lord Jesus Christ and our gathering to Him we ask you brother, not to become easily unsettled or alarmed by some prophecy, report, or letter supposed to have come from us, saying that the Day of the Lord has already come. Don't let anyone deceive you in any way, for that day will not come until the rebellion occurs and the man of lawlessness is revealed, the man doomed to destruction."*

Am I to assume the part that says, "...our being gathered to him..." is the Rapture, or is it not the Rapture? If it is the Rapture, then it tells me that we don't "go" until after the man of sin is revealed. And "revealed" means a full disclosure of the Antichrist, or to divulge or open up to view.

-L.K. in Aberdeen, WA

ANSWER: Second Thessalonians 2 speaks of two things: 1) *"the coming of our Lord Jesus Christ"* which is the day of Christ, and 2) *"our gathering unto Him,"* the Rapture.

In verse 5, Paul acted rather surprised and disappointed. *"Remember ye not, that, when I was yet with you, I told you these things?"* What things did he tell them? First Thessalonians 4:16-17, the clear description of the Rapture!

In verse 7 he says, *"...only he who now letteth will let,*

until he be taken out of the way," that is what is hindering the revelation of the Antichrist.

Remember that Jesus told His disciples that He must leave; otherwise, the Holy Spirit, in His office as Comforter, would not come. In the opposite direction, Jesus cannot come until the Comforter (the Holy Spirit with the Church) is taken out of the way.

CHILDREN RAPTURED?

Dear Mr. Froese,

When speaking with fellow believers about the Rapture, it seems to be clear to them that little children and babies will be taken too. I am not so sure. I have been given Scripture verses in reference to a child in the context of being received into the kingdom of God for eternity.

Little or young child: (Matthew 18:1-5; Matthew 19:13-15; Mark 10:13-16; Luke 18:15-17; Mark 9:36; 1st Corinthians 13:11); Age of understanding: (1st Corinthians 14:20). But do these verse apply to the Rapture?

I received my first-ever copy of *Midnight Call*, March.

I am sorry I missed the first part of "Abraham our Father." Also, I was interested to see the videocassettes, but I would not be able to use them on my VCR here. Are these cassettes available over here?

For a while now, I have felt a sense of urgency in my soul. There is not much time left for the believer to do a work for God on this earth, and show the importance of a closer walk with the Lord and show the love of Christ to those who are unsaved in my family.

Is preparing information for my loved ones who are "left behind," through books and cassettes, about the coming tribulation a lack of faith that they may not be saved in time for the Rapture?

Thank you for all the challenging and informative teaching in *Midnight Call*, and the great blessing received through the audiocassette teaching in prophetic times received through End Time Ministries.

-E.C., ENGLAND

ANSWER: A person cannot be raptured unless he is born again. When our Lord indicated that children, in their innocence, will be saved, that obviously included the Rapture. This event must not be separated from salvation; it's an act of grace, a fulfillment of the work of Christ's resurrection and ascension (1st Corinthians 15:54).

Most of our videocassettes are available in the PAL video system through End Time Ministries, P.O. Box 8212, London SE9 2CH.

Continue to pray unceasingly for your loved ones. The Lord hears and answers prayer in His time.

TWO RAPTURES?

Dear Sir:

In your issue of *Midnight Call*, you have an article on the two-part Rapture. Christ's Church will meet Him in the air, and the Jews will be raptured to Israel. This is something that I have never heard of before and am very much interested in. I would appreciate more information on this subject as well as Scripture references on this. I have taken *Midnight Call* for several years now and enjoy it very much; I also pass it along to one of my friends. He also enjoys it very much and passes it along.

I would like to thank you very much in advance for your wonderful cooperation in this matter.

-C.T., Asheville, NC

ANSWER: I have dealt with this subject at length in my books, *How Democracy Will Elect the Antichrist* and *The Great Mystery of the Rapture.* Here are two verses that may help: Matthew 24:31, *"And he shall send his angels with a great sound of a trumpet, and they shall gather together his elect from the four winds, from one end of heaven to the other."* Notice that the Lord will send *"his angels"* and *"a trumpet."* Who are the elect? Isaiah 45:4 answers, *"and Israel mine elect."* They will not be gathered in the clouds of heaven, but to Israel. All Jews will then be in the Promised Land, according to Ezekiel 39:28, *"I have gathered them unto their own land, and have left none of them any more there."* Notice the contrast between the Rapture of the Jews, when the Lord sends His angels being called *"with a trump,"* and the Rapture of the Church, which we read of in 1st Thessalonians 4:16, *"...the Lord himself shall descend from heaven...with the voice of the archangel and with the trump of God."*

RAPTURE QUESTIONS EXPLAINED

Dear Brother Froese:

I believe that the whole Church is not going to be in the Bride of Christ (who are raptured as stated in 1st Thessalonians 4:16-18). As with the Jewish bride, there will be a shout, the voice of the archangel (the wedding party saying "Here comes the Bridegroom"), and the (not last) trump of God; and we will meet the Lord in the air. This is a time of rejoicing, because it says *"comfort."* Secondly, I believe there is going to be a second Rapture for the tribulation saints (judgment *"so as by fire"*) who are still alive. That is in a twinkling of an eye...no shout, no voice, but it will be at the last trump. Also, it says, *"we will all be changed."* This scene is different from the Bride and Bridegroom (See 1st Corinthians 15:51-52).

My urgency in writing you is that, according to the dates I sent to you previously, the timing caused me to pause with great alarm. Do you see that there is a seven-year period between the Rapture of the Bride of Christ and the appearing of the Antichrist at the mid-tribulation point? Those who believe that the Rapture begins the tribulation will think that the Lord is coming seven years later...but that will be the Antichrist. What a deception for those who don't know Scripture!

-N.N., Murphy, NC

ANSWER: The Church is His Body (Ephesians 1:23, 3:6, 5:30). His Body is the Bride (compare Ephesians 5:25-27). Revelation 21:2 speaks of one Bride. The Rapture takes place at the last trump of God (1st Corinthians 15:52; 1st

Thessalonians 4:16).

The tribulation saints will not experience the Rapture, which includes an instantaneous transformation into the glorious body. In Revelation 6:9 we see them without the body, *"...the souls of them that were slain...."*

Members of the Church will be in the presence of the Lord with their glorified bodies. Then they will stand before the Judgment Seat of Christ, which is followed by the Marriage Supper of the Lamb.

At the end of the seven-year tribulation, the Lord will return with the Church to make an end of the powers of darkness and ordain the 1,000-year kingdom of peace on earth. The saints that come out of the Great Tribulation do not belong to the Church.

ONE SHALL BE TAKEN

Dear Midnight Call:

I was absolutely horrified to see Matthew 24:40 used to describe what would happen in connection with the Rapture! How could you use this reference, which has to do with the Jews, for the Church? The ones taken away are those taken away in judgment and the ones left are to go into the Millennial kingdom.

Why should anyone at the Midnight Call have to be told this? I am ashamed! Think about what the whole chapter (24) is talking about: the tribulation! Nothing to do with the Church!

-S.O., Danville, CA

ANSWER: When reading Luther's translation, I know immediately to which group I want to belong. *"...one shall be accepted, the other shall be rejected."* I most certainly believe that we may use this verse in relation to the Rapture. Also, notice that the reward is rulership (verse 47). In Revelation 5:10, the church is identified as being kings and priests who *"...shall reign on the earth."*

FOLDED GARMENTS

Dear Mr. Froese,

Thank you very much for the video, "Apocalypse," and tracts etc. I do hope the money I send you covers all completely. If not, please let me know.

The video is excellent, but one thing puzzles me: the neatly folded garments left by believers after the Lord has taken them. Forgive me, but would not clothes be left in various positions on floors among bedclothes, as is mentioned?

God bless you all at Midnight Call.

-E.O., Great Britain

ANSWER: The answer to your question is found in John 20:7, *"And the napkin, that was about his head, not lying with the linen clothes, but wrapped together in a place by itself."*

I believe that we will depart in an orderly fashion, for our God is a God of order.

ALL CHILDREN RAPTURED?

Dear Brother Froese:

Greetings in the name of our Lord and Savior Jesus Christ.

I am a fairly new follower of your ministry at Midnight Call and I want to take this opportunity to tell you what a blessing the monthly magazine and *News From Israel* are for Christians in this hour of famine.

May God continue to supply all your needs to keep on the firing line until the day we go home to be with Him. Which brings me to the question I hope you can answer and maybe address in the magazine.

At the time of the Rapture, will all children be taken? This is something that I have thought upon but can't get persuaded with a clear yes or no. I know that the Gospel speaks of children when the abomination of desolation is revealed at the middle of the tribulation, but is that only the children who have been born after the Rapture? What about children of the heathen, like Muslims, Mormons and cults like the Jehovah Witnesses? Will they be taken in the Rapture?

We were discussing this last Sunday afternoon and I really couldn't give a clear answer. Can you help us?

-D.I., Palmetto, GA

ANSWER: Only those who believe in the Son have everlasting life. Upon all others, *"the wrath of God abideth."* To what age children are innocent is not revealed to us in the Scripture. However, we do know that God is not unrighteous and He will deal justly. For those of us who are believers, we must pray continuously for our children that they will accept the only salvation which is found in Jesus Christ and so be ready for the Rapture.

RAPTURE OR DECEPTION?

Dear Brother Froese:

According to the Word of God, there is a great deception that is being spread throughout the world. It is being spread within our churches, our Christian television stations and our Christian magazines. This deception has become so ingrained in most minds that they immediately tune out anything to the contrary. Most have become so attached to this religious security blanket that they refuse to consider that this popular and long-held belief is anything but the truth.

The deception that I speak of is the so-called "Rapture of the Church." It is the belief that the Church will be raptured away prior to the tribulation. It is, quite frankly, nowhere in God's Word.

Please...for just a couple of minutes, open your spiritual eyes and ears to what God's Word says about it.

First Corinthians 15:50, *"Now this I say, brethren, that flesh and blood cannot inherit the kingdom of God; neither doth corruption inherit incorruption."*

In this verse, Paul clearly says that as long as we are in our flesh bodies, we will not and cannot inherit eternal life. I think we can all agree that for us to enter the kingdom of God, this flesh body must be discarded for a new, incorruptible body.

First Corinthians 15:51, *"Behold, I shew you a mystery; We shall not all sleep, but we shall all be changed."*

Again, Paul is saying that we must discard this flesh body for our spiritual body. So...when will this all-important event take place?

First Corinthians 15:52, *"In a moment, in the twinkling of an eye, at the last trump: for the trumpet shall sound, and the dead shall be raised incorruptible, and we shall be changed."*

There it is; we shall be changed in the twinkling of an eye. When? At the last trump.

There are only seven trumpets recorded in the book of the Revelation. The first six trumps are those that usher in the Great Tribulation and the reign of Satan and his locust army. The seventh and final trump...the last trump...is the one that ends the Great Tribulation with the entrance of Jesus Christ on the scene as Lord of lords and King of kings!

If flesh and blood cannot inherit the kingdom of God (1st Corinthians 15:50) and we are not changed until the final trump (1st Corinthians 15:52) then how can you believe that there will be a secret catching away of the Church prior to the tribulation? The seventh and final trump does not sound until the appearance of Jesus Christ at the end of the Great Tribulation.

God's Word is plain. It is true. The Church will not be raptured away prior to the Great Tribulation. In fact, it will not be raptured away at all. Jesus Christ is returning once and for all to establish His kingdom on this earth, not to rapture us all out! But...the good news is that we don't have to be afraid. Just as Noah was protected as he went through the flood, Daniel as he slept with the lions and Shadrach, Meshach and Abednego as they walked in the furnace of fire, so shall God protect from harm those that know the truth of His Word!

In summary, unless you die prior to the second advent, you will be here during the tribulation. There is no such thing as the Rapture. Church history documents the fact that the entire "Rapture theory" began in 1830. Prior to that time, no one believed in a rapture. For additional documentation on this, go to your local Christian bookstore and order, *The Incredible Cover-up* by Dave MacPherson (Omega Publications). Believe me, it's an eye-opener.

In the meantime, God's Word is truth. It is only when we muddy it up with man's traditions that it becomes polluted. And...when it is all over, it is God and His Word that will stand victorious! Hallelujah!

-H.R.O., Gaylesville, AL

ANSWER: Indeed, *"flesh and blood cannot inherit the kingdom of God."* That is why we must physically die or be *"changed."* The latter will occur in the, *"twinkling of an eye."* According to Ephesians 2:6, the flesh and blood is not the real person; the newborn spirit dwelling within the flesh and blood is the actual person.

First Thessalonians 4:16 identifies *"the trump of God."* First Corinthians 15:52 shows that this trump of God is *"the last trump."* This has no relation to any other trump you will read about in the Bible except for the first trump of God. Exodus 19:16 states, *"...and the voice of the trumpet exceeding loud..."* and verse 19 adds, *"And when the voice of the trumpet sounded long, and waxed louder and louder, Moses spake, and God answered him by a voice."* Nowhere in the Bible will you find the identity of God Himself, the voice, and the trumpet except for Exodus 19. It is here that the first trump of God gathers His earthly people to hear the Word of God. The last trump of God is where God gathers His heavenly people to unite with the Word which became flesh. The Scripture does not admonish us to wait for the tribulation or the coming of the Antichrist, but repeatedly warns us to be ready for the coming of the Lord, *"Looking for that blessed hope, and the glorious appearing of the great God and our Savior Jesus Christ"* (Titus 2:13).

LEFT BEHIND DEAD?

Greetings Mr. Froese:

Regarding your new book, *The Great Mystery of the Rapture*, may I humbly take exception to your understanding of the condition of those who are left behind? Please, sir, notice how Jesus Christ states that their condition is one of death. They are left behind, dead! (Matthew 24:28; Luke 17:37).

Mr. Froese, recall with me sir, how Jesus had just stated that at His coming, the people of this world would be in the same condition as those whom He destroyed by the flood in Noah's day, and by fire in Lot's day. Those people were left behind, dead. See Luke 17:26-30, *"wickedness and unbelief."*

Notice sir, how all the wicked are destroyed by the, *"brightness of His coming"* (2nd Thessalonians 1:7-9, 2:8). They are left behind dead! Can there be any doubt? Jesus is quite clear on this, isn't He? See the destruction of the wicked at Christ's coming in Matthew 3:12 and Matthew 13:30. All this occurs at the "end of the age" (the harvest of souls, at His coming [Matthew 13:36-52]). It's all so clear.

This old sin-sick earth will be purified by fire and then recreated. Thank you Jesus for your Word. Thank you Mr. Froese for allowing me to share with you my faith in the soon coming of my Lord and His promise that all sin and unforgiven sinners are to be destroyed. God bless you sir and my prayer for you is Ephesians 1:17-19 and Ephesians 3:14-21.

-R.L., Coldwater, MI

ANSWER: Those who are *"left behind"* are not physically dead. If that were the case, who would worship the Antichrist? Who are the people who will be saved during the Great Tribulation? And over whom will Israel rule during the thousand-year kingdom of peace? You quoted 2nd Thessalonians 2:8, which identifies the destruction of the Antichrist at the Lord's coming, not the people who are left behind. During the Great Tribulation, multitudes will recognize the deception, repent and be saved. Revelation 7:9 speaks of this group of people, *"...I beheld, and, lo, a great multitude, which no man could number, of all nations, and kindreds, and people, and tongues, stood before* *the throne, and before the Lamb, clothed with white robes, and palms in their hands."*

WAIT FOR THE RAPTURE

Dear Arno,

Concerning Mr. G.E.'s request about the Rapture in the June issue of the *Midnight Call*, you left it unfulfilled by the way you responded. The connotation you put on Titus 2:13 excludes a timeframe.

In reality, there is an implied two-fold condition: (1) a looking for and (2) the time of appearing. The first expresses a continuous awareness of the outlook, but the TIME of the appearing, a PROSPECT, [is] not disclosed here.

We all must WAIT for that appearing, whether it is expected now (at any moment), or at some future day revealed elsewhere.

Looking for the appearing at the time of the *"last trump"* (1st Corinthians 15:52) or AFTER *"the revealing of the son of perdition"* (2nd Thessalonians 2:1-3), or AFTER *"the tribulation of those days"* (Matthew 24:29-31), or AFTER *"the 1260 days of the two witness prophecy"* (Revelation 11:18 and 1st Thessalonians 5:9) doesn't change the aspect of our looking for that blessed hope today or yesteryear.

Of course, some of these conditions need a little further explaining to keep them in context, but they still relate to the one subject Mr. G.E. had in mind and was concerned with.

Because you do not use these time-related conditions in your conclusions, the Lord will come in a day, *"when ye think not."* Wake up brother to this reality if you wish to remain credible and a wise servant of the Lord.

-D.A., Raymond, WA

ANSWER: I certainly agree with your statement that, "We all must wait for the appearing, whether it is expected now or at some future day...." However, you confuse the Rapture with the Lord's Second Coming for other groups of people such as the Jews as is documented in Matthew 24, or the announcement of the Lord's literal coming to Israel according to Revelation 11. I am convinced that He could come today and that's the bottom line of my Rapture subject debate. If He cannot come today, then please, somebody tell me why not?

TIME ZONE HOUR

Dear Brother in Christ,

Some time ago, I said to my daughter, a dedicated Christian and a believer in the Pre-Trib Rapture, "It is so close now. The church may not see the year 2000." Her reply was like a dash of cold water in my face. "Mother, you know we are not to set dates. Jesus said no one, including Himself, would know the day or the hour."

How often we hear that statement, always spoken reproachfully, implying that it is a mystery we must not seek to know. It isn't a mystery. It is the biggest lie Satan has sold the Bride. She is being deceived even though

400

many times Jesus warned, "Do not be deceived." As I was deep in prayer, my daughter's words troubled me and I asked, "Lord, please show me the truth."

Let us examine what He said in Matthew 24:36-42. It is plain that He is speaking about the Rapture, "One taken, one left." He said no man knows the day or hour (verse 36). Today, we understand that perfectly though we don't know we knew because we have been deceived.

His appearing will be instantaneous. He doesn't touch the earth. He calls us from the air, all over the world at the same instant. It may be 8:00 a.m. in New York, 7:00 a.m. in the Midwest, 6:00 a.m. in the mountains and 5:00 a.m. in California. All different hours, yet, all hear the trumpet, the shout.

But wait. It may be Monday in the Middle East but Sunday in St. Louis. Different days although all are taken at the same time.

This is a fact, not a mystery. Even our children understand. How have we been so deceived? Plainly, it is impossible for anyone to know the day and hour of our Lord's appearing. Jesus just stated a fact.

-V.O., Craig, MO

ANSWER: I am happy to read that you are waiting for the Lord. The Bible admonishes us, *"Looking for that blessed hope, and the glorious appearing of the great God and our Saviour Jesus Christ"* (Titus 2:13).

Regarding, "the day or the hour," please remember that Jesus is speaking to His people, the Jews; in His land, Israel. This has no relation to the fact that the world is separated into 24-hour time-zones. Your daughter is correct when she says, "We are not to set dates."

But, as I have already said, you are correct by waiting for Him now, disregarding the year 2000 or any other year, day or hour.

MORE RAPTURE QUESTIONS

Dear Arno Froese,

I find your teaching that the Rapture is the next event on God's calendar to be confusing and incompatible with other Scriptures.

A. First Corinthians 15:52 and 1st Thessalonians 4:16 are at the last trump, which is just before the bowls of God's wrath are poured out.

B. Second Thessalonians 2:1-4 says that the gathering together is after the man of sin is revealed and sets himself up in the temple as God.

C. Matthew 24:29-31 says that the gathering together is after the tribulation.

D. In John 17:15 Jesus said, *"I pray not that you should take them out of the world, but that you should keep them from the evil."*

E. In Ephesians 5:27, Jesus said *"...that there will be a glorious church, without having spot, wrinkle, or any blemish."* Such a church does not exist at this time. How can the Church be raptured before it is holy?

F. In Matthew 6:10 Jesus prayed, *"Thy kingdom come. Thy will be done in earth, as it is in heaven."* This has not yet been fulfilled. When is it to be fulfilled? How can it be fulfilled if the Church is not on earth?

G. First Peter 4:17 says that judgment must begin at the house of God. It does not say that the Church will be snatched away and avoid all testing and suffering. Acts 14:22 says that we will enter the kingdom of God through much suffering.

H. First Corinthians 15:26 says that the *"...last enemy to be destroyed is death."* The dead will not be raised until Christ has put all enemies under His feet.

I. Revelation 20:4-6 says that the first resurrection occurs when Christ comes to reign with His people, which is after the tribulation.

J. Daniel 12:1-2 says that the resurrection shall occur after a time of trouble such as never was. That is Post-Tribulation.

K. In light of the Scriptures cited, please tell me how you justify a Pre-Tribulation Rapture? Who is going to teach the Gospel to those who are converted during the tribulation?

-H.E., Sidney, OH

ANSWER: A. Carefully read these two verses and you will find the difference between *"the last trump"* and *"the last trump of God."* There is no relation between the two, nor with the bowls of wrath.

B. Two different events are described: *"The coming of the Lord"* and *"our gathering."* The Antichrist cannot be revealed until verses 6 and 7 are fulfilled.

C. This is not the Rapture because He shall send *"his angels"* with *"a trumpet."* At the Rapture, He comes

403

"Himself" with *"the last trump of God."*

D. We are *"in the world"* but not *"of the world."* No Rapture relationship.

E. The Church is unable to make herself perfect. If the Rapture is based on the merits of our works, you and I would never make it, but praise God, He already did it for us.

F. It will be fulfilled when He comes back with the saints (Church) because He has *"made us...kings and priests; and we shall reign on earth"* (Revelation 5:10).

G. Indeed, the Church has suffered and continues to be in tribulation in various parts of the world, but the judgment has already been fulfilled on Calvary's cross.

H. Jesus destroyed death at Calvary for Himself, then for many Old Testament saints. For us, it will take place when we are raptured, then finally death will be done away with for all who believe.

I. This is the last part of the first resurrection. Don't forget that Jesus was and is the firstfruit.

J. *"The children of thy people"* is not the Church, it's Israel. They are the 144,000 Jews from the twelve tribes of Israel.

K. The Rapture is also called the *"blessed hope,"* the Great Tribulation is not. The 144,000 Jews will preach the Gospel during the tribulation.

CHAPTER 21

RAPTURE TIMING

PRE-WRATH RAPTURE

Dear Mr. Froese,

My name is O.L. and I will soon be 66 years old. I was raised in a Christian home and have never doubted the Word of God. I was taught in my youth to expect the Lord's return at any moment. I continued to believe in an any-moment Rapture well into middle age. I took special interest in prophecy and purchased books written by the leading scholars who were affiliated with Dallas Theological Seminary. These included Dwight Pentecost, John Walvoord, Charles Ryrie, and others over the years. I became knowledgeable and began teaching prophecy, but like all the ones mentioned above, I was unable to satisfactorily answer many questions. I had many questions concerning the Pre-Trib Rapture and every scholar and authority I queried gave me the standard teaching on the dispensations. I already knew all the broad answers that I was given, and I was left with the same unanswered questions. I continued to believe in the Pre-Trib doctrine in spite of my questions.

Then in 1992, I read a book written by Tim LaHaye and it has bothered me for the past eight years. I did not write earlier because I figured my questions would be ignored and continue to be unanswered due to the fact that Thomas Ice is affiliated with Tim LaHaye's prophecy study group and is a contributing editor to your magazine.

I read Marvin Rosenthal's book, *The Pre-Wrath Rapture of the Church,* and was very surprised. I expected to read another book by another date-setter. I was very surprised to find that Rosenthal was most gracious and gave many favorable comments to his former teachers. I took the two books in question and laid them side-by-side and read every passage that LaHaye had commented on. I found that Tim LaHaye not only slandered another Christian, but he lied several times about Rosenthal's book. He slandered Rosenthal by his derogatory remarks, and wrote in such a way as to make Rosenthal a date-setter. He wrote that Rosenthal set the Rapture at twenty-one months into the second half of the tribulation period, which is an outright lie. He then quotes another liar who wrote that Rosenthal set the date at 1,890 days after the Antichrist signs the covenant with Israel, and that is also a blatant lie. I could go on and on quoting non-Christian statements made by LaHaye, but there isn't any need.

I am as educated as any of the most popular scholars and authors. I am completely knowledgeable of all the popular endtime doctrines, and am capable of understanding and dividing the Word of God. The Pre-Trib doctrine is full of contradictions that in no way can be answered without using assumptions and Scriptures out of context.

My guess is that you all know that Rosenthal's interpretation of endtime eschatology is the correct one, but pride and your love of the praise of men is more important to you "experts" than truth. You can all join together and form a dozen groups and write dozens of books and hold a prophecy conference every day and you will still be completely incorrect.

I could go on and on, but I know that none of this is new to you. It is the duty of each Christian to point out the errors of their brothers in Christ when they stray from the truth, and that is what this letter is all about. Any man who (does not) point out the slander and lies that these men (have) committed are more guilty than the original liars.

How you respond to this letter is up to you. May the Lord judge between me and all those who condone and praise liars. I know that I love and accept the truth, but the response to LaHaye's book has shown me that some Christians prefer lies.

-O.L., Norman, OK

ANSWER: In regards to Tim LaHaye's book, you will have to take that matter up with him. Write and explain your view.

In relation to the Rapture, I submit the following: Virtually all students of the Bible agree that the Word of God repeatedly warns us to be ready for the coming of

Jesus. The Lord Himself actually stated that He will come *"when ye think not."* Therefore, any pinpointing of His coming is fundamentally wrong whether your eschatological view is Mid-Trib, Pre-Wrath or Post-Trib.

Maybe an example will help. During the Christian Booksellers Convention, I was interviewed by a woman from a popular publication. When I asked her whether she believed in the Rapture, she stated, "I am Mid-Trib." My reply was, "So then you don't have to wait for Jesus to come today." There was a moment of silence until she finally realized what she had said. Surprised, she asked, "What do you mean?" I replied, "If you believe in a Pre-Wrath or Mid-Trib Rapture, then you cannot wait for Jesus to come today; you must first wait for the tribulation." And that, you will agree, is contrary to the Scripture.

You see, when you read the wonderful passages about the Rapture of the saints in 1st Thessalonians 4:16-18, you would have to ignore the last verse, *"Wherefore comfort one another with these words."* How can you comfort one another if you don't believe in the imminence of the Lord's coming? I am fully aware that I cannot change your beliefs, but please don't try to take away the precious comfort of the simple Bible teaching that Jesus could come today!

PRE-TRIB/POST-TRIB

Dear Mr. Froese,

A year and a half ago, I started to study up on some of our doctrines concerning the Rapture, the Second Coming of Christ, and endtime events.

I started studying the Greek, reading history, and listening to both sides of the fence concerning Pre-Trib, Post-Trib, and fulfilled views.

One question remains unanswered by those who agree with the Pre-Trib view.

The question is this: Where in the Bible is there a Scripture verse speaking of the Second Coming of Christ, or endtime events that say when the Rapture will happen—before or after the tribulation?

The question is not if there is a Rapture but when, before or after?

I will be anxiously waiting your response. May God bless you and all there at Midnight Call.

-G.E., IV, New Milford, CT

ANSWER: Anyone who believes in the Mid-Trib or Post-Trib Rapture cannot wait for Him today because he must first wait for the Great Tribulation. That, of course, is contrary to the Scripture because we are *"Looking for that blessed hope, and the glorious appearing of the great God and our Saviour Jesus Christ"* (Titus 2:13). Incidentally, during one of our prophecy conferences, Dave Hunt once said, "The Post-Trib Rapture is a non-event because all the saints have been executed and no one has a chance of survival unless he worships the image of the beast." So who will be taken after the Great Tribulation if there is no one left to be raptured?

SIGNLESS RAPTURE?

Dear Mr. Froese:

My dear brother, when are you Pre-Tribbers going to decide whether the Rapture is signless or not and stop your double talk on the subject? You slipped into it again in your conclusion to your article, "Israel's Future" in the January 1997 issue of *Midnight Call* when you wrote, "The beginning of the fulfillment of prophecy in Israel is the last great warning sign that the Rapture is imminent."

I thought your belief is that the Rapture is signless and was always imminent. How then, can it have been the last great warning sign presented?

-R.E., Reading, VA

ANSWER: You are confusing the "signs of the times" with the "signs for the Rapture." Matthew 24 and Luke 21 give particular signs of the endtimes for the people of Israel. Israel is indeed the last great warning sign for the Rapture, but don't forget, it has existed since 1948. God's working in, with and through Israel highlights the nearness of His coming for waiting believers. The Rapture itself can occur at any moment with no preceding signs, but right in the midst of the signs of the times.

ANTICHRIST OR RAPTURE?

Dear Sir,

I subscribe to your magazine and agree with you on your Pre-Trib Rapture position. Many Scriptures support that position. However, there is one part of the Bible that

410

concerns me that would disprove the Pre-Trib view. Those verses are found in 2nd Thessalonians 2:1-3. Verse 1 talks about the coming of the Lord and our gathering together unto Him, which I assume is the Rapture. Verse 3 says that day shall not come except there be a falling away first and that the man of sin be revealed, the son of perdition (whom I assume to be the Antichrist).

I thought the Church would be removed before the Antichrist could be revealed. Could you please reply?

-M.E., Patchogue, NY

ANSWER: Second Thessalonians 2 speaks about the "day of Christ" which is His physical return to the Mount of Olives, and *"our gathering...unto Him"* which is the Rapture.

The "day of the Lord" cannot take place unless two things happen first: 1) The hindering element for the full development of darkness must be removed because the Church is the light of the world; 2) The Antichrist, *"that man of sin,"* must be revealed. Only after these events will the "day of Christ" commence.

TRIBULATION

Dear Arno:

I would like to ask one question regarding the Rapture.

I know you teach truth from the Bible. I was reading an article from a man of God who also teaches the truth from the Bible.

He says the Church has to go through (the) tribulation

411

before the Rapture because God wants His Bride to be spotless and without wrinkle. Therefore, the saints have to go through (the) tribulation in order to be ready for the Rapture.

Reading Matthew 24:29-31, *"...after the tribulation..."* God shall *"...send his angels with a great sound of a trumpet...to gather together his elect..."* shows these souls have already gone through (the) tribulation.

Also, Revelation 13:6 says the Antichrist got victory over the saints. So, who are these saints; are they not the Body of Christ, the Church? This also shows the Church going through (the) tribulation.

Please explain to me. I am confused. I expect your reply in the *Midnight Call* magazine. Thank you.

-T.L., Jamaica, NY

ANSWER: If the Church must go through the tribulation in order to be "made spotless and without wrinkle," then Jesus didn't fulfill His work. Members of the Church are those *"...which he hath purchased with his own blood"* (Acts 20:28).

If we must work or suffer to become "spotless and without wrinkle," then it is of works and not of grace.

Matthew 24 is not speaking about the Rapture of the Church, but of the Jews to Israel. Carefully compare Matthew 24:31 with 1st Thessalonians 4:16. *"The Lord Himself"* will come for the Church with *"the trump of God."* But when He comes for Israel, *"He shall send his angels,"* *"with a trumpet."*

The saints mentioned in Revelation 13:7 are Israel,

who will have then experienced a national conversion.

Don't confuse the Great Tribulation with the general tribulation which we all, more or less, experience (Acts 14:22).

PRE-WRATH RAPTURE

Dear Midnight Call,

Thank you for your ministry! I enjoy *Midnight Call* magazine. I renewed my subscription and enjoy the articles! I am writing and would like a reply to a book I don't understand! It's (*The Pre-Wrath Tribulation*) by Mr. Marvin Rosenthal. Two people have "somewhat" explained it. It upsets me very much. I personally believe it is Satan's deception to upset the child of God! I'm told to look for the blessed hope, not the Antichrist! Would you please help me? What could I say to these two people who have read and swear by the book? Thank you again for Midnight Call Ministry!

-I.E., Savannah, GA

ANSWER: Because the very name, "Pre-Wrath Rapture," determines a timetable, it is false. Indeed, we would have to wait for the Antichrist and the beginning of the Great Tribulation instead of heeding the instructions of the Bible to wait for the blessed hope. Obviously, your friends believe in this false teaching, thus, your discussion will be fruitless. Only prayer changes things.

FIRST RESURRECTION

Dear Mr. Froese,

Isn't there only one "first resurrection?" I may not be a mathematical doctor, but I have enough sense to realize that there can only be one "first," so I am puzzled about something, *"...I saw the souls of them that were beheaded for the witness of Jesus, and for the word of God, and which had not worshipped the beast, neither his image, neither had received his mark upon their foreheads, or in their hands, and they lived and reigned with Christ a thousand years...This is the first resurrection"* (Revelation 20:4,5).

Paul said of the Rapture: *"...the dead in Christ shall rise first: Then we which are alive and remain shall be caught up together with them..."* (1st Thessalonians 4:16,17).

Since there is only one first resurrection, the dead rise before our living Rapture and the Scripture plainly shows this after the tribulation under Antichrist, then isn't the "Oz Land" doctrine of a Pre-Trib escape anti-biblical and contrary to the plain Word of God?

-N.R., West Union, SC

ANSWER: There is only one "first resurrection" and one "second death." The first resurrection began with our Lord and includes the resurrection of many of the Old Testament saints (Matthew 27:52), the Church in the Rapture and others such as the two witnesses. Thereafter, the first resurrection is finalized as described in Revelation 20:5-6.

Jesus was the first; the tribulation saints are the last. If you take the element of time away, you have only one resurrection.

414

ESCHATOLOGY

SEVEN-YEAR TRIBULATION?

My Church Brothers:

"Can anything good come from North Carolina?" Is it possible that a country preacher has given us, in absolutely verifiable God-breathed Scripture, a revelation that will crumble a pillar of eschatology?

By building "precept upon precept" from the original Hebrew and Greek, and by allowing Holy Scripture (not current events) to be the interpreter, and by augmenting them with idioms and historians, Pastor Colin Deal has shown us in this unpretentious booklet how we have so misunderstood the book of Daniel—especially 9:27—that we have surely brought tears to the eyes of our Savior.

In exhaustive research, Pastor Deal has endangered other pillars of traditional teaching. He has also cleared glasses which heretofore we had only seen through darkly. Here are some excerpts:

It is generally accepted that the length of the tribulation is to be seven years long. This period is further divided into two periods of three and one-half years each. This view is so prominent and so accepted that seldom, if ever, will one even dare to question it.

The first thing to notice is that the "Messiah the Prince" of verse 25, the "Messiah" of verse 26, the "prince" of verse 26, and the "he" of verse 27 are all the same individual, that is, Jesus Christ. Most people will quickly point out that the "prince" in verse 26 and the "he" in verse 27 are not capitalized, and therefore cannot be Christ. Unfortunately, in the Hebrew, there is no such thing as upper and lower case letters. In other words, there are no capital letters. Thus, the words, "Prince" and "prince" appear identical. You would not know this without a prior understanding of the Hebrew language. This, then, is lost in the translation process. As a matter of fact, it is at this point that the interpretation of the translators takes over, because it is they who have determined to make one capitalized while the other is not.

This three-and-one-half year period is the first half of the last week (or seventieth week) referred to here in Daniel. Then in the midst of this week, or after three-and-one-half years, Jesus was cut off, or crucified. Incidentally, His crucifixion was considered in God's eyes as the final sacrifice, thereby causing "the sacrifice and the oblation" from the Jewish system "to cease" (Hebrews 7:22,27; 9:26; 10:8-12).

In the next portion of verse 27, it begins like this, "and for the overspreading of abomination he shall make it desolate, even until the consummation...." The intent of what Daniel is saying here in the Hebrew is, "because (someone?) has caused an overspreading of abominations, he (the Messiah) shall make it desolate.

As a member of the Body and of your ministry, I implore you to open your mind and let the Holy Spirit prevail. You may then wish to delve further into other equally provocative works by this messenger.

Please be kind enough to let me know your conclusion.

Thank you.

-K.N., Glendale, AZ

416

ANSWER: The Bible says, *"...after threescore and two weeks shall Messiah be cut off, but not for himself...."* Martin Luther translated this, *"And after sixty-two weeks, the anointed shall be eliminated and nothing shall be ...."* My Hebrew Bible reads, *"And after those sixty-two weeks, the anointed one will disappear and vanish...."*

The Romans were the people of the prince who destroyed Jerusalem and the temple. In verse 27 we read, *"...he shall confirm the covenant...he shall cause the sacrifice and the oblation to cease...he shall make desolate...."* Who is this "he?" It is not the Lord Jesus, it is the Antichrist. Daniel 8:11 testifies to this fact, *"Yea, he magnified himself even to the prince of the host, and by him the daily sacrifice was taken away, and the place of his sanctuary was cast down."* Jesus never "magnified Himself." He was obedient unto death, even death on the cross.

REPLACING ISRAEL

Dear Sir:

I am very supportive of the nation of Israel and I believe the promises and prophecies are relative to the restored state of Israel. I preach these things. I am very concerned about the replacement of theologians trying to void these things. Kelly Varner recently wrote a book published by Destiny Image Publishers in Shippensburg, PA, entitled, *Whose Right It Is.*

In this book he mentions, "The Seed of Abraham is not natural Israel but Christ" (Galatians 3:16) in an effort to obliterate the promises to natural Israel. These people say

Israel is no longer relevant to God's plan, and the only way Israel or the Jews can be relevant is for them to be grafted back into the good olive tree.

Varner further states that Elijah and others commonly thought of as Jews are not Jews. We need to counter these lies for the sake of the innocent. What is your view on these Varner assertions?

Dr. A.A., Elizabethtown, KY

ANSWER: Our exalted Lord speaks of replacement theology in Revelation 2:9, "...*I know the blasphemy of them which say they are Jews, and are not, but are the synagogue of Satan.*" A Gentile is not a Jew, nor is a Jew a Gentile. The clear distinction between Jew, Gentile, and the Church can be understood by the scriptural promises given to the Jews. The Church does not have a geographical or political promise, but the Jews do! That is why they are returning to the land of Israel. Also, the Church has already obtained peace through the Lord Jesus Christ. Israel is still waiting for it, "*That he* [the Lord] *would grant us,* [Jews] *that we being delivered out of the hand of our enemies might serve him without fear*" (Luke 1:74). From the destruction of the temple in Jerusalem in A.D. 70 until the Holocaust, fourteen million Jews have perished. Even today, peace is not a reality and to "...*serve him without fear...*" is out of the question at this time. The Bible says, "...*Concerning the gospel, they* [Jews] *are enemies for your sakes*" (Romans 11:28). The fulfilled and unfulfilled promises in the Old and New Testament clearly identify who a Jew is.

RECONSTRUCTIONISM

Attn: Editor

In discussions of endtime prophecy with some of my reconstructionist friends, they will quote Deuteronomy 7:9 and 1st Chronicles 16:15, pointing out that the thousand generations referred to in each could hardly be less than twenty-thousand years.

They conclude from this that the Church has ample time (say 10,000 to 14,000 years) to "prepare" the kingdom for Christ's return.

In context, it could be that both passages refer to natural Israel through time and on into the new heaven and new earth of Revelation 21. This would make the thousand-generation passages allegorical in that they could just as well have been forever, or some similar wording.

One hesitates to assume allegory where it is not obviously intended, but 10,000 to 14,000 years seems to be out of whack with one's impressions of imminence garnered from the New Testament (and related OT prophecy).

-O.L., CANADA

ANSWER: These Scripture references relate to God's faithfulness, *"because he would keep the oath..."* (Deuteronomy 7:8). Also 1st Chronicles 16:16, *"...which he made with Abraham, and of his oath unto Isaac."* This has no relation to the existence of the Church on earth.

THE MILLENNIUM

Dear Sir:

In the March issue of the *Midnight Call* magazine, in the pages of "Letters to Editor," you were asked to explain several questions. One was, "What will people be doing during the Millennium?"

Your answer was, "I assume the same as they are today, going to work, earning money, building homes, having families." This answer indicates there will be little difference in our lives. Please explain to me how your answer fits in with the following verse, *"...the resurrection from the dead, neither marry, nor are given in marriage"* (Luke 20:35); *"...they neither marry, nor are given in marriage; but are as the angels which are in heaven"* (Mark 12:25). To me, this indicates no "families." Matthew 22:30 states the same thing.

You mentioned we'd work and build homes, but the Bible says, *"...we shall reign on the earth"* (Revelation 5:10); *"...shall be priests of God and of Christ, and shall reign with him a thousand years"* (Revelation 20:6). You mentioned Micah 4:3. Isn't God speaking of the nations of the world? I don't believe that God's children who come from heaven with Christ at the end of the tribulation will be rebuked.

You mention we will "build homes." Christ tells us in John 14:2, *"...I go to prepare a place for you."* In studying God's Word, I find many different words describing our lives. Heaven will be glorious. We read about heaven in Revelation 21-22. I am 88 years old and accepted Christ at age 16. I have heard many ministers and read many spiritual books, but never heard of the life you mentioned we'll have in the thousand years. I enjoy *Midnight Call* and read each magazine with opened mind. Please respond with references in Scripture that can be applied.

-M.E., Taylorsville, MS

ANSWER: Neither the question nor the answer is in relation to believers, but to "the people." In other words, those who dwell on earth during the thousand-year kingdom of peace do not belong to the Church. You are certainly correct regarding our position and the Scriptures you mentioned are appropriate. No matter where we are, or what we do, our position is clearly identified in 1st Thessalonians 4:17, *"...so shall we ever be with the Lord."* When the Lord rules on earth, so shall we with Him.

DOMINION THEOLOGY

Arno,

As a new Christian (late 60's), I researched to solidify my base. I labored with Dwight Pentecost's book, *Things to Come*. Without knowing of a bias, I agreed with the Dallas Theological Seminary conclusion of the Pre-Tribulation Rapture, since I was involved with Campus Crusade for Christ at the University of Texas. Hal Lindsey was very popular.

Currently, I am investigating material from a man I used to admire: (his grasp of history, economics and politics) Gary North.

Referencing to *Midnight Call*, November 1995 issue, page 29, I would like some amplification. Dominion Theology, Theonomy, Post Trib-Rapture-after Millennium.

What does all this mean? I am referring to the disagreement with Demar, Leithart, Rushdoony.

-A.N., San Antonio, TX

ANSWER: Dr. Dave Breese has written extensively on Dominion Theology. You can write to him at Box C, Hillsboro, KS 67063. Jesus said, *"...I go to prepare a place for you..."* (John 14:2). No command is given in Scripture that we should prepare the world for Him. Dominion and Reconstruction theology advise Christians to remake this world in the anticipation of His coming. This, of course, is contrary to the Scriptures. The focus of necessity shifts from the cross of Jesus Christ to the ballot box and the courtrooms of the world with a vain hope that Christians will seize political power and force an ungodly population to live by Christian rules. It will never happen.

ALL JEWS RESURRECTED?

Dear Mr. Froese,

About a year ago a friend of mine gave me a subscription to *Midnight Call*. Until then, I had never heard of the magazine. Since then I have enjoyed every issue. In fact, I have saved every issue and have them documented in a database on my computer for further reference. I lead a Bible study in our home once a week and the material in your magazine may be helpful in the preparation.

I believe that the Scriptures tell that a born again believer, from this age of grace, will be resurrected or translated to heaven upon the return of Jesus Christ for

His Church. I believe that our resurrected bodies will be flesh and bone, not unlike Jesus' resurrected body.

However, a question has come to mind about the Old Testament saints with respect to their resurrected bodies and to where their place of resurrection will be. Joseph left specific instructions that his bones be removed from Egypt and carried to the Promised Land (Genesis 50:25). Moses took them (Exodus 13:19) and they were buried in the Promised Land (Joshua 24:32).

This prompted my question? As a Christian, I believe at the time of resurrection, God will find my bones no matter where they are buried. Why, then, was Joseph so desirous to have his bones buried in the Promised Land? Why were his instructions remembered after so many years in captivity and Moses and the people so obedient to Joseph's wishes?

To me, Isaiah 26:19, Ezekiel 37:12-14 and Daniel 12:2 indicate that Old Testament saints will be bodily resurrected to the land that God promised them. Their resurrected bodies will be like the resurrected body of Lazarus and those who came out of the tombs after Jesus' death (Matthew 27:52-53).

Mr. Froese, I would like to know your thoughts about this. Remember I am not concerned with the Body of Christ made up of both Jew and Gentile, but only the blood descendants of Abraham.

-A.C., Oroville, CA

ANSWER: Joseph, the great grandson of Abraham, knew of the promises; subsequently, he wanted to be identified with the land. This was symbolic because we don't read of other Hebrews who came out of Egypt in their coffins.

Ezekiel 37 is speaking of the national resurrection of Israel, which means that the Jews who have returned, and continue to return to the land of Israel today, are coming out of their "graves."

In the Diaspora, there was no hope of a future for the Jews to be established as a nation. Thus, we read, *"...I will open your graves, and cause you to come up out of your graves, and bring you into the land of Israel"* (Ezekiel 37:12). Israel will experience national salvation, while the Gentiles will experience individual salvation. The chosen people are not complete outside of their Promised Land.

The resurrection described in Isaiah 26:19 and Daniel 12:2 has no relation to Ezekiel 37. A distinction between two groups is made in verse 14, *"They are dead, they shall not live..."* and verse 19, *"Thy dead men shall live...."* Daniel 12:2 also identifies these two groups: 1) *"some to everlasting life"* and 2) *"some to shame and everlasting contempt."*

The resurrection saints who rose after the Lord's resurrection (Matthew 27) belong to the heavenly citizens, and I believe they ascended with the Lord, because "He led captivity captive." However, Lazarus was a demonstration of the fulfillment of prophecy and although the Bible does not provide this information, I believe he too died.

GIFTS OF THE BODY

Dear Mr. Froese:

Your ministry means a lot to me, and to many others also, it's certain. May God bless your work continually until He comes.

There's been some fear in my thoughts concerning the Great Tribulation, but the Lord has been kind in comforting me about these things.

Last August, I received an unsolicited magazine called *Zion's Fire*. Perhaps you've heard of it, and of the reason given by the editor for discounting that the Church will return with Christ (on white horses) to defeat the enemy and his followers. He argued that the translation of the word "saints" (1st Thessalonians 3:13) should actually have been "holy ones," contending that Jesus would be accompanied by the angels only. This troubled me deeply, yet God still made provision for me with His peace. Still there remained a desire to explore this contention.

I'm not a Bible scholar, nor a translator of Greek or Hebrew, so there is a great deal I need to learn, and I know this.

I prayed that God would help me to better understand the Rapture event and at what point in Revelation history it will take place.

One sleepless night, our Lord kept running a thought through my mind regarding the lack of logic for a mid- or post-tribulation Rapture, saying, "the Body of Christ."

I realized that He was pointing out that Jesus suffered physical, mental, and spiritual pain for our sins.

According to Ephesians, we are members of His Body,

425

of His flesh and bone!

Doesn't the Father see His only begotten Son when He looks at the Church? Since these things are true, those who tell us that the Church must endure part or all of the tribulation seem to also be saying Christ's body must receive the wrath of God again. But that can't be so. Upon His death, Jesus said, *"It's finished."*

There are other important reasons to believe in the Pre-Tribulation Rapture, but this reason filled me with assurance. I have written you this letter because I haven't heard it from prophetic ministries before, and I wondered if it is new?

Even if you have heard and even ministered it before, it was a very loving gift to me. I had resigned myself (after the confusion of the article) to accept God's plan for victory even if it means my family and I would battle through the Great Tribulation, but He graciously revealed the faithfulness of His trust.

I hope you will find a few minutes to respond. Thank you for your time.

-A.N., East Lansing, MI

ANSWER: Your analysis of Christ's suffering for His Body really drove the point home. The words, *'It is finished,'* are in fact, a vital statement regarding the imminence of the Rapture. Thank you very much.

PHYSICAL OR SPIRITUAL PROMISES?

Dear Mr. Froese:

I was surprised to read in the *Midnight Call* that its departed founder, Dr. Malgo, was a Post-Tribulationist. In his book, *Biblical Counseling*, on page 34 of the June issue he says, "At present, we are passing through that hour of temptation which Revelation 3:10 speaks of."

I believe most Pre-Tribbers interpret Revelation 3:10 as a reference to the Great Tribulation. If so, then Dr. Malgo is saying that we are presently in the tribulation and since the Lord has not yet returned that event must be Mid or Post-Tribulational.

Secondly, I find your answer to the second letter on page 36 unconvincing. Specifically, God said Abraham and His seed have been given the promises (Galatians 4:16,19). The seed is clearly identified as Christ; therefore, all who are in Christ have been given the promises. The chapter, of course, concludes with the clear and statement that, *"...if you belong to Christ, then you are Abraham's offspring, heirs according to the promise."* If that doesn't say that the Christian Church inherits whatever is embodied in the promises to Abraham, the words have no meaning and the interpretation of Scripture is left to whatever meanings one will allow.

-BO.E., Reading, PA

ANSWER: In regards to Dr. Malgo's response in the June issue of *Midnight Call,* apparently you did not notice the first three words in the second paragraph. "...However, spiritually speaking..." Dr. Malgo, never was – nor are we

427

– Post-Tribulational.

The spiritual aspect also applies to the matter regarding Abraham and his descendants. The Church does indeed inherit the promise, but not an earthly one, as is the case with Israel. We are saved spiritually, not physically. Our flesh and blood has no physical, geographic or political promise. While Galatians 3:28 states that there is *"neither Jew nor Greek"* and *"...neither male nor female..."* there is no physical application; otherwise, you would have ceased being male after your conversion. In the same way, a Jew remains a Jew and a Greek a Greek as long as we are here on planet Earth. The Church is God's heavenly people and Israel is His earthly people. Don't mix the spiritual with the physical.

ENDTIME EVENTS

Dear Dr. Froese:

A couple of my godly Christian friends worry about who will preach the Gospel after the Church is raptured. I keep telling them that the tribulation is the time of Jacob's trouble (the Jews before they get saved), and that there will be 144,000 of God's elect (Jews) who will preach the Gospel on earth–the remnant of Israel sealed, supernaturally protected on earth (Revelation 7:3-4). Revelation 14:1-5 apparently shows these believers with the Lamb in heaven. Somehow they have trouble picturing Jews preaching about Jesus.

Some of the saddest Scripture in the Bible is Amos 8:11-12. Although Amos and Hosea preached to the northern kingdom of Israel before they were captured and dispersed by Assyria, I have a feeling that these verses might very well be a parallel as to how things will be for the world right before and during the tribulation.

I base my "feeling" on the lackadaisical attitude of many faithful church-goers who have little knowledge of God's Word. A daily devotion to them is reading a page from publications like *Guideposts* (although there is nothing wrong with that) in lieu of reading the Bible.

Many consider the Bible boring and/or difficult to understand. They figure that head knowledge is OK, but as long as they love and know Jesus as Savior, there is no danger in their lack of Bible knowledge.

-N.A., Oklahoma City, OK

ANSWER: In searching the Scriptures, I have not found any verses indicating that we are to make preparation for those who are left behind after the Rapture. Israel has already experienced Amos 8:11-12, but the finale will take place at the end of the Great Tribulation. I suggest you read the last seven verses of the book of Amos and note the conclusion, *"And I will plant them upon their land, and they shall no more be pulled up out of their land which I have given them, saith the LORD thy God"* (verse 15).

If somebody "loves and knows Jesus as Savior," he will not consider the Bible boring, but will feast on the precious Word of God daily and eagerly await His coming.

TRIBULATION SAINTS

Brother Froese,

I am from the mountains of western North Carolina, an area where churches stand strong in traditional teachings, which can be a good thing.

The problem is that I have difficulty understanding one of those teachings. It is believed here that only the Jews (respectively) can be saved during the seven-year tribulation period that is soon to come to this world. I have difficulty in accepting this teaching. Here is why:

1. The churches here believe that the term "fullness" (or times) of the Gentiles means that when the last Gentile is saved, the Rapture will come about. But Luke 21:20-24 shows the time of the Gentiles to be well into the tribulation period. I believe the tribulation occurs after the Rapture of the Church. I also believe that the Rapture begins with the tribulation period because when the Holy Spirit leaves with the Church, then the evil which is here now will spread (2nd Thessalonians 2:7).

2. Romans 11:25 shows (I believe) that the Jews are blind until the fullness of the Gentiles is complete. This also points to the latter part of the tribulation period because when the "eyes" of the Jews are opened they will cry out to Jesus and He will come. I believe that this is the reason for the tribulation; their knees must bend to Christ—not to the nations of this world.

3. Revelation 7:9-14 shows a group of people clothed in white—which no man can count—standing before the throne. White robes depict salvation before the throne, and verse 14 says they came out of the Great Tribulation. They were saved in the latter part of the tribulation

period. These Christians are from *"all nations, kindreds, people, and tongues,"* not just Jewish people.

If you can show me where I'm wrong, then I will have a better understanding of God's Word. Please keep in mind 2nd Thessalonians 2:10-11, which seems to show that only those who have already rejected God's only Son, Jesus Christ, will not find salvation in the tribulation period. I give you the right to use any part of this letter as you see fit.

-L.R., Tuckasgee, NC

ANSWER: Revelation 7:9 makes it clear that all people from *"...all nations, and kindreds, and people, and tongues..."* will be saved. Therefore, the assumption that only Jews will be saved is an error.

1. There is a distinct difference between Gentiles who are saved, Gentiles who reject the Lord Jesus Christ, and as we have just seen, Gentiles who are saved during the Great Tribulation.

2. Based on Romans 11:25, the time of the Gentiles continues even after the fullness of the "saved Gentiles" has been completed.

3. Revelation 7 speaks of the tribulation saints and should not be confused with "Christians." The Rapture takes away the Christians who will be in the presence of the Lord forevermore. Their destination is the place John described in Revelation 21:22, *"And I saw no temple therein: for the Lord God Almighty and the Lamb are the temple of it."* The tribulation saints *"...serve him day and night in his temple..."* (Revelation 7:15). However, all are glori-

431

ously saved through the shed blood of the Lamb.

Those mentioned in 2nd Thessalonians 2:10-11 have deliberately rejected God's truth. As a result, they believe a lie.

AFTER THE RAPTURE

Dear Mr. Froese,

I am always a bit disappointed when I get to the last page of *Midnight Call*, as I want it to continue and not wait another month.

Therefore my question: I know that once the Rapture occurs, we're outta here and with Jesus, and our loved ones in Christ, in heaven. What always amazes me is that when millions (are) gone in the blink of an eye, how can the world continue as we see it?

Just think of it: Perhaps your son, daughter, husband or wife just ups and disappears. Firemen, policemen, judges, pilots, store clerks, bankers and TV newsmen, just gone. Crashes and smashes, fires and world-wide horror await the people left.

What explanation will CNN give to the world?

When people are on the verge of madness with loved ones gone, how can they just pick up their lives and go on?

Apartments and homes empty, hospitals packed with perhaps no doctors, heart attacks from just the fear of what has happened, insanity run amuck – with the National Guard unable to hold back the flood of thieves.

Why should I even worry or think about this? Well, no

explanation has been written to satisfy my curiosity. The only thing I read about is the coming Antichrist who will solve all their problems.

I'm sure God wants to spare us the chaos that will be world-wide; however, since I'm still in this world with a God-given mind, can you enlighten me, and perhaps others? Love your magazine, especially "Letters to the Editor." God bless you.

-W.R., N. Miami Beach, FL

ANSWER: In 2nd Thessalonians 2:11, we read, *"...God shall send them* (those left behind) *strong delusion, that they should believe a lie."* We know that Satan is the master of deception and will appear with many *"signs and lying wonders."*

I could well imagine that the chaos caused by the sudden disappearance of the saints may be explained away as an alien abduction or some other supernatural cause. Peter Lalonde deals with this subject at length in his book, *Left Behind.* His new video, "Apocalypse," also reveals some possibilities.

The distinction between those in heaven and those on earth is recorded in Revelation 12:12, *"Therefore rejoice, ye heavens, and ye that dwell in them. Woe to the inhabiters of the earth and of the sea! for the devil is come down unto you, having great wrath, because he knoweth that he hath but a short time."*

I am sure this doesn't fully satisfy your curiosity, but neither does it mine.

CONCLUSION

LETTERS TO THE EDITOR

The letters you have just read are only a small representation of those we felt would best serve as instruction and edification for the Church of Jesus Christ.

It would be presumptuous to think that we could answer all questions in such a way that this book would serve as a guide for counselors in any ministry. That is not our intention because we are fully aware of the uniqueness of every individual. Just as no two flowers are ever precisely alike, no two people are ever identical on all levels. For that and many other reasons, questions will never cease; the more questions we have, the more answers we receive, and the more answers we give raise even more questions.

However, the fact that we have questions proves our uniqueness as individual creatures of God, each of us with our own capacity to reason, analyze, and think. This simple fact alone exposes the folly of the widely practiced worldwide theory of evolution. By definition, evolution cannot create individuals.

Man's ability to make decisions based on our intellect sets us apart from God's other creations, such as animals. The vast differences between our intellectual capability of analyzing certain situations and circumstances is demonstrated in the book of Job. Each of Job's friends assessed his situation in his own way. Notice how diametrically opposed some of those analyses were. In chapter 38, God, the Creator of heaven and earth, posed 83 questions to Job, to which he could only answer, *"I have heard of thee by the hearing of the ear: but now mine eye seeth thee. Wherefore I abhor myself, and repent in dust and ashes"* (Job 42:5-6).

Therefore, all of our questions and answers must not be based on circumstances, our capacity to analyze things, or a philosophical understanding. Instead, our foundation must always be the Word of God. In his book, *Keys To Bible Prophecy*, James C. Morris made this profound statement, "We do not gain an understanding of the Bible from external information, we gain an understanding of external information from the Bible" (page 99).

Through the years I have learned that the more I occupy myself with His Word, my understanding of many issues has seemed to melt away like the snow in the sun.

The Lord's disciples had many questions, of which some were not answered; however, the disciples continued to seek, debate and analyze. In spite of the fact that they did not receive a complete and final answer, their questions kept giving birth to new questions, until one day Jesus said, *"I will see you again, and your heart shall rejoice, and your joy no man taketh from you. And in that day ye shall ask me nothing"* (John 16:22-23). That is a striking statement because it would seem that a more appropriate response might have been, "in that day I will answer all your questions." But that is not what He said. Why? Because He is the answer – in person – to all things. He is the originator of all things. When we see Him as He is, all of our questions will be answered. As a matter of fact, I think they will all disappear.

Thus my final admonition for each child of God is Proverbs 15:33, *"The fear of the LORD is the instruction of wisdom; and before honour is humility."*